The Hidden Master

20 oct 2011

The Hidden Master

From 'I' to 'Itness
on
Vimalaji's Teaching'

Christine Townend

MOTILAL BANARSIDASS PUBLISHERS
PRIVATE LIMITED ● DELHI

First Edition : Delhi, 2002

ISBN: 81-208-1886-5 (Cloth)
ISBN: 81-208-1889-x (Paper)

Also available at:
MOTILAL BANARSIDASS
41 U.A. Bungalow Road, Jawahar Nagar, Delhi 110 007
8 Mahalaxmi Chamber, 22 Bhulabhai Desai Road, Mumbai 400 026
236, 9th Main III Block, Jayanagar, Bangalore 560 011
120 Royapettah High Road, Mylapore, Chennai 600 004
Sanas Plaza, 1302 Baji Rao Road, Pune 411 002
8 Camac Street, Kolkata 700 017
Ashok Rajpath, Patna 800 004
Chowk, Varanasi 221 001

Printed in India
BY JAINENDRA PRAKASH JAIN AT SHRI JAINENDRA PRESS,
A-45 NARAINA, PHASE-I, NEW DELHI 110 028
AND PUBLISHED BY NARENDRA PRAKASH JAIN FOR
MOTILAL BANARSIDASS PUBLISHERS PRIVATE LIMITED,
BUNGALOW ROAD, DELHI 110 007

CONTENTS

PREFACE

In my youth I vaguely imagined that enlightenment was something that happened to Buddhist monks who went and sat in caves for years on end, and after, emerged as radiant gods, never again to live as a human being, but to smile enigmatically, detachedly, at the foolishness of lesser mortals.

Through the wonder and magic of life I was able to meet a human being who had become enlightened, or who had passed through the process of self- realisation, of moksha, of *satori*, or the third initiation as it is called by the Theosophists. And, as I questioned her, and learnt from her, I began to understand that self-realisation is not some mysterious process dropped from heaven upon a selected few, but that it is a component of human evolutionary unfoldment, a process through which thousands of human beings have passed, and through which increasing numbers will pass as the millennium progresses. For this reason, more information is required about this transformation of consciousness, which, in ancient India was treated as an exploratory science.

I had met, through the gift of circumstance, an ordinary human being who was also a god, who illustrated for me through the example of her life and her Teaching, that self-transformation is the birthright of every human, and that there is a direct path, a scientific enquiry, which can bring about an inner revolution, a radical shift in perception and awareness, in the human psyche. I began to realize that this inner-revolution was so profound, so irreversible, that the person who underwent such a process could never be the same again, and yet, this process was entirely private; it was an inner transformation. In much the same way as the caterpillar became the butterfly, quite surprisingly, without any manipulation on its part, but merely co-operation, so also the human consciousness emerged from its bondage, and realised itself as universal and unlimited, free from time and space, and ego.

In recent years there has been an increased interest in the subject of enlightenment. Among the plethora of claims, and the multitudinous information, much confusion, contradiction, and misdirection is to be found, perhaps deterring some from going further in their inquiries, due to the emotional and exaggerated stories that are told.

In this book is recorded the story of my meeting with a Master, and the information which she shared with me, as a result of my probing and inquiry. I lived and worked in India whilst concurrently pursuing the quest for spiritual truth. This is not a biography, but my observation of certain processes which take place in consciousness. I hope it will provide useful material, some debate and discussion as well as inspiration for all those who have seen that the future of humanity does not lie in creating more and more wealth and material comfort, but in scientifically examining the inner processes which revolutionise consciousness, and thus perception of, and behaviour in, the phenomenal world.

Christine Townend,
Help in Suffering Animal Shelter,
Jaipur, Rajasthan, India.

CHAPTER ONE

MY FIRST MEETING WITH VIMALAJI

My heart is no more on this earth.
Nor is there a sense of belonging here.
I am far away from everywhere.
There is neither land, nor sea, nor skies;
There is neither light of the sun, moon or stars;
There is neither life, nor death where I am;
There is neither me, nor you, nor I and mine[1].

Because my friends had invited me to go with them to India in 1975, I went with them, and because I went with them, I met a realised person in Pondicherry. She lived in a small room in the grounds of a temple, and she radiated light, and, because, when I returned to Australia, the realised person, whose name was Diana, continued to communicate with me, and because she advised I should study the books of Vimala Thakar, I did so. And because I read the books, and because I was in India (after going on a field trip to slaughterhouses), and because I had a few days to fill before my plane departed, I went to Mt. Abu which was a hill station in Rajasthan where Vimala Thakar lived. And, when I was in Mt. Abu, I met a guide, and because I asked him if he knew where Vimala Thakar lived, and because he knew, he led me up back lanes, behind a park, and I followed him, until we came to a house, which had a high fence, and a gate.

He unlocked the gate and pulled it open. I had no time to protest, to hesitate, or to be afraid. I did not know whether

---

[1] Thakar, Vimala, 'Poem', *The Invincible,* Vol. IX, No. 1, Jan-March, 1992; 24.

she would be there, and I assumed the guide was authorised to march boldly into the interior of her garden, so I meekly followed.

I was taken up a path, through a garden, with trees and flowering things, up a stairway and onto a verandah. Sitting on the verandah were two women, in saris, reading. And behind them was a view of Mount Abu, with haze. One of the women seemed older than the other. She looked at the guide and me for a while, and then she said in a very calm and measured voice to the younger person: 'Kaiser, who is he and how did he get here?', and the younger woman said, 'He's a guide,' and we were all stopped and surprised to be inflicted upon each other at that particular moment in time

The older woman had deep and endless eyes, which penetrated me, so that I was exposed and did not have any backing. It seemed she had materialised out of essence into the chair, like myths of coaches and concealed princes.

I was suddenly there, on the verandah, without expecting it, standing confronting her privacy, as she looked up from an unfinished conversation with the woman standing beside her. I immediately sensed that this intrusion was not in keeping with her schedule, that I had disturbed something important, deep discussions, urgent plans, matters relating to the destiny of the world, and I, uninvited, unasked, without even a preliminary phone-call, was catapulted into her seclusion.

I thought perhaps she would expel me, or perhaps I should take my leave. I was hesitating between motion and non-motion, turning and non-turning, when she took the initiative by looking towards her companion, and saying, as if I did not exist, 'How did he find the way?' Perhaps she was herself asking the questions in order to have time to install composure in order to calm the tossing, restless, excitement and nervousness, which must have gone in spokes and in pricks from my being.

'Are you Vimala Thakar?' I asked, and could not speak at all, and mumbled and muttered, and said, 'I don't know what to call you or whether it is alright to be here.'

'Yes, it's alright,' she said. 'I am Vimala. Please sit,' and was silent, and lost, although words had come and gone.

So I thanked the guide, and pressed money into his hand which I knew was over-generous but I was worried about his health.

'How can I help you?' Vimalaji asked.

'I read your books,' I said, 'And I wanted to see you to ask about meditation.'

She waited and did not say anything at all. She just waited, and continuously waited some more, as though she was so full that everything would flow out and spill and engulf the world if she opened at all.

'I had a whole lot of questions, but I can't think of any of them,' I said. 'I've been to the slaughterhouses. It's the most terrible thing.'

'Why did you go to the slaughterhouses, dear?' She asked this as though she wished to give me time, to fill the moment, so that I could again gather myself into coherency. But the more she spread her being through me, the more I was dispersed.

'There is a man living in South India, Professor Ramaswamy. He's campaigning to have the transport and slaughter of animals improved. He asked me to help because I am president of Animal Liberation in NSW. He took me and showed me...'

And I began to cry, and I could not speak, because all her love was mixed with all the hate, the blood, the violence, the suffering of the animals which I had witnessed. And all the tears which I had controlled, and which I had not shed at all, suddenly began to flow uncontrollably and the crying would not stop, and it continued for a long time, while the great being just sat, quite blissfully and serenely. Then, finally, when the crying had finished, Vimalaji spoke.

'You shed tears for the state of the world,' she said. Again she was silent, and then she said, 'My tears have dried, but your tears have not yet dried. When I was young,' she said, 'I campaigned against the cruelty of the slaughterhouse. I know exactly how you feel. It is caused by religion. Religion is the root cause. But you can do something. You can fight for change.'

'But it is so entrenched, and I don't live in India.'

There was more silence which endured continuously and seemed never to end. Then from the depths of her being came words. 'You will return to India to work for animals,' the words said.

I did not answer. I was washed clean. I could no longer speak. Everything seemed glorious. There was much time which was empty and not filled. Everything stopped and started continuously so that the world was just jerks and pieces taped in place.

'I have read your books,' I said. 'I have tried to observe myself but I cannot control the thoughts.'

There was silence during which she assessed and assembled information without doing anything at all. She seemed to have vanished, to have abdicated to some other, more substantial world, leaving myself sitting in isolation on the stone verandah with the hills and purpleness all splashed and scattered below.

When time had gone, and come again, and marched on the spot, and then run away, she said, 'There are three stages. First you watch yourself, and then this watching will melt into the state of observation. The thoughts will melt away, and you will enter the Silence. In the state of Silence, many Energies are activated. The Energy of Life will be perceived. It is like growing older. It happens gradually and the difference between the stages is not pronounced.'

I did not understand at all. I felt out of depth, confused. There were many things I had wanted to ask, but none of them seemed important now, so I just apologised again, and said, 'Well, I should go.'

Vimalaji did not resist this offer, but merely continued to brood, to be the receptor and transmitter of some magic, which came from hats and wands. And I felt myself be nothing and just a bubble in consciousness, which would burst and vanish at any time. I was crass and noisy, like fax machines that always emit, even if ignored and left in a corner. I was a weeping, demanding, eternally voicing person, that babbled and judged and was so preoccupied with the noise of life that I had never stopped to listen.

'Well, I will go,' I said, once more, feeling uncomfortable and insignificant in what I realised to be a moment of great import. I did not know then that this meeting, the sparking of fires, the touching of radiance on unseen levels, at that precise stopping in time, would alter and affect whatever had been and would be. There was an extraordinary inevitability, an unavoidable flowing, a dance, in which Christine was just a blown point.

I remained, however, an embarrassed human, shocked by the immensity of my intrusion, by the way I had marched in, uninvited, stomping, weeping, flinging myself in front of this enormous monument to stillness, babbling and uncontrolled, disturbing what may have been prayers for the universe and movements of history. So I looked at my feet, which were dirty, in dirty sandals, and apologised for weeping, and went.

Vimalaji did not stop me going, but merely continued to be vacant in the pond of deepness, sunken in her chair, with the view behind of distant hills and winding roads, and India, with haze and purple.

It was dusk, and I returned to my hotel room. It was winter. People were going home. This ancient pilgrimage centre, where sadhus once came to meditate in seclusion in the caves surrounded by forest, had later become a hill station for the British, and now tourist resort, with shops, hotels and taxis which blew horns, with shouting men leaning from windows of jeeps.

I could not ever be happy again, it seemed, because of the way the cattle would die. I could not know how any creator could allow such suffering to those that supposedly were loved. If creation entailed the invention of such murderous, greedy, fiendish animals as humans, it seemed hardly worthwhile at all. The dreaming philosophising of the Upanishads seemed unable to answer this most fundamental question. Although doubtless it was written somewhere in inscrutable Sanskrit, the words would have been meaningless to me anyway, because of my bitterness. Everything that I had accepted because it seemed sensible, now appeared too grand, too lofty, to abstract to address the immediate urgency of life.

I sat on the bed in the hotel room. I closed the door and the window to shut out the noise of traffic, and wrapped myself in some blankets. Then I thought, 'Who am I to understand anything? I know nothing, and never will know anything.' And as I thought this, I was weeping with the burden of my own worthlessness.

Then from outside, from some external source, something seemed to strike down at me, perhaps a sword. Immediately, I felt that I was being transformed into a column of fire and in this state I was able to see that I myself was God. In me resided all power, all glory, all answers, all triumph, all love, and all bliss. I was the source of the being of existence. All the world issued from Me, a universal unlimited nothingness. Its mistakes, its cruelty, its blunders, its destruction were just surface scratchings on the stillness of eternity. I was coming down from somewhere with everyone rejoicing because there was some being who had taken the gross material of the universe and decided to make it live. To make it live would involve suffering of this embryonic form, and the being would have to put all thought, all attention, all moments, all love, all will into the effort of making it grow. The purpose of making it live was not just so that it could know itself, but so that the very matter of which it was made would be transformed and elevated by the transmutation of growth.

I sat for a long time. I wondered whether I was just mad and deranged, and hallucinating. Perhaps it was the onset of dementia. Perhaps diarrhea and heat had affected me. And yet, because of this temporary but total transformation of my whole being, my whole nature, my whole mind and all my emotions, I could not accept that this event was just extraneous stimulus of errant brain-cells.

After a long time, which may have been hours, when I was earthly again, I walked through the streets. I seemed split in two, with that body which was called Christine crouching in reverence before the mighty radiance of the Self. I thought that everyone was staring because of my burning. I was so effulgent, I could not hide myself. Perhaps already my madness was being noticed in wild eyes, in lurid motions, even though I felt my body was just slipping and gliding in a quite unoteworthy way.

At the side of the road a man stood, selling small carvings in soapstone. Among his offerings, arranged on the top of a stone wall, was a miniature representation of Shiva, the creative and destructive aspect of the godhead, represented by a phallus, a thrusting, rounded white column. But what intrigued me most was that Shiva's vehicle, in the form of a small bull, knelt before him. This reverent, crouching animal worshipping something which was so great that it could only be represented by a symbol, seemed to explain my own experience exactly, for Christine's personality was like the bull which knelt before the flame of unlimited being.

And when I saw the carving I knew at once that I was not mad and raving, but that long ago some other Rishi, some other sage, had formulated this universal experience in art. So I bought the small piece for an exorbitant sum, because I was overwhelmed with gratitude that this poor man should stand here selling statues all his life, just so that I could walk past and know I was not mad.

I went back to my room and I read the *Mundakopanishad*. 'He is within our own hearts. He has lodged Himself in the food-sustained body of men and rules both body and life, even He that sustains the whole universe and all its glory. The unruffled spirits contemplate on Him and realise his deathless form of absolute joy.'

Then I was overwhelmed with gratitude that the knowledge of India could be there for anyone to read, and that it had said, and explained, that I was not an imagining hallucinator.

And I knew then that whatever I gave to India could not be enough, because I had been given more. And I somehow knew that the Silence of Vimalaji had been projected into me, so that I could know and understand that Silence in which she lived, that Silence which was the reality of life.

....

After my meeting with Vimalaji, I returned to Sydney and continued my work for Animal Liberation. During that time I had to give many talks to the rural community who resented the allegations that they did not care for their animals properly. On a particular occasion, I drove over 700 kilometres to a country town to speak to a farmer's organisation. I spoke to the meeting, comprising mostly of graziers, on the need for proper care and attention for Australian sheep, and referred to Christ's parable of the love of the good shepherd for his sheep. For some reason this talk particularly irritated the audience. And, as I drove home the next day I began to realise that I was losing interest in the work which I had been voluntarily doing for over fifteen years. I wanted to investigate Vimalaji's Teachings. I wanted to know this point of consciousness which was called Christine. I wanted to verify whether it was really true that by following certain practices one could enter some unknown state called 'silence', and another state called 'meditation'. Obtaining agreement from my husband, I rented a small fibro cottage in the Blue Mountains, about two hours' drive West of Sydney. I had set aside two weeks to begin the exploration, the inquiry, into the reality of life.

The cottage was located in Leura, and there were veiws of
ancient valleys, and worn rocks, and crushed blue forest, and
vastness and the streets were silent and swathed in mist, and
there were roses in gardens and wooden archways with
clematis and green lawns, and fat dogs on leads.

I wanted to experiment for myself, to discover through my
own experience whether enlightenment was possible. I had
nothing left, no alternative, but to accept the word of
Vimalaji and Diana that such a state could be obtained, and
that it was obtained through constant self-observation. I felt
very much alone, and I speculated that the rest of my family
and most of my colleagues would have thought I was crazy if
they had known what I was doing.

But then I thought about Diana, and about Vimalaji, about
how they were hidden, and even some people who met them
did not recognise what was within them. And I thought about
the long history of spiritual inquiry which had originated in
India thousands of years ago, when great sages had taught
the ancient wisdom which was later recorded by their
disciples in the Vedas and the Upanishads. Nobody knew
when these teachings were first given, but the latest date
which historians gave was five thousand years. Tradition had
it that when the Aryan people swept down into India,
perhaps from Europe, and established a sophisticated
civilisation in the Indus Valley, great sages had emerged
from the Himalayas, where They lived in retreat, in order to
share Their understanding of life with these people, who
were to become the repository of this esoteric truth, to hold
it, on behalf of the world, despite whatever might dim or
submerge it, so that it remained a hidden light, forever
waiting to be uncovered once more.

And it seemed to me that despite the pollution, the crush of
traffic, the chase for material well-being among the affluent

middle class of India, there was still this hidden spirituality to be found. But it was not to be found among the fake gurus who stood up and did *namaste* [2] in front of adoring, swaying fans, like movie stars, but it was there, hidden, to be found in the true realised beings, who never proclaimed themselves, never advertised themselves, in fact, often even veiled their personalities to hide their shining radiance, so that they looked like ordinary humans, and could not be distinguished from the crowd, from the ocean of living beings that swarmed across the soil of India.

So I sat in the mouldy cottage on a mattress which smelt of marmite, perfumed by the sweat of too many bodies, and I tried to look at myself, so that my body and mind and being was outside and separate from the point of consciousness which was observing.

At this stage of my life I had no understanding of the term 'enlightenment'. I did not even comprehend that Vimalaji's terminology of 'inner revolution' and 'total transformation' related to the same process. I had studied the Theosophical literature, and the books of Alice A. Bailey. She was an Englishwoman, and the knowledge contained in those books had been dictated to her telepathically between the years 1925 to 1950 by a Tibetan Master dwelling in the Himalayas, whom she had met through unusual circumstances[3].

In these books - an interpretation of the ancient wisdom written for Western readers - enlightenment had been given the name of 'transfiguration', or the 'third initiation'. Due to the fact that many of the states of consciousness and structures of the psyche simply do not have words in English

---

[2] Indian traditional greeting in which the palms of the hands are pressed together, much as in prayer.
[3] Bailey, Alice A., *The Unfinished Autobiography*, Lucis Press, U.S.A., 1973.

to describe them, the Tibetan Master had drawn upon
Sanskrit terms, used from Vedic times[4] and also had
developed His own terminology or code-words as a short-hand.
This meant that it was easy for readers to take His
words at their face value, rather than look for the meaning behind the symbol. This was exactly what I had made the mistake of doing. Later I learnt that Vimalaji also had a set
of code-words, and once these had been 'cracked', through relating them to one's own understanding, I began to see the depth
and brilliance of her Teaching.

But at this time, I still had the idea that enlightenment was
something that happened to the physical body. This was only
partially correct, and as long as I thought in this way,
although I did not know it then, I would remain stuck and
trapped in the sticky, matt, human separative consciousness.

According to the Tibetan Master, there were two initiations
'of the thresh-hold', the first being when a belief in 'God'
was born in the human heart. At this time control of the
physical body, usually indicated by awareness of physical
fitness, and a lack of interest in consumption of drugs,
alcohol and meat, together with sexual restraint, also
demonstrated. At the 'second initiation', control over the
emotional, or astral body was demonstrated, and the person
never again could be swept away by passions such as anger,
jealousy or fanaticism. However, it was the third initiation
which marked entrance into 'the kingdom of God', in which
the human became a 'soul-infused personality', an
enlightened being. This was my simplistic understanding of
the situation, and, although correct in a superficial and a

---

[4] *The Vedas* are the recorded teaching of great spiritual Masters or *Rishis,*
who lived and taught in ancient India many thousands of years ago. The
exact date of origin of these scriptures is not known.

technical way, it entirely missed the essential point, which was that the third initiation involves a transformation in the psyche, in the soul or consciousness, and therefore a loss of all sense of personality, all sense of 'me' and 'I' and ego. I did not understand that according to Vimalaji's Teaching it was not something which the body/mind called at birth 'Christine' could cause to happen. All she could do was to make conditions conducive to its eventual occurrence.

However, a knowledge of the technicalities of 'initiation' was something that was probably required in any case, for it was necessary to understand the invisible structure of a human being, the structure that would undergo change as a natural result of enquiry, of the search for truth. Those who had studied the powers of the mind and the consciousness over thousands of years, and who had documented their findings, had always talked of a second physical body, now being identified by science, sometimes called an etheric body, an electrical force-field which interpenetrated the gross material body, and which was the prototype of which the heavy muscles and bones, nerves and organs, gelatinous eyes and fleshy tongue were just a crystallisation, a poor and weighty duplication.

When blocks and misdirections of the flow of energy through the etheric body occurred, sickness then manifested in the gross material body. The science of acupuncture, developed so many centuries ago, used the principles of knowledge of the flow of the *prana* or life-force, or the electrical energy of this etheric, invisible, but physical body, to treat illness in the gross physical body.

According to the Tibetan Master's teachings, and the Theosophical literature, the invisible, etheric body consisted of a web or network of interwoven threads of energy in the region at the top of the head, of which the fontanel was the symbolic physical representation. During the process of psychic development, as a human being learnt to live in the state of meditation, the downflow of energy from the spirit and the upflow of the energy, (the *prana*, or *shakti* as it is often called in India) which had rested dormant in the etheric body, resulted in a rupturing or tearing of the web, sometimes rapid, and sometimes taking years or life-times. When this web was finally dissolved, the human being had achieved a continuity of consciousness, for he or she was consciously and continuously connected to the 'buddhic plane'. This buddhic plane was said to be the etheric body of the planetary logos, the Christian 'God', in whom we lived and moved and had our being. Later I was to understand that it was at this level or layer of electrical vibratory activity that 'at-one-ment' occurred, for if the individual could adjust to the tremendous velocity of this electrical force-field, this buddhic plane, this undivided, unending, eternal, infinity of universal consciousness, then there could never be separation again, then the sense of being a separate entity, a separate person would be forever lost, would fade away.

Once the conscious connection was established (through dissolution of the etheric web) then the individual had access to all the energies that were existent in the body of the planet. These were the material expressions of that creative Intelligence. They were not Intelligence itself, but emanations of that Absolute Intelligence, that Absolute Ground of Existence. The Spirit or Father in Heaven, as Christianity termed it.

The destruction of the 'etheric web' (an old-fashioned and clumsy term, but I know of no other) had several consequences, the least important being the development of supernormal powers, and Vimalaji frequently stressed in her books that these powers could actually be a deterrent and a block to further progress, if the person became absorbed in the wonder and glory of their manifestation.

Indeed, I suspect it was for this reason that Vimalaji never mentioned such things as 'etheric web', or serpent power, or 'kundalini', for these were all the sensationalised words which could attract people to the glamour of enlightenment, obscuring the true meaning, the true purpose, which was for the individual psyche to become universalised, and thus to lose its sense of personal identity.

The esoteric importance of the destruction of the 'etheric web' was that at last in the physical (but invisible) structure of the human, there was no longer an obstruction, no longer a gap in consciousness between soul and body/mind, there was no longer a fluctuating state in which the individual sometimes felt separate, and sometimes felt connected to the Unicity. The electric Fire of Spirit, with which the soul was already linked, could flow directly into the body, emotions and mind of the human, and with that downflow of universal, infinite Intelligence, the individual person lost all sense of ego, for it was now a movement of the Cosmic Intelligence that took place through and in the bodies of the person.

Yet this was only one way of explaining the process. Viewed differently, it could be understood and visualised with different symbols and descriptions, and, I was later to learn that the technicalities were secondary to the sense and feeling, the inevitable determined and dedicated seeking, which drove the inquirer onwards to the goal, for, in the final analysis, the mind and knowledge had nothing to do with the search. The search, the endless questioning, the constant adjustment of understanding, the ceaseless probing of the psyche, sensing and identifying changes in consciousness, shifts in perception, dimensions of awareness, forsaking that which had been useful, and moving into new fields of endlessness, like opening windows which had been sealed with dust, pushing and nosing like a dog, following one's instinct, desperately smelling one's way, using all the inbuilt equipment of one's being, in an almost frantic, totally determined search for the clues, feeling, tuning and re-tuning, as the dog locates indication after indication that he has found the route home, never fully understanding, always surprised, wonder-struck and amazed, the comprehension following the experience, and the previous knowledge then becoming understandable.

And thus, in my first feeble attempts as a sniffing dog, in my fortnight alone in the Blue Mountains, I puzzled over Vimalaji's books and words, desperately seeking direction as to what to do, what process to follow, how to best proceed. I did not even quite understand what it meant to observe oneself, yet this was her recommended starting point.

'You cannot do without this psyche, the conscious, the sub-conscious, the unconscious. We cannot destroy it; we cannot wish it away. We cannot fight it out. It is going to be there,' Vimalaji had pointed out[5]. I read these words again and again, and realised that this was an important clue. It seemed that I, Christine, did not have to make an effort to transcend my human nature, my human mind and emotions, but rather that I needed to understanding the nature of bondage, as

---

[5] Thakar, Vimala, *Towards Total Transformation*, New Order Publishing, Ahmedabad, 1970; 23.

limited by and attached to the structure, body and mind, which was called Christine.

'When a person dies, that is to say, the body is dead, the death of the body does not mean destruction of those vibrations that were floating around in the ether. They are there. Your predominant, basic fundamental *vasanas*, fundamental thoughts are there,' Vimalaji has explained. 'If there is an urge to set oneself free of this unending cycle of birth and death due to unfulfilled desires and thoughts, what do you do? You learn to live without the movement of thought [6]'.

Vimalaji had explained that one's individual memory was, in fact, merely a part of the collective and racial memory, using the Sanskrit term *parabdha*, that which has been begun before, which was set into motion before, to explain how each person had appropriated a small part of the universal consciousness, for which that person had responsibility. 'If you make silence – that inner, unconditional relaxation, your abode, and if the consciousness is there in the emptiness and responds whenever necessary in such a way that it does not create any new attachments, any new bondage for itself, then there is nothing left to be reborn. That is why it is said that the person who lives in the state of meditation puts an end to the cycle of birth and death [7]', she had said.

Vimalaji had also explained that to seek enlightenment, to lock oneself away at a certain time of one's life, was not selfish at all, but indeed a contribution to the world:

---

[6] Thakar, Vimala, *Through Silence to Meditation,* Vimal Prakashan Trust, 1998; 29-30.
[7] *ibid;* 32.

By allowing a psychic mutation to occur in our beings, we
would be reducing one area of violence from the globe. By
offering our life for that psychic mutation to take place, we
might be creating a living cell of a new life-style, a new way
of living. We might be setting into the orbit of human
consciousness a spark of love and compassion. So let us not
forget that we are embarking upon the adventure of a religious
enquiry, not for petty little self-centred ambitions of
cultivating kundalini power, shakti patha and having astral and
occult experiences. But we embark upon that enquiry on
behalf of the whole human race.[8]

The process of psychic mutation, of liberation began,
according to Vimalaji, with the ability to be able to sustain
the state of Silence, defined by her as 'non-action of the ego,
the total relaxation of the 'self', the 'me.' To enter the
dimension of Silence was a tremendous step on the path of
human evolution, it seemed, for a radical change in the way
life in the world was perceived, was viewed, came about in
the first moment that the dimensional shift occurred. Silence
was not 'meditation' yet - it was the discontinuity of the
movement of knowledge, experience and all the garbage and
junk which we dragged with us through life, which we held
in our chattering minds, in our trembling emotions.

I stared out the window. There was a wind, and leaves were
blowing. There was electric air. I found it almost impossible
to observe myself. I walked down the street, and I was
confronted by the vast hole of the Jamison Valley, shaped as
though a giant caterpillar tractor had gauged great scoops of
earth from a cosmic mining site. The canopy of eucalypt
forest thrown like a sheet over the black hole, sunken in the
middle, with lumps here and there, shimmered and was sharp
and brilliant, dazzling with wind.

---

[8] *ibid*; 49.

I was still struggling to understand the complexities of Vimala Thakar's books. What was Silence? To reach this Silence, did she mean that a person just watched their own behaviour whenever they remembered to do so, and then, in moments of reverie, analysed the antics of this ego? Did she mean that self-observation was merely a method of being detached, of viewing life without emotional involvement? Or was it something more intense, more sustained, than this?

'Life is a mystery that contains Silence which is free of movement,' Vimalaji had written. 'Silence is the total negation of movement. Life contains that silence, that stillness, that state of unconditional freedom from movement or motion, and it also contains mind, which is constantly moving[9].'

'Silence which is free of movement,' she had said. I thought about that statement for many hours. It seemed that she was implying there was a state beyond the mind, where there was not the movement of thought. The state of silence must have been greater, or wider, than the mind itself. I thought of what Gurjieff had said:

> You can know consciousness only in yourself. Observe that I say you can know, for you can know it only when you have it. And when you have not got it, you can know that you have not got it, at that very moment, but afterwards. I mean that when it comes again you can see that it has been absent a long time, and you can find or remember the moment when it disappeared and when it reappeared. You can also define the moments when you are nearer to consciousness and further away from consciousness. But by observing in yourself the

[9] Thakar, Vimala, *The Mystery of Silence,* Lectures held on the 5th, 6th and 7th of June 1976 in the Hoorneboeg, Holland, Bookfund Vimala Thakar.

appearance and the disappearance of consciousness you will
inevitably see one fact which you neither see nor acknowledge
now, and that is that moments of consciousness are very short
and are separated by long intervals of completely unconscious,
mechanical working of the machine...
..You do not remember yourselves... you are not conscious of
yourselves. In order really to observe oneself one must first of
all remember oneself.[10]

I had been spending many days watching my thoughts. In the
moments when the thoughts were truly observed, the person
called Christine became objectivised, became an outside
thing, a swinging appendage.

It was clear that the the thoughts were there, and they came,
but they were not necessarily something to do with Christine,
who herself seemed to be just a larger and more grotesquely
obstructive thought-form. The thoughts seemed to come
from outside, to blow towards one, to invade one's watching
consciousness. There was certainly a core within Christine
which was not touched by thoughts. If there was some part
of the mind which was not touched by thoughts, this must be
the unmoving part of consciousness, and the thoughts would
be the part that moved, the conditioned, habitual patterns
from the conscious and unconscious mind, from the
collective mind of the whole human race, from all of
accumulated history and culture and birth. What was there
before the thoughts came upon Christine? What would
happen to this consciousness when the thoughts were
stopped, when the consciousness was left in its unmoving
purity? This was what I wanted to discover more than
anything else in the whole world, and to discover it, the
experts had said, you had to observe yourself.

---

[10] Ouspensky, P.D., *In Search of the Miraculous,* Harvest/HBJ Book, USA,
1977; 116.

Again and again, throughout that first week in the small, cold fibro house, with the grey-green, rough, worn carpet, the cream fibro walls and ceilings, the stained beams running across the ceilings, the old, round Hallstrom fridge with the door which did not shut properly, so that you had to press a chair against it, the permanently dripping tap, and the vinyl, marble-patterned table with chrome legs, I struggled to bring my mind back to a state where it was watching itself. At first I could only remember to watch myself for a minute or so. I developed all sorts of tests and tricks to help me to remain alert. I would give myself 'tests' as to how long I could remain without a thought intruding upon the consciousness, or else I would offer 'rewards' of a tea-break after a new record in thought-absence had been achieved.

I noted that, in her books Vimalaji had emphasised that self-observation was not the same as concentration. In concentration one fixed one's attention upon a particular object, such as a candle and stared at it without letting other thoughts intrude. But in self-observation it was important not to attempt to bully the mind, not to do violence to the mind, she had explained. I noticed that this was correct, for as soon as I started to force my mind to stop watching thoughts, it became recalcitrant and its power seemed to grow. However, if I merely observed the thoughts, as I watched them they would begin to vanish, to evaporate of their own accord, like ash flying through air towards you melts as it is burnt.

Once I understood the difference between observation and concentration, I was able to objectivise the thoughts, and when they became objective, my mind seemed to be watching itself, to be watching the thoughts coming, and to be able to stop their advance. I began to challenge myself as to how long I could maintain this state of mind in which I kept all thoughts outside. I imagined that I was the one inside, and that the thoughts were flying towards me, and, by asking them politely not to enter my field of consciousness, they seemed to fade in the greyness of the space in which they floated.

I grew to know every crack on the wall which I sat and faced, grew to know the movement of the sun, how by eight in the morning it came through the kitchen window, by midday went behind the carport, and from two in the afternoon began to move across the living area, by four thirty vacating the house, which rapidly began to grow cold, necessitating additional jumpers and coats be added to the layers of clothing already extant.

As my skills in observing my thoughts began to increase, I decided to test whether I could walk round the block whilst at the same time observing myself. There was the smell of log fires, the mist, the green, wet gardens, the old wooden cottages which had been so lovingly restored with picket fences and English trees, with rhododendrons and azaleas and weeping cherries, and pine hedges. But none of this I noticed very much, for the mind was watching itself, it was absorbed in the attention of being empty.

But what was Silence? This was not silence. Christine was still Christine. I was still stuck in myself. I still had that sticky, human, captured feeling. I was still a mind, a human mind, which had simply learnt a new trick. It was interesting but not sensational.

Then, suddenly, when I was sitting on the kapok cushion one afternoon I seemed to pop out of myself, and occupy another place, somewhere above, in another removed dimension. There was no word that could describe the event. It was utterly unlike any experience I had ever known before. I was lifted, and entered a completely different range of consciousness in which the whole phenomenal world seemed far away, and I, aloof and detached from that world, gazed blissfully at the events and appearances which seemed to be occurring behind glass, far away. So this was the Silence that Vimalaji had described! It was so qualitatively different a perception that it was easily identifiable, and yet all words, and all descriptions seemed completely inadequate and totally useless.

And I saw that it was called Silence because although everything was still there, and although everything was still making all the noises that were made before, and although I was perceiving all the noises, they seemed to come from far, far away, like whale calls echo through ocean.

I was filled with a sense of incredible power. I could do anything, know anything, be anything. I was perceiving life in a radically different way. Nothing was the same as before. It was like staring at a 3-D picture. All the patterns, all the shapes were the same, but suddenly the flat, matt texture of the page turned into a deep, vibrant, radiant picture which, although seen with the same eyes, on the same page, was entirely different. The deeper radiance was hidden within the external pattern. I was exultant, amazed, and deeply surprised.

An extraordinary exhilaration filled my being because I had, of my own accord, and by means of my own effort and endeavour, verified what Vimalaji and Diana had described. I had proved privately and to myself that there was another state of consciousness beyond the human. I hypothesised that this state was that in which one thought and acted as a soul, rather than as a personality. The soul, or psyche, the consciousness, could either identify with the movement of thoughts, the bright, lively patterns of material life - it could be drawn to that colourful world of events, or, it could 'wake', it could know itself as it was, as the son of the father, a pure, reflective magnetic field which beamed down the electric fire of spirit into the world of form. I saw I was that Soul, that Angel of the Presence, and not at all Christine.

Over the following day the feeling gradually faded, and the usual state of human consciousness returned. I continued to struggle to again return to the Silence. As I managed to maintain the state for longer periods, I noticed an extraordinary phenomenon, an unknown feeling had become perceptible. It seemed to permeate all my being, all levels and layers of existence. I felt it in my body, as though every muscle was being massaged by gentle hands, as though I was standing under a waterfall, the gentleness of the falling water tingling on my bare skin. It was a delicate, stroking, blissful, tangible tenderness. I did not know how the feeling had come, nor what it was. I had not expected it, nor anticipated it, nor did I now understand it.

Initially I thought that it was an activisation of endorphins, releasing opiate-like substances into the brain, due to my own mental gymnastics. But there was an added quality, an additional note, an addendum, an inseparable component which came complete with the physical blissfulness and relaxation. I knew that this Energy was all-pervading, eternal and infinite. It was an inseparable Love which permeated and interpenetrated all levels and layers of the being, physical, emotional and mental. How could I know that it was something that had always been there, and would always be there, and I had simply not noticed its existence before? I had no idea. I was perplexed and awed by the sacredness of its touch. I called it the 'One Unicity'. It was a feeling only. It was a perception perhaps, or an awareness. It could be felt only when one entered the Silence. There was nothing I could say about it except that it was THERE. It WAS, and It was in me!

I walked through the bush. There were crumpled rocks with moss, and small streams with ferns. There were tiny birds which appeared on branches, and disappeared, and then were somewhere else. There were twisted banksias trees with frayed attempts at flowers, and everything was ancient, and paused, and singing, and I was just a person who touched, and went, while the great saga of evolution, of muds and heavings and thrustings of life, shaped the landscape. It was time for me to go home. I stared at the ancient rock cliffs, the blue valley far below. I had to return to the world, and I did not know if I could maintain the new state of consciousness that I had discovered over the previous two weeks.

But my understanding was still too limited, too narrow, to be able to grasp the true implications of what I had experienced. Whilst the practice of self-observation had succeeded in connecting Christine to something great and all-inclusive, which I had felt and perceived in every muscle and nerve of my being, I was as yet unable to interpret my experience, nor to relate it to the place and circumstances in which I found myself working and living in the world. So long as I thought of myself as an individual soul, as an individual existence, I remained trapped in the swinging, swaying mess and muddle of colour and noise and action which constituted the phenomenal, material world. Without understanding, the experience was null and void.

I had made the mistake of thinking that nirvana, that Samadhi, could somehow be captured and tamed by the mind, that you could still be a person, and at the same time liberated.

. . . .

Having touched, however briefly, that infinite, all-pervading Energy, I now began to arrange my life so that it consisted of a series of guilty escapes where I ran away whenever I could, either to my mother's unit on the north coast, to empty flats or to vacant rooms. These periods of retreat contributed to my understanding, but, as I was later to discover, I had to pass through many changes and upheavals, before I could again confront the nothingness of Christine.

It happened that, in 1989, whilst in England with Jeremy, my husband, on an animal welfare visit, I had contacted Crystal Rogers, an Englishwoman in her eighties, who had founded a small animal shelter in Jaipur, called Help in Suffering.

I well remember that meeting. She was a thin, autocratic woman, with penetrating eyes, and wavy white hair.

'Call me Mishy,' she said, 'That's the name everyone calls me in India. If you call me Crystal I feel like a film star.'

I asked her about the shelter, and she was friendly and remote, seemingly in another world of dust and dogs. How I envied her, that she had been able to spend so much of her life in India, working for animals, and how I longed that she would suggest to me that I might like to help, but no such offer was forth-coming.

In 1990 Jeremy and I attended a conference of the World Society for the Protection of Animals in Basle. I wrote to Mrs. Janine Vogler, President of Animaux Secours, who had been raising money for Help in Suffering. She invited us to stay with her in Geneva, and to see her shelter, and, after the conference, we did just this.

Little did I know then how that meeting would change our lives. As we walked on the mountain with her, she explained to us her concern. 'Our society is still sending money to Help in Suffering,' she explained. 'But I am so worried. I don't know what is happening there. I cannot go myself to check, but the manager and his wife have left, Mishy is no longer there and I'm afraid that the animals are not in a good condition.'

Janine knew that I had made several trips to India, both with Professor Ramaswamy, and with Annabella Singh, who was a director of the World Society for the Protection of Animals. I am not quite sure how it happened, but I agreed to go to Help in Suffering within a few months, to represent Janine, and to report to her as to the condition of the shelter, for she was reluctant to go to India herself.

I found the shelter was run-down, with dying puppies and dogs lying in excrement. Upset, I rang Janine, who suggested I could become managing trustee. She said she was not willing to send further money unless I was there. I met the Indian trustees, and in October 1990 Mishy signed a document which declared that Raja J.K. Atal and myself were now the Joint Managing Trustees of Help in Suffering.

In 1992 my husband Jeremy, resigned from his legal partnership, we sold our family home invested the money, and came to live and work as volunteers in India, in a small cottage in the grounds of Help in Suffering. In an unexpected and surprising way, Vimalaji's prediction had been fulfilled. And we were there, in Jaipur, in my beloved India, surrounded by animals, and their voices and their being, and now I was only twelve hours by bus from Mt. Abu, instead of seventeen hours by air. And I wondered whether I had come to this place so that I could be closer to Vimalaji.

CHAPTER TWO

AN INVESTIGATION OF SILENCE

There happened a marvel.
In between two thoughts
The austere beauty of
Sheer nothingness shone [1].

For eighteen months Jeremy and I were so busy establishing the shelter and setting up a spay-vaccination programme among the street dogs of Jaipur, that I had no time to sit in silence nor to visit Vimalaji. But finally the opportunity presented itself.

Jeremy and I went to Udaipur in October 1994, when we were contemplating establishment of a shelter there, and at that time I managed to persuade him to take me to Mt. Abu. Thinking about it now, it seems stupid that I had not written to Vimalaji to inquire as to whether she would be there, and I turned up at the office, to meet Kaiser Irani who was Vimalaji's personal assistant, and also editor and publisher of the books.

At that time I did not know Kaiser very well. She did not look very Indian. She was tall, with a fair skin, and spoke fluent English. She kept herself in the background, and it was only later that I was to find out the pivotal role she played in bringing Vimalaji's books before the public, and in assisting with arrangements for the large numbers of visitors who constantly streamed to *Shiv Kuti*.

---

[1] Thakar, Vimala, 'The Beauty of Nothingness', *Friendly Communion*, Vimal Prakashan Trust, Ahmedabad, 2001; 34.

Kaiser explained to me that Vimalaji was holding talks each day for a group of people who had come from Norway to hear her speak on various matters which had been submitted in the form of written questions. Only with their permission could Jeremy and I listen to the talks. Kaiser agreed to ask them on my behalf, and kindly, they gave permission for two strangers to participate. Again, I had crashed in when I had not been invited. Again, I was welcomed.

Jeremy and I sat in the room with a group of perhaps twelve Europeans. It was a very large, very cold room, for it was winter. Along one wall were glass-door bookcases containing hundreds of books. At the front an *asana*, or meditation divan, was arranged with a microphone and recording equipment. Those who had come to hear sat either cross-legged on the floor, or on chairs behind.

Soon Vimalaji entered. It was over four years since I had first met her. I was full of my own importance, of the magnificent and sacrificial work I was doing, and of the great spiritual achievement of having touched and felt the Infinite Unicity which surged through my being from time to time.

Vimalaji did not appear to notice anyone in the room, and seating herself on the *asana*, indicated to Kaiser to turn on a cassette. The sound of serene and haunting classical music of India filled the room, and we sat in silence for about fifteen minutes until Vimalaji began to speak.

She spoke very slowly, very clearly, in fluent and articulate English, with a compelling magnetism. She talked for more than an hour without once referring to notes, without once hesitating, although often she appeared to sink into silence, and be temporarily absent from the room. It was only much later that I was to realise that I was still viewing Vimalaji through the veil of all my own prejudices and limitations. I saw in her at that time what my own restricted consciousness allowed me to see. I still thought then that she was a human who had done something incredible and somehow become enlightened, and that as she knew the secret, she was able to impart it to others, was able to be a real teacher through her own experience.

She began by saying that she was fortunate indeed to have been asked the question by the group of Norwegian friends, which was 'How can we change ourselves instead of trying to escape from the realities of life[2]?'

'...When you ask yourselves how can we change, it is better to go to the fundamental and see that the 'I' consciousness, the 'me', the self, the ego cannot be changed. It is not like organ transplantation, human organs are transplanted, new ones are grafted. A new 'I' cannot be planted. In other words, the content of your consciousness cannot be changed,' she began.

'Human consciousness has a content of conditionings. The 'I', the me, the ego is only the conceptual monitor of the structure. So the content of thought, the content of conditionings, the content of memory in ourselves cannot be changed. If you want to change from one pattern to another, that can be done, but that is changing the pattern, not changing yourselves. We must understand the implications of what we want to do.

---

[2] This talk was later to be published in *The Invincible,* Vol. XI, No. 1, Jan-March, 1995.

'The content of consciousness is thought structure. The 'I', the 'me', the self, the ego, has been there through the conditioning of millions of years. We are the products of human civilization, we are the products of human culture of millions of years. It cannot be changed in ten or twenty years. The conditionings are there in the physical structure, in the bone structure, in the muscular structure, in the glandular structure, in the nervous structure.

'...If these points are clear, please accompany me, let us take one step further. The content of thought structure, the content of memory, the content of consciousness – conditioned consciousness – cannot change. We can make any amount of efforts, but it is still there. So what will we do? It is a beautiful situation, if you really allow yourselves to come to that point. People do not allow themselves to come to the point of real crisis, they go on playing games with themselves, they exercise self-deception and therefore the crisis does not come.

'We are sitting in this room, a handful of us, let us imagine that you and I are at that point of crisis. We are convinced, we have seen, we have understood, we have realised that the content of consciousness, the conditionings of millions of years contained in the blood stream, in the nervous system, cannot change. What is the alternative left to us? Is there an alternative? I dare say: 'Yes, there is.' That alternative is to allow the whole content – the sensual system, the verbal system – the whole momentum to relax completely into non-action. We are not asking it to change; we are not asking it to acquire anything.

'... I am exploring another way of living where there will be
no desire to escape, where there will be meeting life as it
comes, not rejecting anything, not running from anything. .

'... Whatever time you can spare, please do sit ... if you are
thus seated, then whatever comes up – the content of
memory – gets exposed to your perception. Let them get
exposed, you are not there to change them, but you are just
perceiving – not as an act of will, but there is a perceptive
sensitivity. Life is an energy that has perceptive sensitivity.

'So there is exposure, which is a movement of the past. You
have not voluntarily brought it about, you are not related to
it, your conscious effort is not related to it. It comes up on its
own and, being alive, you have the perceptive sensitivity...
Please do understand with me, because if is a perceptive
sensitivity. Seeing understanding, hearing the sound – all
these are the movements of life wherever it is. So when you
sit down quietly, close your eyes and you allow the exposure
of the unconscious, subconscious to take place, then without
your conscious effort, the seeing also takes place.

'What does such a seeing lead to? The seeing, the
perception, point out to your Intelligence the details of the
contents, the details of your conditionings which you had
never seen before. You had read about them but you had
never seen them before. In yourself, the lust, the sexual
obsession, the violence, the kindness, the gentleness, the
pettiness, the excellences, the weaknesses – everything
comes up. When you sit before a mirror the mirror carries
the reflection of what you are, in the same way when you sit
there quietly with yourselves you get acquainted with the
factual content of yourself. There is not silence yet, but a
quietness, peacefulness, steadiness is there. No images,

nothing, because you are alone there. If you allow such an encounter to take place, then throughout the day when you are with people, you will be conscious of the anger, you have seen how it has come up and do not allow the anger to spoil your relations. So the first thing would be that the quality of your relationship will go through a change without an effort of the will. This encounter and exposure brings about a change in your behaviour without your knowing. My friends, this is what Vimala had gone through some thirty to forty years ago. Perception is a tremendous, powerful act. It is not a casual seeing, it is not a casual looking it is a total action. It is a movement of your total being.

'Now in that encounter day after day you see the repetition of certain thoughts, desires, tendencies. You see them day after day and you realise that the memory, the thought, the conditioning, contains repetitive, mechanistic movement and then the identification, the attachment to the past disappears because you are not interested in repetitive, mechanistic things. Mechanistic repetition has no glow of life, they have no warmth of life, so attachment to them disappears without renouncing anything. You do not have to go in for renunciation, you do not have to decide and say: 'Ah, I'm now going to be detached'. There is no attachment, there is no detachment. You know what is what, and therefore a new relationship with your own consciousness, with the content of consciousness, comes about. When there is no attachment to the content, when there is no identification with the content, then the past – the conditionings, the memories, the thoughts – lose their grip. This is the third thing that happens.

'Friends, when such a total exposure and encounter is gone through, nothing more remains to be seen. The contents have been seen, therefore their movements suspend themselves. Everything has been seen, you do not act upon it, you do not even touch it; Therefore there is a cessation, a discontinuity of the exposure and a beautiful silence comes to life. A beautiful, spontaneous, total relaxation of the conscious, sub-consciousness, and the unconscious does happen. If it has happened here,' she said, gesturing towards her own body, 'It can happen there. Those who allow the mutation to occur in their lives, it is bound to be there. It is a scientific thing. It is not the privilege of any individual.

'Now there is Silence – not the steadiness, the quietness. The undisturbed placidity that was there is the beginning of a new quality of Silence. Nothing to be seen, therefore the perceptive sensitivity also subsides. No seer, and no seeing, and seen. It is a beautiful state of Silence. It is the state of your Wholeness.

'If you are really interested in changing yourself, then allow the Silence to come to life in you. There is the release, the activisation of energy, a new vitality. Everything will happen by itself. You have to take the step of giving yourself an opportunity and going to the point where Silence comes to life in you. That unconditioned energy is not like the 'I', the 'me', the ego. It has nothing to do with civilization or culture, it has no biological or psychological inheritance; It is born of Silence. It is born of Emptiness. It is virgin in every individual, the energies born of Silence in you are unique to yourself.'

When she had finished speaking, as the roomful of people sat, immobile and unspeaking, purged by the velocity of her words. I felt ecstatic, elevated, and I wanted the magic, the serenity and bliss contained in that protected room to continue forever. I did not want her to leave. I did not want to go back into the outside world and face the battles of India again. But Vimalaji gave a slight nod of her head, slipped from the *asana*, and left the room quickly, before anyone had a chance to speak.

Kaiser was standing outside on the verandah, helping someone with arrangements for repair of recording equipment. I was so full of myself. I thought that I had reached that state of Silence, I had tasted it, and I was superior to the others for I had understood.

I asked Kaiser whether it would be possible for me to meet Vimalaji some time privately and ask her a question. She said she would ask Vimalaji, and would let me know the next day after Vimalaji's talk.

The next day Kaiser said to me, 'Vimalaji will see you after she has finished the camp. Until then, she wants only to think about the questions which these people have asked her to answer. Will you be able to wait for a few days?'

I said that we would be able to do so, and, after the camp had finished, Kaiser told me I could see Vimalaji.

After taking off our shoes, Kaiser led me up the stairs to the house. I had no fear. I thought I was clever, for I had located, and could feel, the One Unicity. I thought I was far in advance of everyone else. I was so interested in my own achievement that I took interest in Vimalaji only inasmuch as she could answer my question, and help me on my way.

'And how is Christine?' she asked.

'I'm very well,' I answered.

'And how is your work?'

'It's growing all the time.'

She was sitting in a small room which had several chairs at one end, and, behind the chairs there were some large windows which looked out over Mt. Abu, for the house was elevated, seemingly built on a rock outcrop.

At the other end of the room was a desk, with a few papers tidily placed, and behind this was a door which seemed to open into a large kitchen.

'Do you have something you wish to ask me?' Vimalaji said.

'Yes,' I replied. 'There's this feeling in my body. I don't know what it is. It feels like standing under a waterfall, the flesh tingling. It feels as though I'm being massaged all over, like this,' I said, in despair of being able to describe what it was that I felt, rubbing my legs with my own hands.

She did not answer immediately, but thought for some time before asking me a question: 'When did you first notice this feeling?'

'I began to notice it after I went away in 1989 and meditated in the way which you suggested.'

Again she was silent. 'Do you feel it all the time?'

'I only feel it sometimes. It comes and goes.'

'It is the Thatness,' the said. 'The Thatness is being felt by Christine.'

'I can't believe it,' I said.

'Why dear? What it is to not believe?'

'It seems so miraculous. One strives for this for so long, and it has happened.'

She smiled and said nothing. She must have realised there was so much I did not understand. She must have known, by some inexplicable means, that I was not yet ready to go further than this. Later, when I was to think about this meeting, and to regret the time I had wasted, I understood that there was a time for everything, and my time had not yet come.

. . . .

It was to be over a year before I again went to Mt. Abu in March 1995. Jeremy and I had met Kristin, a close friend from school days, in Udaipur, and then travelled together to Mt. Abu. On the afternoon that we arrived I went to *Shiv Kuti* and met Kaiser who remembered me. I asked her if Vimalaji had any groups whom she would be addressing, and Kaiser said no, but asked if I would like a private meeting. I answered yes, and Kaiser rang Vimalaji's house from the office below. She said that I could meet Vimalaji at nine the next morning.

Kristin and I arrived there a little before nine and soon were called up to her room. When I saw her sitting so composed and so serene on the low divan in the front room, my eyes filled with tears, and I saw from her penetrating glance that she had recognised my joy and relief from being again in her presence.

She asked how I was and I said, well, which was not correct, because at that time I had been suffering from stomach problems, and, being unable to eat much, had lost much weight. I introduced Kristin to Vimalaji, who smiled at her, and then asked me, 'And how is Christine's inquiry?'

I tried to explain: 'After having realised – I mean touched ....'

'Realised,' she corrected, smiling.

'After having realised that inner Silence, I feel there is this huge abyss between the outer world, which I have turned from, and yet am stuck in, for I just can't stay in the Silence during normal activities.'

I was feeling very shy and spoke with a soft voice, and she had to ask me to repeat myself.

She seemed to understand exactly what I was trying to explain, even though my words were so clumsy.

'You see, dear,' she answered, 'first there is the period of self-observation – this happened when you went away on retreat. Then there was the period when you first touched It, but now there is a period where you have to get to know It. Have your really explored it? Have you really got to know It?'

'Yes,' I answered, and then, 'No. When it comes it's effortless but the mind intervenes all the time. Maybe I should go away again to get to know it?'

She paused for a long time and did not actually answer this question. Much later, when I wondered why it was that she had not answered in the affirmative, and why I had wasted so many years rushing hither and thither, I realised that perhaps she had foreseen the future, had known what I still had to face, had understood that the time had not yet come to fruition.

After this, Vimalaji turned to Kristin and asked her how long she had been in India. Kristin replied, 'Only a few days. We met in Udaipur and drove here.'

'I'm sorry,' she said to us. 'I feel it must be so difficult for you. I can't hear your reply, but please don't think there's anything wrong with what you said. It's just the reoccurrence of an old ear injury from a car accident many years ago.'

Then there was a pause, and she asked me, 'Is there anything more that you want to ask? We have set aside an hour for Christine.'

'Would it be possible just to sit in Silence with you?' I asked.

'If only everyone who visited asked such a question,' she answered, smiling.

She asked Kaiser to take the phone off the hook, and to make sure that no-one interrupted.

'For how long do you wish to sit in silence?' she asked. 'I have set aside until ten for Christine.'

I looked at my watch, and saw that it was about quarter past nine, so, not wanting to be greedy, I suggested quarter of an hour.

'Please sit comfortably,' she said. 'Move the cushions as you wish.'

So Kristin sat on the floor and I sat facing Vimalaji across the small room. If I opened my eyes I could see her still serene face. But I felt absolutely no self-consciousness and immediately sank into bliss and tried to learn to understand everything she was communicating to me which was basically to glorify, so it seemed to me then. We were mutually rejoicing. Neither could stop and it was quarter to ten when I opened my eyes and saw her eyes were already open.

Then she said to me, 'Thank you for the wonderful gift you have given me.'

I was feeling very depressed and stressed at this time, and it seemed extraordinary to me that a realised being who pushed and pummeled everyone who came into her presence with wavings of love, could even hint that I had given something to her. Her humility, her encouragement, her compassion filled me with a new confidence which, at least temporarily, replaced the feeling of insecure failure which had been haunting me over recent months.

I mumbled in response, 'Oh no, it is I who have drunk from you.'

'How long as you here for?' she asked, as we stood up to go. And it was in this moment that she gazed from the profundity of her eyes into the eyes of Christine, so that it was nothing to do with jelly and aqueous fluids and retinas, but more a meeting, a transmission between some other, higher sheets and drapings.

'Three more days, I think,' I croaked from fields of other places. And then I wondered if I could ask her if I could return for another session. But I knew that did not need it for she had already given me everything, and we left without speaking further.

Afterwards, outside, I asked Kristin whether she had thought that Vimalaji had said I should go away alone on retreat. 'I don't think she did say that,' Kristin commented. 'She could see you were very stressed.'

And this remark of Kristin's made me realise that I was nothing, and just at the beginning and before I could do anything else, I had to learn to be serene like Kristin, who was able to enjoy life, and not want anything at all.

. . . .

By now, my attitude towards Vimalaji was beginning to change. I longed to be with her, but it was still out of a selfish motive, for every time I met her I was filled with an ecstatic bliss which lasted for days. I suspected that she deliberately 'injected' this energy of love into my being. But apart from my first meeting with her in 1989, I remembered most vividly the after-math of a meeting I had with her in December 1996.

I had taken a room in a hotel nearby and had been reading the book, *Ego*[3] I had found the answer to one of the questions of my inquiry – why should the state of Observation or Awakeness be called 'silence' when there was in reality not silence, but the perception of that blissful stream of massaging love, which was felt in the skin, the bones and the flesh. This was not a silence, but a state of communion, in which the Energy seemed to fill the being with love.

> You call it emptiness because thoughts do not move. We have equated the whole consciousness and the content of consciousness with thought, knowledge, experience, memory. So when that movement is discontinued, we call the other empty. It is a relative term. In that aliveness and alertness there is the flavour of awareness, which is not attention, attentivity . That alertness is not dependent upon yourself creating a subject, and trying to relate to the world as an object. IT is a non-subjective and non-objective state. It is a non-attentive alertness where there is no observation and no attentivity [4].

I could not equate these words with my own experience of a tingling, blissful sensation in the body, a sensation that some great void, some huge moving Presence that was existent in all material objects, penetrating and infusing all muscles, all flesh, all leaves and branches and stones and feathers. Vimalaji talked about 'unity of Life', of 'Wholeness of Life', of 'Intelligence'. I wanted to be able to apply these definitions, these terms, to the energies I was perceiving. I

---

[3] Thakar, Vimala, *Ego*, Vimalaji's informal Communion with Bombay Inquirers during Friendship Festival at Mt. Abu, 23-27 November, 1993, Vimal Parivar, Bombay, 1995.
[4] Page 16, *ibid.*

felt that unless I could correlate my own discoveries with her own, there would be no endorsement, no verification that I was moving in the right direction.

After a few days of sitting cross-legged on someone else's bed, with a puppy I had rescued, whining in the bathroom, I decided to see if I could make an appointment to meet Vimalaji. I walked up the road past the small stalls selling saris and lengths of cloth, cheap battery toys, and Kashmiri boxes. Kaiser was working in the office, in the same building as the meditation room, with an entrance from a verandah.

After we had exchanged greetings, Kaiser said that Vimalaji was ill with bronchitis, and could not see me.

'Will she go to a doctor?'

'She does not go to a doctor. She says that if she sits in total relaxation she will be healed.'

'I don't really need to see her,' I said to Kaiser, 'And I really don't want you to trouble her if she's not well.'

'If you come back tomorrow, I could let you know,' Kaiser said.

I still hardly knew Kaiser. To me she was someone friendly, but important, who should not be troubled by small details.

I returned the next day, and Kaiser said, 'You can see her, but you will not be able to ask questions. Vimalaji might not be able to answer.'

As I walked up the steps to Vimalaji's house I felt very afraid. Perhaps this fear was a result of the recognition of her power and sacredness, a recognition which had emerged gradually with the passage of time. But when I was shown into the room, and saw Vimalaji sitting deeply still, flowing with radiance, the fear vanished and my eyes filled with tears of relief to be in her presence once more.

As Kaiser had explained might be the case, Vimalaji did not speak, so I said, 'I would be happy to sit in silence in your presence if this would be alright'. So Vimalaji said, 'Wonderful,' in a voice that did not sound at all croaking or wheezing, and Kaiser and Vimalaji and myself sat together in silence for perhaps twenty minutes. Finally when I opened my eyes, Vimalaji also opened hers, and smiled at me in a way which penetrated every fibre of my being.

As I stood up to leave, Vimalaji asked, 'How is your work?' and I answered, 'It is expanding,' with a gesture in which I spread my arms wide. I did not want to say anything else, for I felt it was causing her pain to speak. It did not ever occur to me to ask after her health. I somehow assumed that because she was realised she would not suffer, and that she had all biological levels of health at her command. I thought that because she was superhuman, she was above and beyond all ordinary, mortal things. I had no understanding of the fact that a realised person still had to live in the world with whatever physical equipment happened to be available.

Then she asked me, 'And how is Christine within?' It took me a long time to respond. Kaiser turned and looked to confirm that I had heard the question, but then I replied, when the right words had come to mind, 'This individuality has not yet been dissolved.'

After a silence, Vimalaji asked, 'Why?' and I answered, 'I think I'm ambitious for liberation, and that this is wrong.'

'Is it ambitious? Or is it a desire from within to be with one's Source?' Vimalaji asked, and was smiling, and calm, and beaming everything that ever was collected through herself so that it was intensified and projected and overwhelming. Then there was some more silence, and she said, 'Look. It's Christmas time. My Christmas gift to you is to pray for your liberation. It will come.'

Then I mumbled, and said I could not thank her enough, and I felt that Vimalaji gave me answers in dreams, or in her books. Then Vimalaji held out her open hands to me, and I put my hands in those of Vimalaji, and she held my hands and everything from the whole of space and universes flowed into me. Stumbling from the room, dazed by the brilliance of light which filled the world, and all of Mt. Abu, I walked away. And it was then that the Fire descended.

I had made notes at the time:

> Now, while I have every answer within me I am going to try and describe It. It is absolute intoxicating love and tenderness which is so powerful and drenching that you are almost immobilised. It is hard to walk, hard to speak, because the love is everything. It is not the heart love, as it permeates all the nadis and whole body thrills to it. While this all-permeating bliss is pouring, It is all-absorbing, like being in love, but there is no "I" to be in love. It is simply an enveloping adoration that is poured into every atom of life. It is the dazzle inside everything. The words 'It doesn't matter' or any other thing to do with thought have no relevance in this state. Nothing means anything except for the pouring onto and through everything. It is there to perceive, has always been there,

but 'I' failed to merge in it. Now I know what merging
means. I had written a question to ask Vimalaji and this
is the total, final, complete answer:

. . . .

The brief realisation of a blissful inner union only served to
make the daily events of life with all their pressures and
difficulties more torturous and demanding. The
understanding of the condition of Oneness that could occur
in the being, only served to emphasise the uncomfortable,
circumscribed human consciousness and its limitations. I
knew now there was something more, yet it seemed to be my
dharma to work from morning to night at an animal shelter,
without any moment where I could sit alone, and thus my
life was dual, externally satisfied by the achievements of our
work, and internally empty and bereft.

In March 1998, while I was in a garden with friends, in
Kalimpong, in the foothills of the Eastern Himalayas, where
Jeremy and I had started a new animal shelter, I was
unexpectedly attacked by a large Tibetan Mastiff. These
dogs were traditionally used to guard the yak and mule trains
which came from Tibet with goods to trade, and were known
for their unpredictable and dangerous behaviour.

The dog came from behind and leaping into the air, seized
my neck and lower face in his mouth, crushing his jaws
together. I remember thinking that I did not want to have a
scared face for the rest of my life, but after that, I have no
memory of the events of the following few minutes.
According to those present at the time, I knelt down, and the
owner of the dog, fortunately remaining calm, called to the
dog, rather than trying to pull him away. If the dog had

shaken his head just once my neck would have been broken and the carotid artery would have been severed.

There were no proper medical facilities in Kalimpong, but the doctor to whom I was taken seemed to have been inspired by some miraculous luminosity and exhilaration. After initially refusing to stitch the wounds, because it is well-known that dog bites become infected and have to be left open to drain, he finally agreed that he would have to stitch the open tears or my face would be hideously scared. He poured bleach into the gaping wounds. He flourished scissors and needles with confidence, slicing off a flap of torn lip, throwing my very flesh into the waste bin.

However, I was not troubled at all by any of the events. I had a conviction that the outcome would be good, and I felt that I was completely removed from the body, looking down on the surprising events that unfolded. My dear friend, Aldona, a vet working at the animal shelter, who had healing powers, nursed me through the first few terrible days until I could return to Delhi. I was afraid I would lose my lower lip, and never be able to speak again properly, but Aldona passed her hands over my body, and I felt a tingling, like an electric current, and I believe through her spiritual gift she healed me.

After a few months when I had recovered from the shock of this attack, and my face had miraculously mended itself without the loss of my lip, I wrote to Vimalaji. In the letter I said that I believed that I was meant to die at that time, but that divine intervention had taken place, and I had been saved.

Vimalaji wrote back:

Dear Kaiser and myself were shocked to read about the attack
on you by the Tibetan mountain dog. We are very grateful to
Life that you have recovered so well and so fast.....I'm
keeping reasonably well and will be staying at Mt. Abu till the
end of 1998. Let us hope that you can carry on your life
mission with the same vitality as you had before the attack.
With warmest greetings, Vimala Thakar.

....

In Udaipur, I looked from the hotel room at the view of the
lake. I was filled with gratitude that I should be given this
two weeks alone. The lake was silver grey, with rows of
golden lights around the periphery and the hills behind were
olive green and grey in the fading sky, which had pink
streaks, and pale turquoise where clouds were meant to be.
The statue of Chetak, the warrior horse, stood illuminated on
a distant hill. The central island of grass and trees, white-
walled, seem to float in the grey water. In the gardens of the
hotel puppeteers were struggling to erect a coloured tent
against the evening breeze, and on the highest peak above
them the monsoon palace, a white and ancient castle, was
floodlit against the evening sky.

And then the morning came, and I went in a taxi to the bus,
and I took the bus, and it went along narrow roads, through
hilly, desolate country with stonewalls, and buffalo with hips
protruding. The bus driver's girlfriend, wearing a purple
polyester sari, sat in the front with him, and the bus driver
stopped to buy a garland of marigolds, which he placed in a
temple as an offering to the god, in order to ensure a safe
journey. There were thin white cows, and twice the bus

stopped at a dhabi where the passengers ate hot *roti* [5] and vegetables thick with chili.

And then the bus climbed the hill, and when it was evening I was in Mt. Abu, and I went to a hotel, which was cheap, which Kaiser had said was good, and I stood at the window, and looked, and had a headache. But most of all I was grateful that I could be here alone for two weeks, for I could see across the hill-tops, the very trees under which was the house in which Vimalaji lived.

I bought harpic and cleaned out the bathroom, and washed the floor. The walls also were dirty. It looked as though people had spat food on them, so it was necessary to clean them to remove the sticky brown collections scattered over the surfaces.

Anita, the cook, had set up a bed in the kitchen. Her comb and facial oil were ranged next to the cooking utensils. She put oil into a deep pan, and then threw in semolina, curry leaves, mustard seed, green chili and coriander. After it had been stirred for a while, she threw in water, and soon it thickened into a wonderful mixture. 'Upma,' she said, pointing to the contents of the bowl proudly. She then made chai by boiling together milk, sugar, tealeaves, fresh ginger and crushed cardamon seeds. I sat on a table outside the kitchen, enjoying the food. A man came and sat next to my, 'What is your country?' he asked. 'Do you like India?' Do you have a husband? Do you have children? When he had satisfied his curiosity he said that Mt. Abu was very sacred because in past times many holy men had lived in the caves and achieved *moksha*, enlightenment.

---

[5] Flat unleavened Indian bread.

During the ensuing week, I sat in silence from morning to night, taking off time only to eat my meals and to walk around the lake. But still I was making the mistake of imagining that I was an individual consciousness, a psyche, a soul, and that all Christine needed to do was transform herself from a body and become instead a glowing angel. I thought I had finally understood everything, and that I would become enlightened. And thus I was greatly mistaken, and still needed to understand much more.

There were many times during the fortnight when I underwent orgies of bliss, sunken in enraptured states of euphoria for hours at a time. But I knew that without understanding the meaning of these states, and without being able to allocate direction and meaning to the Energy which was perceived, without being aware of its origin and source, it was an ephemeral and empty experience.

This type of euphoric meditation had been described by the Buddha, for whom discernment was an important part of awareness or mindfulness. In the *Nibbana Sutta*, an important point was made that if a person remains beset with directed thought and evaluation, paying attention to perceptions dealing with sensuality, then 'that is an affliction for him.' Even when a person is 'beset with attention to perceptions dealing with rapture', it is not true *samadhi*. Even if the person enters and remains in the sphere of the infinitude of consciousness, and 'his mind is beset with attention to perceptions dealing with the sphere of the infinitude of space, and that is an affliction for him.' In fact, the *Nibbana Sutta* points out, 'even if the person is in the sphere of neither perception nor non-perception, dealing with the sphere of nothingness, that is an affliction for him.' So long as there was any trace of ego, any interpretation of any state, it was not the Thatness, it was not the Transcendental, not the Absolute Ground of Existence, but merely a body/mind interpretation of what Thatness might be, and therefore duality, and not Unicity.

As yet, I remained perplexed as to the correct discernment of the Energy which I perceived. I feverishly studied all Vimalaji's writings, and all parallel Teachings, including Alice A. Bailey and Sri Nisagadatta Maharaj, Paul Brunton, Sri Aurobindo, Ouspensky and Joel Goldsmith, and Sri Ramana Maharshi, all of whom I recognised as realised beings, and I thumbed through chapters, comparing paragraphs, staring into space, dreaming and puzzling over the complexities and meaning of the human structure and of the relationship of the mind to enlightenment.

I wandered down to Karnak Dining Hall for lunch. It was an old and shabby restaurant, full of worn wooden tables and chipped chairs. Between twelve and three a Gujarati Thali was served on a stainless steel tray with small dishes, placed before you. Waiters came and distributed generous servings of spiced vegetables, sweet smelling rice, pickles and desserts, and hot fresh breads. I watched a waiter run his finger round the lip of a serving bowl to clean it, and then shake off the gathered food on his finger, into the bowl.

I walked back around the lake. It was swathed in a monsoonal mist which cooled the earth, and veiled the paths and trees in that mystery which had once been jungles, and caves, and water and tigers, of towering rocks with ferns in niches. There was the sound of pumps raping the aquifers – a kind of monotonous droning, machine-like friction and as I walked I thought, and puzzled about the perceptions and experiences through which I was passing, and it was like an exam, or a deep philosophical exercise, to try to fit the understanding to the perceptions.

It was this Fire that I now wanted to know about. Was it the soul, was it the spirit, was it something outside, or inside, or both? Was it *Buddhi*, as the Theosophists and Vedic sages called it, or was it merely endorphins pumping out opiate-like substances? The more I thought about it, the more I realised that although the endorphin release might be a factor in the sensation of bliss, it was not in itself the reason for, or cause of the bliss. I came to this conclusion because whilst feeling the tingling, one was also apperceiving an infinity of being, one was able to understand that the bliss was a part of, or exudation of, or expression of a being, a limitless and all-pervading vibration.. The bliss could not simply have been produced as a result of endorphin release because it was a result of understanding, a result of awareness. There was something behind the bliss, for in the state of bliss, in that dimension, came new understanding as the whole consciousness was widened and deepened. If the release of endorphins had merely been a response to a mind free of thought, it would be felt only at the physical level, in the flesh and the bones of the body. It would not have contained within it the recognition of an Existence or Presence.

This bliss, this One Unicity was felt in the mind, and it was felt in the consciousness, and when it was a true feeling, and not just a dreaming, mystic state, then it contained awareness and discernment. The production of endorphins, if this was indeed what was happening, was the physical result of the electrical activity of Life or Spirit. This magnetic force-field, when contacted by the lower self, conveyed not only wisdom, not only love, but also the physical sensation of bliss.

Each time I had an experience such as this, I learnt something deep about the nature of the universe, something which could not be fully described in human words, for it was so vast and so far-reaching that it was beyond words, and beyond minds. There seemed to be this truth which was perceived at a super-conscious level, and it seemed natural that this should be so. The mind of thought could be superceded by a mind without thought. In the mind without thought, without vibration, without movement, there was the potential to perceive finer and subtler waves of sound and light, there was a receptivity, a connection made, with a new dimension.

It was this that I thought as I walked up the path which wound up the hill, past a troupe of monkeys to Swami Narayan Hotel.

But still I puzzled over this Fire which Vimalaji had once shown to me but which would not reappear. I sat again in the room, staring through the window at the view of distant hills, of treetops, and the old gardener, who came out every afternoon, hobbling on a stick, wild with rage, almost falling over in his rheumatic haste to chase away with stiff limbs the fat cows who ate the grass on his master's tennis court.

I began to read again and to think deeply about everything that Vimalaji had written on Silence. This word, this state, which Vimalaji called 'Silence' was obviously the key to everything. All that Christine had thought she had understood before now seemed useless. I decided to begin again, to learn again, to investigate this state of Silence, as though I had never heard of it before.

Firstly, Silence was the state which was entered when the mind stopped moving. I knew from my own practice that the movement of thoughts could be stopped through observation of the thoughts, and when there was freedom from thought, another dimension of consciousness appeared, or became active. In this state of consciousness there was a tremendous freedom, a tremendous power, a tremendous removal from ordinary existence.

As long as there is the desire and ambition to acquire knowledge and experiences .. there is no possibility whatsoever of silence coming to life. ..Silence .. is a voluntary but choiceless non-action; a total non-action. Beyond the known and the unknown, beyond the visible and the invisible, lies the area of silence, the unknowable. The unknowable is absolutely and fundamentally different from the known and the unknown. That which has never been named, mapped out, chartered, that which never has been measured and shall not be measured by the human mind, do what it will, there lies silence. The negation of total mental movement, cerebral movement, is absolutely necessary to understand, to encounter, to live and to have one's being in that silence – limitless, motionless.

.. one has to be aware all the time that the *word* silence is not the thing that is silence. The dictionary meaning of the *word* silence is not the content of silence ... every discovery has a newness and uniqueness – when a person discovers some meaning, that meaning is virgin. It has not been touched by another person. .. Now if silence is total unconditional negation of cerebral activity, how does that happen? How can the brain voluntarily go into total negation of movement?

..Consciousness is a multidimensional thing, it can move in a multidimensional way. Now, if it is understood that there still is a possibility for this brain though it is conditioned, cultivated, cultured, trained to behave, that its whole content is a variety of habit patterns, to become

quiet, to go into abeyance and non-action, then we
proceed further [6].

It seemed to be true that there were three major Energies or
vibratory electrical fields, from which life on earth had
originated. There was that vibration which was called
'Shiva' or the 'Father' in Christianity, the Spirit, the
Absolute, the Monad, in Theosophical literature. This was
said to be the infinite, all-pervading, unlimited and eternal
vibration, or consciousness. This was also sometimes called
'Thatness'. Astrophysicists had now declared that there was
an interstellar medium, a gas which filled space between
stars. And there were WIMPS, weakly interacting massive
particles of anti-matter, concerning which we were told 100
billion passed every second through our bodies, floating
through the earth, and the scientists said that most of the
universe was made up of something no-one had seen, that
ninety nine percent of matter we did not normally perceive.

Could it be that from the stillness and non-motion of the
Thatness, the moving colours and forms, the soul, the
consciousness emerged as a blanket or field of vibratory
activity, which became separated into myriad units, each
connected to the other?

What else was Silence but the individual soul awaking to its
reality as a form or expression of that which was behind, the
Father, or Spirit, the Absolute, unmoving, infinite. Silence
was the cessation of thoughts, and with the cessation of
thoughts came the understanding that one was not, and had
never been, a body/mind.

---

[6] Thakar, Vimala, *The Mystery of Silence,* Bookfund Vimala Thakar,
Holland, 1986; 18-20.

However, even though I seemed to be grasping the nature of silence, I remained confused and puzzled about many questions. It seemed that, no sooner would one query be answered, than another would arise. During my days of solitude in Mt. Abu I grew increasingly confused as to where the focus of one's attention should be placed during the practice of silence. For years the question had troubled me as to whether the centre of consciousness should be focused above the crown of the head, which seemed to be the seat of Silence, or whether one should feel the heart, the burning center of love, a Fire, between the shoulder-blades. Then again there was a third centre of energy, which I felt as somewhere in the human heart, a centre which emanated a feeling of trust, rest and surrender, of love and completion. I could feel these three points of concentrated energy, and yet they were not visible to physical sight. How were these congregations of energy, each of a different nature and vibration, linked to each other and what was their role in the practice of Silence?

If the soul was the symbol of love, then surely the heart centre, which was a coagulation of compassion and understanding, must have been an outlet for the soul in the unseen layers of the physical body, much as threads of invisible nerves, knitted and bound together, which emerged from some finer, interpenetrating layer or force-field, thus inter-connecting the different levels of being. And yet it was said that the centre above the head, the radiant crown, the halo, was the seat of the soul, whose whirling circular force field of colour and vibratory sound was called, in the Theosophical literature, the causal body or the solar angel.

I knew now there was a 'spirit', or unmoving dimension of homogenous consciousness from which everything proceeded and to which everything returned; as the *Gaitreya* had described it, there was a Father in Heaven, who was Spirit, who moved upon the face of the waters, and caused the universe to manifest, this *Shiva*, creator of the universe and also the cause of its final destruction when the vibratory thought-form was withdrawn. I knew because of my own direct knowledge, that there were these layers of consciousness of some great Thatness in whom all lived and moved and had their being. I had felt, time and again, this One Unicity, this infinite, all-pervading, eternal persistence, which loved and endured and gave all Its attention and all Its thought, and yet I had been unable to place this Thatness, this O.U., in the context of my own existence. There was the Spirit, the Absolute, the Thatness, and there was herself, Christine, and I did not know how they connected. This Absolute, Whose expression or quality Vimalaji called Intelligence, because she did not want It labeled with emotive, religious terms that had been tarnished and distorted throughout the centuries, this Absolute Ground of Existence must have been something of even finer substance than the Soul, I speculated.

The One Unicity which I, Christine had felt pervading my body must have been the perfect Inner God, the Self, the Soul, which was also the moving consciousness, the form or attribute of compassion and love through which the un-embodied Absolute expressed Itself and which Vimalaji called 'Intelligence', and the Theosophists called 'love-wisdom' or buddhi, or the universal oversoul, Christ Consciousness. Vimalaji had once said to me that the vibrations of the ultimate Reality were felt by the sensitivity that only Silence could produce. This then was the Son, Silence was the one between, who came forth to link both Spirit and Matter, the third in the trinity, just as the inner nucleus had to be connected to the outer, spinning electrons by magnetic force.

It was cold and raining. A breeze blew through the open windows. The trees were washed with the monsoon coolness. The spit on the pavements swilled into the gutters. Everything dazzled with the cleansing and drenching of clouds.

Why had I not understood all these matters previously? I was uplifted and exhilarated to think that I had discovered the meaning of Silence. Soon the rain stopped and the sun came out. I walked down to the lake feeling full of bliss. There were crowds of shouting people on holidays, clothes on hangers blowing in the breeze, a cow eating something on a roof, a boy unlocking drains choked with muddy water. Plastic bags of rubbish lay on the road, and a car drove round the narrow mall surrounding the lake, horn blowing, music blasting from the interior, shouting youths leaning from the windows. New hotels were being erected on every piece of open land. I was watching the destruction of this ancient, sacred place, I was witness to the irreverence of new wealth.

After several days had passed, I gathered my courage and rang Kaiser. When I heard the voice of Vimalaji at the end of the line, I was speechless with awe. Something in my attitude towards her had changed. I could no longer think of her as a person who could be casually visited and plied with questions. I was beginning to realise that she was extraordinary, that she was human, and yet more than human. I don't know how it was that this realisation was born, but it was flourishing, and filling my being, so that I could not find a single word to say.

'You can speak,' Vimalaji said in a deep, serene voice.

'I'm overawed,' I answered, thinking it was best to be honest. There was no sound from the other end of the line, and so I said, 'I didn't want to trouble you.'

'Did you want to see me?' Vimalaji asked, and the voice was from gods and clouds and not at all ordinary mortals. I was filled with relief, with waves of love, with a terrified awe and sense of worship.

'If it would be possible,' I replied.

So Vimalaji said that I could see her the next day at four p.m. and when the time came, I walked through the market and clamour of selling, and came to the gate, which was large and made of wrought iron. I put my hand through the slat, and lifted the catch. There was a garden, which was full of peace, and the office to the right, from which Kaiser came, smiling. Together we took off our shoes at the foot of the stairway, which led upwards to the house. There were rocks on which the house was built, and little plants grew in cracks. It was an old house, of plastered stone, which loomed from the outcrop of ancient hardened larva on which had been built. I was so afraid that I could hardly walk up the steps. Something had happened, and I could never again think of Vimalaji as anything but a God.

There was a screen which hung across a door, the veil of the temple. There was a voice which came from inside, and we entered. Vimalaji was seated on a divan, white-wrapped, cloud-lost, with greatness of eyes, like mirror-rooms of palaces where light turns and turns in the darkness. I was moved by some other current, not nerves or ganglion, but the

ever-renewing, ever-rejoicing, ever-bursting, burgeoning
swelling of radiance which bubbled and pounded like jets
from high-speed waterfalls and everything was pulsing, so
that Christine was rendered speechless in the void of
nothingness which shook the room.

After a while, Vimalaji spoke, as statues stir when eyes are
blurred and it seemed that the heavens waved, and stars
swayed, and Christine was just human and lost in the power
and the glory, and no word would come. Vimalaji looked
gently, and asked, 'Would you like a cup of tea?' but I was
so pacing and restless and beating, that I could only say, 'Oh,
no I couldn't drink it,' because my hand would have shaken
and I would have dropped the cup. So Vimalaji said, 'please
sit down', and I sat opposite her, and was so close to her in
the small, warm room that I began to sweat because of my
fear and awe and discomfort. And I wished I could have
been kneeling at her feet, and not sitting as an equal.

Then Vimalaji asked, 'How is Christine's health? She looks
very thin,' and she was so gentle, but still I could not speak
except to squeak, 'I'm fine'. Then I tried to say, 'When I'm
in your presence all my questions go away.'

Vimalaji smiled and said nothing. Then again I tried to
explain that I worshipped Vimalaji but the words did not
come out. So Vimalaji said, 'Well, if you are here for a few
days more, you are welcome to come back again, and today
we can talk about other things.' She was so matter of fact,
and so human and yet this indescribable, invisible radiance
poured through her with such a tremendous velocity that I
was like a burnt shriveled leaf blowing in hot air on summer
days.

'Maybe we could just sit without talking,' I replied, recalling how in the past we had spent blissful times in silence. But this time it did not work. No Silence came to my mind. I was restless, agitated and uncomfortable, and I opened my eyes. I was hoping that Vimalaji would say something, but she did not do so, and so I asked her, just to make conversation, if she believed that animals had individual souls. Vimalaji then spent a few minutes speaking in a calm, serene voice about the fact that in each animal was a point of individual consciousness.

After that, I asked her if she believed that there was a Lord of the Animals.

'Not in the sense of an individual God,' she answered.

Then I told her the story of how I had become the managing trustee of Help in Suffering, and wanted to live in India, but Jeremy was a lawyer with obligations to his partnership. I told her how there seemed to be no solution, and that one day a sharman from a village had told me to pray to Lord Hanuman, and how, half an hour after my visit to the Hanuman Temple, Jeremy had rung, and offered to come to live in India with me, and I felt that Lord Hanuman had heard my prayer.

'It was the appeal of the heart, the surrender which had brought an answer,' she said after sitting in silence for some time.

Then I said, 'It is eight years since I first touched that One Unicity and yet still this individual Christine has not been dissolved.'

'It is an achievement,' Vimalaji said, 'That you have reached this stage. Many do not.'

'But why can't I become enlightened?' I demanded, still restless and striving and mad.

After a long time Vimalaji asked, 'When did you first become aware of the feeling of the Thatness?'

'After I first met you in Mt. Abu in 1989 I went away and followed your books, and I feel it sometimes, but it comes and goes.'

Again for a long time Vimalaji was silent, and then she spoke. 'There are two ways,' she answered, 'One is through Bhakti Yoga, and the other is through Gyan Yoga, Bhakti yoga, through the heart, through trust, through faith and love, and Gyan, through understanding. Maybe you could pray to Lord Hanuman.'

Kaiser and I laughed. We thought it was a joke, and I was embarrassed and squirming when Vimalaji did not smile, but continued seriously, 'Sometimes a great upsurge of faith, of surrender and of devotion, will be effective if the ground has already been prepared, if the seed has been sown.'

And I was amazed at her humility, that she should suggest praying to Lord Hanuman, when all of Lord Hanuman's power was retained within her also.

Then she was silent for a while and she asked, 'What are the conditions of your life?'

'They are frantic,' I answered. 'There is never time to be alone with oneself.'

'Then this could be the problem,' Vimalaji responded, and said nothing, and seemed to be in another place, and consulting other books which were in clouds and stratospheres. Then she continued to speak and said, 'Yes, I can see Christine running here and there, trying to persuade the people to be kind to animals, and the Indians not listening. I can see her busy life.'

'That's so right,' I answered.

Then Vimalaji said, 'The Energy would be dissipated by the demands of everyday life. It would be restored, when you sat in silence, and then again it would be fractured.'

Then she thought some more, and again consulted distant records, and spoke. 'If Christine really wants it so much, if it is the only goal in her life, it will happen.'

I was surprised and amazed by such a prediction. Gradually my awe and terror began to fade. 'You must go away alone for three months, if you really want the sense of personality to be lost in the universal consciousness,' Vimalaji said.

Then she asked Kaiser to bring some books, which she gave to me, and I thanked her, and Vimalaji said, 'We would like you to come to see us again before you leave,' which I knew was a generous offer, because she was always occupied with many visitors and many tasks, so I said, 'Thank you,' and left, and as I went I said to Kaiser, 'I feel embarrassed that I could not speak,' and Kaiser said, 'Oh don't worry, People

are often like that the first time they meet her. Do come
again before you go if you wish.'

So I said goodbye and went away in a state of misery, and
thought that I would never go to see Vimalaji again, because
I could not speak in her presence, and was crass, and caused
disruption and discomfort and discord. But when it was the
next day I thought that this would be allowing defeat to rule,
and I could not be a failure, and I should return to Vimalaji,
and be sensible. And again I rang, and again Vimalaji
answered the phone, and this time I said I would like to visit
again, and Vimalaji said, come at 5pm, so I went, and this
time I was not at all disturbed.

Vimalaji smiled, and said, 'What is it that Christine would
wish to talk about? This is your time,' and I answered that I
would like to sit in Silence. I tried to explain that I was
trying to adjust and intercept the radiance and fire that
streamed from Vimalaji, I wanted to understand, to be able
to touch, to taste, to smell that vibration, and Vimalaji said to
Kaiser, who was also in the room, that it was her greatest
satisfaction that Christine should ask this, as most people
wanted to talk.

'How long would you like to sit in silence?' she asked me,
and I suggested fifteen minutes, and Vimalaji asked if I
would like to sit on the floor, because she could tell that I felt
uncomfortable to sit at the same level as one so great, for this
was an Indian practice, which had become also an instinctive
feeling within Christine, and Vimalaji knew that it had
contributed to my discomfort at our last meeting.

This time, because there was stillness within me, and
because there was so much love because of the patience and

understanding and gentleness of Vimalaji, I was able to receive the Energy which poured through her and which was transmitted to everything that might have been anywhere nearby. And I was removed into clouds and stairways and exaltation with wings and trumpets and not at all in an earthly place. Sometimes I opened my eyes and looked at Vimalaji's face, and saw that her eyes were almost closed, and that there was the slight, pure smile of Buddhahood which held her lips in a place which was of temples and gods and pagodas in mountains. And Christine sat immobile, and did not ever want to speak again. Then two helpers came into the room, and they also sat on the floor, and finally they stopped, and they smiled at each other, and then Vimalaji asked, 'When will you be leaving for Australia?'

'In about a week,' Christine answered. 'Do you know that you had told me two days ago that I should spend three months alone in silence? Well that day I had news that my aunt had died, and left me some money which would enable me to do this,' I said.

For a long time Vimalaji was silent, and then she said, as if directing words which came down a pipe from clouds, 'You see, dear, if there is a step to be taken the means for its fruition will be provided so that it can be fulfilled as is intended.'

Then again there was silence, and then again she spoke. 'Kaiser and I were very grateful to you that you had shared with us the horrifying experience of the dog attack, and we learnt something wonderful from this. Christine would not have been given more time here, had it not been intended that she would take the next step. It is intended that Christine

should further develop. There is no doubt that this will
happen for you.'

So then I thanked Vimalaji for pointing out to me that I
needed to be alone for three months, and I said that this was
what I had wanted to do for a long time, but I had never been
brave enough to do it, because I thought it was my karma to
keep working, and Vimalaji smiled, and wished me a good
journey to Australia, and I went, and, after I had been in
Australia, and had returned to India, I went to Mt. Abu for
three months of silence and solitude as Vimalaji had
recommended.

CHAPTER THREE

THE PROCESS OF INQUIRY

Life is one, indivisible, homogenous wholeness
... It means that in this Cosmos every expression
of life is inter-related to every other expression of
life. There is inter-relatedness and inter-
dependence of all expressions of life. .. No
sustainable society can come into existence unless
this organic inter-relation among all the
innumerable expressions of life is noticed,
perceived, analysed, appreciated and recognized
in every human activity [1]

Some monkeys called to each other in the trees, and outside
two shouting boys galloped their ponies along the asphalt
road. I was in Mt. Abu, in the Swami Narayan Hotel, in the
same room which I had occupied in July, and which I again
cleaned with Harpic and Ajax. This time I had come in a
taxi, with several suitcases containing food and cooking
utensils, so that I could prepare my own meals in the room,
which was large, with a wonderful view, and a very cheap
rent.

I thought that I would not bother Vimalaji at all. I was still
afraid of her. I did not know if I would be struck dumb again
if I was close to her. I decided that it was enough that I was
in a room which looked over the treetops and rooftops and
hills, and from which I could see the location, perhaps even

---

[1] Thakar, Vimala, *The Invincible*, Vol XI, No. 2, April-June, 1995: 19-20

the rooftop, of that house in which she lived, in which light was sucked from the universe and poured in torrents and columns through her being. The whole of Mt. Abu was lit and fluorescent and translucent and radiant because of the presence of Vimalaji, that central point, which expanded and magnified and multiplied and doubled and intensified what was already there, but which became more fanned and more spread and more dense and defined and detectable due to her existence, in a house, in Mt. Abu, in Rajasthan, in the world. And it seemed miraculous and incredible that she existed, and I began to realise in a way which I had not understood before, that this Vimalaji was human, but also more than human, and contained within herself the inter-galactic skies, and all the past and future.

So I made myself begin to sit in silence, and I took notes of everything that happened, so that I could be dispassionate and factual. At first the old feelings of panic and fear emerged, and I felt restless and afraid. I had no idea what, if anything would happen. I had come as an act of faith, more because Vimalaji had said I should come than for any other reason. I began to doubt everything – whether I had come to the right place to meditate, whether I was doing the correct practice, whether I could ever again feel that 'Fire' which filled and flooded the being. I realised I still had no understanding about anything. I wondered how I would sit for hour after hour, day after day, week after week, knowing nothing, ignorant and confused.

I knew now that I had to first enter the dimension of Silence, and that in that dimension the energies of Life could be perceived. I had felt this Energy, but I had not yet discovered its meaning or association with the person, Furthermore, I was puzzled and bothered by two seemingly contradictory pieces of knowledge. Should I focus the point of consciousness above the head, or should I focus it in the heart? My failure to understand or interpret the correct practice disrupted my attempts at silence because I was confused as to which energy should be the centre of attention.

There was a process that had become apparent to me over the years, which seemed to follow a pattern. A question would arise in my mind, as for example, 'Should the consciousness be focused above the head or in the heart?' I would then puzzle and brood over this question, reading material from spiritual books, staring at charts and diagrams. When the answer came, it resulted in a new sense of freedom, of understanding, of expansion of consciousness. Perhaps this was the technique which Zen Buddhism extolled, and perhaps also, this was the reason why Vimalaji called it an 'inquiry', because the quest for enlightenment was a continual questioning into the nature of reality.

Another question which had often puzzled me was Vimalaji's answers to two of my letters which had been sent with a time lag of several years between them. I had these two answers in my notebook, together with my letters which had evoked the responses, and I sometimes read them, puzzling over her two answers which seemed to contradict each other. I felt that my failure to fully understand the difference between the first and second answer indicated an important lapse in my comprehension.

My first letter had said:

> Dear Vimalaji,
> Since meeting with you in February (1994), and receiving your confirmation that the all-pervading

feeling felt through all 'my' bodies is that Unconditioned
Silence, I spent six months puzzling as to how this
Energy related to myself. I felt it but did not know my
relation to It, except that It was in me and through me
whenever I thought of It.

Now I am writing to ask you, can it be correct that this
Unconditioned Silence is the Perceiver of the
consciousness, that this all-pervading, unbounded Energy
without any borders, is 'my' self – the One Self –
looking 'down' on this world of forms and
consciousness? It seems to be that this unconditioned
Silence observes the soul – the consciousness – as once
that consciousness loved and observed the body/mind. It
seems to be that I am God, and this soul or consciousness
is my perfect form. This is all so extraordinarily amazing
and miraculously unbelievable but I cannot conceive of
any other answer as to what is this Unconditioned
Silence. So I thought I will write to you about this most
private and sacred thing, and ask you is this true that this
limitless, loving, tender Energy is my Self, the Perceiver
of the consciousness. It can't be the consciousness
because even though that consciousness can be without
thoughts, that consciousness has a different Energy
which is not boundless, but seems to be focused
somewhere above the head. Even this soul itself must be
just a concept, just a body observed by this 'Father in
Heaven'. This means even that soul, which seemed to be
a perfect Being within myself, must now be superse4ded
by a still greater Limitless Absolute.

So many people must write to you with so many
questions but I thirst for an answer from you who know
and understand.

She had answered:

> Dear Christine,
> Arrived here yesterday. Received yours of 11 October.
> Hearty congratulations for correct understanding. Inner
> emptiness or Silence is figuratively called 'heaven'. The

omnipresent, omnipotent, seeing Intelligence is called, 'Father'. Some call it 'Mother', some others, 'It'. Vedanta terms it 'That-ness'. That is our real nature; our existential essence.

Forms containing consciousness have that unbounded intelligence as the core. It is the cause and substance of creation.

With much love, Vimala

I read again the letter which I had written to her two years later on a similar theme:

For a couple of years now I have been feeling the all-pervading, unlimited Thatness which permeates this body and mind. I know there is this Absolute, or Thatness, because I feel its bliss in all levels and layers of my being.

But although it is not difficult to recognize this impersonal energy behind everything, although it is not difficult to know that It is in my body and mind, because I feel it is infinite and permeates everything, it is very difficult for this individual's sense of consciousness to recognize that it is, in itself, divine. Surely it is divine because God is in everything and even a grub is a manifestation of deity. But it seems too amazing that each human being in itself is an embodied God.

I have read Advaita and Buddhist philosophy which seems to stress that the soul or consciousness, is itself impermanent and merely the form for the Spirit, and therefore a concept only. In the end the soul also passes away and all that is left is the Absolute, or Spirit, or That.

So my question is concerning the blissful loving attentiveness which I feel in my body and consciousness, but which is not consciousness or soul, but is perceived by the consciousness. It seems to be so impersonal; I cannot imagine it is my Self. It is just this great loving nothing which is everywhere. But it seems totally apart from me as a conscious point of life.

If this individual consciousness is just a concept, or form for the all-permeating Energy to express Itself, then it is impermanent and not to be worshipped. The Spirit, or Thatness is too impersonal to be my Self. So what is it within myself that I can worship? You are divine and others have been human and became divine individual Gods. Is it the consciousness which becomes divine when it merges with the Spirit or Absolute? Does the impersonal Thatness become an embodied God when the consciousness somehow accepts It as Itself and inside itself?

Can you please comment on this which seems to be so incredible; that in order for the being to be united and merged with the Absolute behind the soul, the Absolute which has created this soul, this form or body of light, must turn inward and worship the Father, the Source, meaning this being, myself, must actually worship myself, because that source of everything is myself.

Her reply had mystified and confused me, even though, at the time, I had thought I understood:

Dear Friend,

Received yours of July 24/96. many thanks for the same. Life is Energy. It permeates every expression including human beings. There are innumerable energies working in us. Biological energies, psychological energies and cerebral energies are limited by the material form. Hence they are called personal. In fact there is no personal energy and therefore no impersonal one.

It is the centre of cognition, i.e.; the 'I', the 'Me' or the Ego which tries to appropriate the psycho-physical energies and calls them personal. The same ego feels baffled when it notices the movement of an unidentified

energy in the body which it cannot account for or
control.

My dear, there is nothing to worship and nothing to
discard. One understands the nature and mechanism of
life and remains a perceiver of the whole phenomenon.

It is not possible to say more in a written letter. Life is
Divinity. The act of living is the worship of the divine.

With much love,
Vimala.

So the seemingly contradictory content of these letters was a
continuous enigma which refused to be solved, and it re-
surfaced again with a greater intensity now that I was
intensively investigating the very source of consciousness
and being. The question of where to focus the point of
consciousness seemed somehow connected to the greater
mystery concerning the nature of one's being. In addition
there were other lesser questions which came and went and
solved themselves more easily.

At this time, my major exploration was centred on the
question of the fire which I felt between the shoulder blades,
and how this related to the Fire which had consumed me
after that extraordinary meeting with Vimalaji in 1996.

The heart was always spoken of as the centre of compassion,
of interconnectedness, of love and total merging. If this was
the heart (and, Diana had said, 'Always feel the heart') then
should not one be absorbed in this blissful, unconditioned,
undivided love? It was also said that the heart was magnetic,
and through its love it drew down the Spirit. Perhaps; but
then, there was also the other centre, the other point of focus,
that heavy crown above the head, that seemed to expand and

press down, that point through which the total removal occurred, through which one became merely the Perceiver, staring down into a three-D world.

The soul or individual consciousness was the sphere of Energy or force field which became 'awake' in the state of Silence, I reasoned. Vimalaji's 'Silence' was equivalent to the Theosophical or Christian terminology of 'soul consciousness', or Ouspensky's description of being 'awake'[2]. The state of awakening was in fact the state in which the soul became aware of Itself, instead of being asleep, and letting the dream of daily living in the world, seduce it into thinking that this pattern and noise of material living was the reality. Perhaps when that soul was awake, the vibration of the Atma, or Spirit, or Absolute, the Thatness which filled the soul, was also perceived in the brain itself. The soul (or individual consciousness) transmitted the 'word', the vibration of Atma – that infinite, eternal, all-pervading One Unicity. It could do this when it was no longer attracted to the vibrations and shoutings and perturbations of the physical world, and turning from the noise, became a still reflector which could act as a mirror, and beam down the infinite to earth.

And yet, I could not describe it in this way either, because the Infinite Absolute Thatness was always present and all-permeating. It had never needed to be perceived in order to exist. I had a distinct conviction that, whatever this Energy might be, It was something which had waited for me, which had always loved, which had always been present, which had always been watching. It was not a being in the sense of a human being, but it was some vast, neutral, loving consciousness. It was indisputably, definitely, unarguably

---

[2] Ouspensky, P.D., *In Search of the Miraculous*, Harvest, USA, 1977.

there. I could feel it, sometimes weakly, sometimes strongly. It was miraculous and extraordinary. And I had not known it existed, until I had first touched it in the small fibro cottage in the mist, with the smoke from the fires and the scent of pines.

I wondered how it was that, if the Thatness had always existed, and always been watching, and always been loving, how it could be that a human being could not sense, could not touch, could not perceive the Thatness, had no idea of Its existence. And I speculated that perhaps it was through the practice of self-observation, when thoughts became dissolved, when the soul became awake, that a thread of energy descended from that point of consciousness above the head, into the individual consciousness, thus connecting it to the wider, greater universal consciousness. In a sense, the human being became plugged into that Energy, and to be plugged into that Energy the human being needed to have the ability to completely still the mind, or soul, or individual consciousness, the one between, the Son, the reflector. In other words, in the state of Silence the *antahkarana* as the *Vedas* called it, the inner thread of light energy, was constructed, so that the Cosmic Infinite Thatness could flood the individual consciousness and take control of operations.

That Son, that soul, that consciousness, was a mediator, like an adaptor which stepped down the voltage, so that one highly vibrating frequency could be perceived by another slowly and heavily vibrating field of energy. That soul was in fact the great gift, which every human had embedded within themselves, and yet it was not the Highest, even the soul itself was an imagined reality. The Real, surely, was that which was permanent and which would endure forever, and the unreal was that which was changeable and impermanent, which could cease to exist at any moment. The soul was not the ultimate inner God!

The soul, which I had thought to be the Self, was only a temporary Self, it was a connection, a sensor, a presenter, a form, even though invisible to human eyes, it was the psyche, with all its brilliance, its skills, its creativity, its powers of clairvoyance and clairaudience, which began to express itself in the world of forms as it awoke from its slumber, as the centre of the being became focused in that dimension of Observer and Perceiver.

As this became clearer to me, I was partially, but not fully, able to understand Vimalaji's two letters. Her teaching always emphasised the fact that there was no individual consciousness, no individual ego, and one of her purposes for doing this was to help her students to avoid the mistake of building a super-ego in a super-conscious form.

I sat on the bed and stared out the window at the view below. Only a couple of weeks had passed, and I was enduring long bouts of depression, of total frustration. I watched a bus draw up outside the hotel, and from its interior scores of school children tumble, shouting and jostling, each carrying a small pack of belongings. There were two teachers who went into the office below, and soon the group of seething, shouting, laughing children, were ushered by the manager and teachers into the large, open room two storeys beneath. Even though it was far below, I could hear the sounds of their yelling and jumping traveling through the walls. It was clearly some school excursion, and the children had been put into the dormitory, which was kept for pilgrims. Soon I could hear the children playing ball in the courtyard below, calling to each other, cheering, and chanting, the sounds rising and echoing. I began to worry about whether I should move. But I had spent so much time examining the hotels of Mt. Abu, and only those, which were beyond my budget, might possibly have provided the silence I required. I decided to stop worrying about the noise, and to make it known to Vimalaji and Kaiser that I had arrived.

I had a large packet of dried fruit, which I had brought from Australia for them, but as I did not want to see Vimalaji in person, due to my fear of her, I decided to leave the dried fruit, with a card, at the office for Kaiser. I walked down the winding single lane road, which ran through some small areas of rock and natural growth, with rapidly encroaching houses, and, just before reaching the lake, passed one of the large, whitewashed Brahma Kumari buildings[3]. As there were always sounds of cooking utensils being bashed and scraped, I assumed that this was the kitchen area for this complex of building owned by this sect with followers from all over the world, who came to stay, to study and to meditate, consuming vast quantities of limited water resources, much to the chagrin of the local people.

I walked around the lake, past the small image of Hanuman set into a stone wall. The image was painted orange and had been smeared with oil, so that the stone recess had turned black. A sweet smell emanated from the burning incense and rose petals which had been scattered at Hanuman's feet.

As I approached Vimalaji's house there were lurchings and chippings of terror in my stomach. Try as I might, I could not suppress my terror as I moved towards her abode. As I

---

[3] The Brahma Kumaris are a spiritual movement with centres in many parts of the world where followers go to study the teaching of their founder.

reached the gate of the house, I saw a young slim Indian woman, who smiled radiantly. I recognised her as Achana, who seemed to be some sort of helper for Vimalaji. She was the one who had slipped into the room once, and sat with us when we had been meditating in silence.

She smiled at me, and I asked her if she could give the packet to Kaiser. She said she would do so, and took it. Then I hurried away, returning to my room. It was spacious and sunny. I made tea on the spirit stove which I had brought with me, and drank it.

Not long afterwards, I heard a knock on the door, which was now very clean because I had wiped all the greasy fingers and strange spatterings of adhesive grey stickiness from the white paint. I opened the door and saw that it was Kaiser. I was so happy to see her, and asked her into the room. She handed me a plastic bag full of fruit, and a box of sweets from Vimalaji, together with a letter which said,

> Dear Friend, This is to welcome you for your Sadhana of Silence and Solitude. We are glad that you have launched upon this adventure of Self-discovery.
>
> One begins with the discovery of the true nature and structure of Mind. One goes through an encounter with the movement of the Ego, which builds up a conceptual nest of 'I' and 'Mine'.
>
> It begins with the physical and extends it to the psychological. When one sets one's being free from the shackles of 'my-ness', there is Wholeness. You belong to the Wholeness of Life, to the global community of living beings and perhaps to the multi-versal cosmic Intelligence. Please contact dear Kaiser in case you need any help during your stay at Abu.
> With deep love,
> Vimala.

I was overwhelmed that Vimalaji should bother to send me these objects of welcome.

'It's blessed by her,' I said to Kaiser.

Kaiser smiled. Although we had met each other on many occasions over the years, the encounters had been brief, and I knew little about her or about Vimalaji's life.

I asked Kaiser if she would like tea. She declined and expressed concern that I would not be able to prepare proper food in a hotel room, with such limited equipment. She said it was not good to eat out, because you never knew whether the food was clean.

'I could speak to the cook, and arrange for her to prepare you meals without too much oil,' she said.

There was a plastic chair, which had been covered with grease marks, and which I had washed, so I asked Kaiser to please sit, and I squatted on the bed opposite. Kaiser was wearing a salwar suit. I did not ever see her wear saris.

Kaiser looked around the room, and dispassionately viewed my strange collection of assorted utensils assembled in a corner on a plastic stand which I had purchased. 'You must eat properly,' she said.

'I've got heaps of everything,' I answered. 'Look, I've even bought a small table and these cooking things.'

'Vimalaji says we have a duty to eat well and thus look after our bodies properly,' Kaiser said.

I was rather dismissive, as I simply was not interested in
food. My mind was so focused on my inquiry, I was so hot,
and afire, and burning with the passion of the search, that I
could not be occupied with any other issue.

I felt very comfortable with Kaiser, and not at all awkward.
It was easy to talk to her, and she was responsive, and full of
information. But I was so fanatical about the proper use of
every minute of my precious three months alone that I did
not even want to waste my precious minutes in an exchange
with her.

How was your journey to Australia?' she asked.

'It was good. We saw our grandchildren, our sons, our
mothers, and friends.'

I looked at her sitting in the plastic chair. She was slightly
hunched. Her dark hair had grey streaks and was unruly.
Even her clothes looked crushed. She was such a natural
person and I began to feel that we were somehow united in a
common journey.

'How did you meet Vimalaji?' I asked her.

'You see, Vimalaji was invited to speak in many places all
over the world, and she always responded to those requests.
Sometimes I would say to her, 'But what if no-one comes to
the talks, after you've traveled so far?' and she would answer
that it was her responsibility to respond, and it was the
organiser's responsibility to arrange for the listeners. About
twenty years ago she came to Canada, and I went to listen to
the talks. I was married at the time to an Indian, and his job
had brought us both to Canada. When I heard her speak I

thought she was so exceptional, I asked her if I could go and live with her and work for her.'

'She must have been delighted?'

'She advised me to wait for two years. If I was still interested then we could talk about it, she said. So, after two years I was again in India with my husband, and I went to Mt. Abu. He met Vimalaji but was not interested in staying there. So we agreed amicably to part ways. We had no children.'

'But it must have been difficult, as an Indian woman. It was very brave.'

'There was only one thing I wanted, which was to be with Vimalaji, so it was not difficult.'

'And you are her personal assistant?'

'You could say that. I transcribe the tapes, go to Ahmedabad and supervise publication of the books.'

'And you do typing for her, and act as a filter between her and the public.'

She smiled.

'And how is it that Vimalaji lives in Mt. Abu?'

'You see, she was in the land-gift movement. Do you know what that was?'

'It was led by the great saint, Vinoba, and the people walked from town to town, asking the rich landlords to give land to the landless villagers.'

'Yes, well Vimalaji was a leader in that movement in the fifties. But during her work for the land-gift movement she was in a car accident in Assam, and her ear was injured very badly.'

'Yes, I remember reading about this in the small book she had written. This was just after she had met J. Krishnamurti, the spiritual teacher who was so famous all over the world. She met him, and he offered to heal her ear, and it was healed.'

'She wrote to the leaders of the Land Gift Movement, and said she was dropping out. Her things had been stored with them, and when she said she was dropping out, they found a place for her in Mt. Abu, and wrote and told her.'

'Why at Mt. Abu?'

'The house was empty. A saint had been living there, and nobody else wanted to occupy it, because they said there were ghosts. The trust offered the house to Vimalaji to live in.'

'I know hardly anything about Vimalaji's life,' I said. 'I've only been interested in her teaching.'

Soon Kaiser said that she would leave. I followed her down the steps, which were cement, with cement walls, which were stained in random places by people who had spat chewed *pan* with liberty and abandon, as though they were contributing to the design and décor of the otherwise ugly stairwell, past the patches of cactus, watered and weeded lovingly, in small garden insets among the tiles and cement, and out the gate, which seemed irrelevant as it was never locked. I watched her start her motor scooter, and vanish up the road, clothes billowing, hair flying.

I walked up the stairs again, averting my gaze from the mottled patches of stained spit, and then I read once more Vimalaji's letter, and was liberated by the contents, and I saw that all the world was a creation of a mind, including whatever Christine thought or did, which meant that every small thought was just a floating thing that drifted and went, as did the whole thoughtform of Christine. Only the One Unicity remained, endured, persisted, loved, and observed the creation that had emerged from it.

But you could not escape the outside world, nor your own ego. It was attached to you, and you swam in it, and you were a point which was blown like the dupatta which billowed from Kaiser's neck, so you could not ever quit until the time had been ordained, but you could recognise that you were not the body, not the thoughts, and, when you had recognised this, then you were free. Because when you saw what you were not, you could become what you truly were. And this I had yet to find, but I knew I would find it, and everything would be completed and triumphant.

If I could stand firm in the One Unicity, feeling only Its vibration, then it was easy not to be enmeshed in the movings and beckonings of the material world. And that was all I needed to do, for hour after hour, day after day, and everything would be shown to me, and then I would understand.

At first my attempts to just BE did not proceed well. It was very subtle, the feeling which permeated all levels and layers of the being, and it seemed to evaporate, to vanish like mist when the sun shone, as soon as some other thought entered the mind. The One Unicity, its infinite, all-filtering, all-presence, was so subtle that you could not feel it if your bodies were coarse, if they had not been refined and developed, so it seemed.

Then I thought, what if I never succeed in attaining liberation, and I have to go back into the world without having realised my true nature, and what if I fail? And I did not realise that I was seeing my life from a backwards projection, and from reversed positions, because there was no Christine who could fail or could not fail.

I had brought with me one of my old notebooks, which contained my observations on previous realisations and many quotations from many books I had studied over the years, quotations which seemed relevant to my inquiry, my struggle to find the truth, my quest for understanding. For a human was a person pulled in two directions, the inner consciousness became transfixed and seduced by the outer movement, the colours and patterns of the physical life, the senses were drawn outward, and, instead of the conscious witness remaining as an interested and detached observer, that witness, that mind, became enmeshed in the muddle and flashings of daily life, tricked and deluded into an entangled encounter with the forms and shapes which the senses had presented, and which the brain had interpreted.

I went jogging round the lake, and thought frequently of Vimalaji's words, 'Wholeness responds and eliminates the division.' There was nothing for Christine to do but to trust in that Wholeness. The ego was interfering and causing this person given the name Christine to worry and demand and agitate. There was only one way to escape the hell of the ego, which was to allow it to be dissolved by the Wholeness itself. The ego could not be fought, it could not be suppressed, it existed and was dominant. Only if it was transcended, if it was ignored, if its petty little world of noise was turned from, only then would the Reality bloom.

As the days passed, I began to feel more definitely once more that Energy which I had named the 'Fire'. This was an ecstatic physical bliss which was felt in the body as though someone was massaging the flesh, which tingled and became totally relaxed with the tremendously tender electrical force which permeated every cell and nerve. This Fire was somehow different from the abstracted and blissful state which I had called the One Unicity, which Vimalaji seemed to call the Wholeness. In the state of Wholeness, although the physical tingling was included, there was also something greater, deeper. In the state of Wholeness, one perceived the unending, undivided, unlimited love and understanding, which was unrelated to time or place or mind.

I pondered deeply on the significance of these Energies, related and yet able to be separately perceived. I pondered relentlessly about the other streams of energy which seemed to be emitted from the centres or chakras in the body – not the physical body, but that 'etheric body', that underlying invisible system of energy points.

You could focus all your attention above the head, and you felt as though you were carrying an empty stone, which was pressing, and that you were sitting there, in that cave, above and removed from the concert of life. Or, you could put your attention into that place which seemed to be somewhere near the heart, or throat, which was a centre of intense, unconditional enduring love. And so I continued to remain confused as to where the attention should be focused. Yet I was determined not to disturb Vimalaji, and, in addition, I felt too afraid to meet her again face to face.

Over ten days had passed. I was feeling ill, and not eating. From the moment when I woke in the morning until the moment when I fell asleep at night, I sat alone in my room, observing myself. 'This is going to be my greatest test ever,' I thought.

Kaiser came again, and this time she brought an electric pot which could be used to boil rice or noodles or soup. She said she had given it once to Vimalaji. It came from Mumbai and it was still new and unused.

'Vimalaji had suggested I should lend it to you,' Kaiser said.'

'I wonder if she knew that I was not feeling well, and not eating much,' I said.

Kaiser said nothing.

So I thanked her for the cooking pot, and said it would be useful and that I would look after it carefully.

Then Kaiser told me where I could buy curd that was clean, and *panir*[4] which was safe to eat, and she told me about the sweet shop, and she said that Mt. Abu would become very

---

[4] pressed, sliceable cottage cheese.

noisy next month, which was *Diwali*[5], when lots of people visited during their holidays.

And after we had talked for a little longer, Kaiser went.

The next day, I was in a state of extreme stress, and had to stop sitting in silence. I felt agitated and afraid, as though part of me was fighting against myself. I decided that in this unsteady state it was not wise to force myself to meditate, and instead, I took a day off. I walked down to the market, down the winding road that ran among the trees, which branched to the left at the back of the Brahma Kumari Ashram where the workers lived in shacks with their goats and dogs. I rang Jeremy from a small telephone booth, hoping that there would be no emergency which would result in an enforced return to Help in Suffering. But he said that everything was going smoothly. Then I bought coriander and spinach and tomatoes from the hawkers who lined the sides of the footpath. They had come in from the villages with their fresh produce in baskets, and they were always surprised to find I spoke Hindi. The old women joked and bargained. I enjoyed the exchange. Later, I sat in my room and re-read some of Vimalaji's books.

The next morning I woke early and began to meditate. 'This is true hell,' I thought. 'There is no way out. I cannot turn back, and I cannot seem to go forwards.'

After drinking some tea, I went jogging. As I walked down the flights of stairs I suddenly woke up. I saw. I became alive. I was somewhere above myself, vividly, vibrantly awake, looking down at the world which I saw so sharply, so keenly, so intensely, that as I crossed the courtyard and went

---

[5] The festival of lights, an important Hindu celebration.

down the steps past the pots of cactus, it was someone else
who did these acts, and I, gloriously detached, wrapped in
effulgence, watched from afar. This was the same state I had
experienced when attacked by the dog. It was a different
state from that of feeling the Fire, in which one was still in
the body, and perceived the Fire which permeated every
muscle and nerve.

My whole being was scrubbed clean of any sense of being
human. In that state I jogged round the lake, through the
mist, nodding at a man who was jogging in the opposite
direction, patting the dogs which had become my friends and
which greeted me every day, and only as I returned to the
room, and began to think of asking for a cup of ginger and
cardamon tea, did I begin to descend into the human state
once more.

In the state of awakeness there had been no time. Everything
was already completed, already finished, already perfected,
even though it was not so. Whatever I was to become, had
already happened. Everything was beautiful because it was
not in time, it was already completed in the eyes of the
universe. Therefore there was nothing to worry about,
nothing to take action about, nothing to initiate, for
everything was happening and would continue to happen,
and you were somewhere watching, but not at all involved.

I assumed that when the false identification with the
body/mind had suddenly ceased, the consciousness became
clean and still, unruffled by the vibrations of thoughts, and
was then able to be itself, untrammeled and unpolluted by
the distractions of material life. When it was awake as itself,
there was no Christine. It was an individual consciousness
which was a completely separate entity from the ego which

constituted Christine. I was no longer Christine, but something else. I had made a terrible mistake all my life in thinking that I had been an entity called Christine when in fact I was this watching, God-like being.

But still I had not grasped the full truth. I had not realised that there were three stages of perceiving, that there were three withdrawals or recessions to be made.

After a couple more days I suddenly realised, or experienced, another truth: the being which was awake, the real entity (as distinct from Christine), was in fact only an entity in as much as it was a point of consciousness, or speck of fire within a great, unseparated network or sphere of Life through which that fire of love, compassion, tenderness, and attention interpenetrated and circulated. Never again could there be a sense of separation. It was only the entity, the I-thought, the thing called Christine, that thought there was a separate ego. In fact, forever this had been an illusion, a terrible mistake. The animals, the earth, and Vimalaji herself were all interwoven and interconnected by this same fire of love, the perpetually enduring One Unicity which filled every atom of the air and sky and sea and earth. Christine was nothing but an impermanent shell of emptiness, filled with the Fire. Now at last I understood why Vimalaji had given a different response to my second letter.

I looked out the window. It was about six pm and the sun was setting. The distant hills formed a black horizon and the sky blazed with a plethora of wildness, red, purple and lilac pulsing and singing in space. To realise that Christine was nothing, and had only been a mistaken thought was so logical, so obvious, that nothing could be said. It was just there, just being. It just WAS. Nothing you could think or not think could change this ISNESS.

I read the words which Vimalaji had spoken with a new understanding: 'the total Energy is at the disposal of the person who has made Silence their abode,' and 'The vibration of the ultimate Reality is felt by the sensitivity which only Silence can produce.'

But now I was beginning to realise something even more complex and extraordinary, as I contemplated on the biblical statements of the Christ, particularly those from St. John. If the Father was Spirit, or Purusha, the unmoving consciousness, the absolute ground of existence, then the Son was the universal consciousness, comprised of the sparks of individual souls, the many consciousnesses which comprised the form or body of the Spirit, which was of too fine and rarified a vibration to be perceived by gross matter. This was why the bible had said, 'No man comes to the Father but through Me (the son).' Only by that in-built, inherited, intermediary consciousness could a human being grope towards the infinity, and finally detect that delicate radiation.

To live utterly in the Silence meant to not allow admittance at all to anything of the world, including the sense of loss. To be in the state of silence was to be in another dimension, a subtle world impossible to describe, a viewing through a telescope of another, separated, outside world.

CHAPTER FOUR

THE WHOLENESS OF LIFE

No-one has arrived at inner peace and happiness
through attachment and desire ... If you are
attached to material things like a bank balance,
house, motor car, etc., they will possess you and
keep you in constant fear and anxiety about the
possible loss of those things.[1]

For me, the most difficult part of the exercise was first thing
in the morning, on waking, when I tried to reach the state of
Silence. Because it was a dimension that was without ego,
this meant that, in order to enter that dimension, the ego and
all the physical world with it, had to become powerless, a
removed principle. In the centreless Silence, one had to be
devoid and detached from the three *gunas*, that was, the
energy of matter.

'Now that I have started seriously watching myself I see that
I am hardly ever conscious as a soul, as one who is awake,
let alone continuously, so I still have a long, boring path
ahead', I said to myself.

The next day was to be *Divali*. I stared out the window and
continued to speak to myself. 'Pre-Divali check-up: Is it
correct that there are three energies to be felt which merge,
and that they should all be felt? There is the Silence, that is a
sense of removal and wonderment. Secondly, in that state of
Silence there is the feeling of the One Unicity which moves
through, and penetrates everything. Thirdly, there is a sort of
submitted personality, humbly worshipping the Wholeness,

---

[1] Thakar, Vimala, *The Invincible*, Vol. XV, No. 1, Jan-June, 1999; 24.

but all these three are merged together in one fire.' I was thoroughly confused. Nothing that I thought or reasoned made any sense at all.

I was suddenly moved to go down the stairs into the manager's office, and ask him if I could use his phone to ring Vimalaji. He was helpful and friendly, and immediately pushed the phone across the desk towards me. It was a stark office, with nothing more than the desk, two plastic chairs and some photos of Swami Narayan hanging on the walls. I rang Vimalaji and she answered the phone.

'It's Christine speaking,' I said, 'I wondered if I could ask you a technical question.'

'Of course dear.'

'When that Silence is felt, in that Silence, the Wholeness or Infinity is felt. And does one concentrate on the Thatness, or just try to stay in the Silence?'

There was a silence for a moment, and then she replied in a deep, measured voice, 'It would be better if you could come to see me, and we could discuss this. It is rather difficult to answer on the telephone.'

'I would like to do that,' I answered.

'When would it suit you to come?'

'Any time.'

'I would be free between four and five thirty this evening,' she said.

'Well, four pm would be good,' I answered.

So I was going to see her! I felt I had had no say in it. I had been projected down the steps and towards the telephone. And, even though I had resisted seeing her for more than three weeks, even though I could almost see her house from the window of the hotel room, it had not helped to make her usual and ordinary, but she had just grown more enormous and more mythical, and I was afraid.

In case I would not be able to speak, I wrote my question on a piece of paper, revising it several times until it said what I wanted it to say:

> Silence: It is experienced as a different dimension of consciousness from that of the physical consciousness, which seems to be far away, behind glass. The witnessing consciousness is not a personality, but is aware of the abstraction from matter. Physically it is felt as the whole top of the head spins and stretches. There is a sense of miraculous surprise and wonder at everything that is going on 'down below.'

> Wholeness: It just always has been, behind all manifestation. It is infinite and all-pervading and it cannot be divided so it just IS. On a physical level it seems to be like a fire which is lovingly massaging all the body but is particularly felt between the shoulder blades and up through the head.

> There is also another energy, which maybe should be superceded now, which seems to be associated with the personality, which is somewhere in the throat or heart and which is a feeling of 'I know', 'I trust'.

> I would be grateful to know whether the above understanding is correct, and I am confused about the

'technique' (if one can talk in such terms.) Does the
person first need to evoke the Silence, and stay in that
state whilst also feeling the Wholeness, or does the
person let go of the dimension of Silence, once the
Wholeness is felt, and just allow that fire to consume?

Incidentally, the state of silence has never been
continuous for me, although Vimalaji says that one needs
to live in this dimension continuously, so does this mean
I need to first perfect a continuous abode in the Silence?'

It was a muddled groping towards the truth. All sorts of
energies were beginning to be felt, energies about which I
had no idea, could not place in any context, nor connect even
to the descriptions in Vimalaji's books.

I walked down the winding path, alongside the lake, where
holiday makers were rowing small boats on the rapidly
diminishing, increasingly odorous waters, and then through
the small bazaar to the wrought iron gates of *Shiv Kuti*,
which were closed. I lifted the latch and went into the
garden. The office was closed, and I was not sure what to do.
I took off my shoes, walked up the stairs to house, and
hesitated. Still Kaiser had not appeared, so I rang the bell,
and heard a voice call out, 'Come in.'

I went inside, and saw Vimalaji seated in a chair in a small
front room, and although my heart was racing with terror
(which I could tell she knew) when I entered her presence I
began to feel relaxed, and even to think that she looked like
an ordinary human, except for the enormous eyes like
satellite dishes for receiving distant messages. They seemed
to be tuned to something far and distant, and yet at the same
time, all the attention of the universe was focused on myself.

'And how is Christine's *Sadhana* progressing?' she asked.

'Not too well,' I answered. I felt hot and uncomfortable to be so close to her. It was almost more than I could bear.

'Why is that?' she asked.

'I've been getting confused, and in a panic, maybe because I've been trying too hard or something. Actually, I've written my question on a piece of paper, in case I lost my tongue again in your presence.'

I handed her the piece of paper. I had to remind myself that I was a fifty-four year old woman and not a school girl standing before the headmistress.

'Could you pass me my glasses please, dear?' she asked me.

I was so perturbed by the impact of her presence that I could hardly bring myself to carry out such a simple task, even though I could see the glasses on a desk to the left of the room. I picked up the glasses and handed them to her. I felt triumphant in that I had managed the first step, which was to retain my cool in the face of such an awesome responsibility as touching and holding the glasses of Vimalaji.

She began to read out what I had written slowly and deliberately, causing me considerable embarrassment, because I did not like what I had written. After she had read the first paragraph, she stopped and asked, 'The Silence is an abstraction?'

'Oh, it's just my bad words, my attempt to try and describe what I thought Vimalaji meant by those words.'

Then she read the next paragraph, and said, 'What is this feeling between the shoulder blades and up through the head?'

'Oh, that's just how it seems to feel physically,' I answered, apologetically.

'Have you read this somewhere?' she asked. She sounded very severe, and I was afraid and ashamed of what I had written.

'No, it's just my attempt to describe the feeling,' I said.

She did not say anything, but continued to read until she had finished.

'Well,' she said, looking surprised, 'Well, Christine never was continuously in the state of silence because she has never had the opportunity. It's not something you live in as an abode. It just is.'

'I'm confused about these energies and which one I should be feeling, and maybe I was trying to analyse it too much - and what does Vimalaji mean when she talks about Silence?' I asked.

'Silence is that state where movement of the thoughts ceases,' she answered. I was totally confused and Vimalaji continued. 'For now you should stop trying to analyse the energies and just sit.'

Then, surprisingly, she completely changed the subject. 'Kaiser is not here right now,' she said, 'She's gone out with two young children and their mother. Can you believe that the little girl was eight and wanted to go and look for God. Luckily the mother found her packing her bags and brought her here to see me.'

'It's good that she was brought here,' I said.

Then Vimalaji was silent again. At that moment Kaiser came into the room, said hello to me, and went to make tea, at Vimalaji's request. Again Vimalaji read the sheet of paper which I had written and then pondered it in silence.

'The state you describe is not that of the personality, the personality is not there but the mind is still there, and this causes a sense of resistance and negativity. Often people say they have a feeling as though they are dying,' she said.

'Maybe this is the same as the feeling of being totally removed which I have,' I replied. 'Also, there was a feeling of panic which might be the last kicks of this ego.'

'It will kick, because it will know it has lost its power. It knows it cannot be got rid of, the personality will always be there, but it will not have the power. It will now be ruled by the Wholeness.'

She was silent, and then spoke again. 'But this is very early, this fire. How can this be happening so quickly?'

'I don't know about this fire. I thought it was the physical effect of feeling the Wholeness.'

'How did this happen so fast?' she seemed to be asking herself, almost incredulously. 'When did you first begin?'

I was surprised that she had not seen, with clairvoyant vision, whatever incomprehensible condition might have been present in the bodies of Christine.

So I explained to her that I first met a realised woman when I was thirty, the first time I came to India, that she had been called Diana and that I had loved her deeply. I explained that Diana had written to me for fifteen years before she died, and that I had begun to sit in silence a couple of years before meeting her in 1976. I explained that it was she who recommended to me that I should study Vimalaji's books. 'Then I came to Mt. Abu in 1989 and first met you, and wept in your presence. Do you remember?'

'Yes, I remember, but it was not weeping. It was remorse for the state of the world.'

She looked again at the paper. 'This is the state of meditation you are describing,' she said. 'This is *dhyan*. This is the state of meditation.'

She saw that I did not understand the Sanskrit term and did not proceed further with the explanation.

Soon Kaiser brought in the tea, in teacups, on a tray. It was sweet, rich, milky tea and it tasted very good. As we were drinking it, the phone rang, and Kaiser went to answer it.
Left alone again with Vimalaji, I asked her, 'So I should not try to feel the Silence feeling?'

'Let that go. Just relax in the Wholeness. Just forget any reasoning. Afterwards you can try to analyse it,' she answered.

Soon Kaiser came back into the room. 'Are you comfortable?' she asked Vimalaji, after greeting me, and re-arranged the cushions of the chair.

I thought that I also should have worried about Vimalaji's comfort, but I had somehow assumed that a person who was enlightened never felt uncomfortable and never became ill. In that moment I understood that so long as there was a body which anchored the individuated divinity to the world, that body would suffer the same laws as all corporeal matter. It was a body born from other human bodies. This in fact made her presence all the more extraordinary because she was a point of consciousness which had moved beyond the human state, and yet remained in a human form.

'Kaiser was only saying this morning that we had not heard from Christine for more than eight days,' Vimalaji said, seeming to suggest that I had operated on some higher, invisible dictate.

'I did not want to bother you. I thought it was enough to be in the same place, and to absorb the vibrations which come from Vimalaji and which fill Mt. Abu,' I replied.

'You cannot bother me, dear,' she said. 'When I was with Krishnamurti we spoke often. Could it be a trouble when we are doing *Sadhana* together and maybe one of us is ten steps ahead of the other? It is good to talk.'

Then, in order to demonstrate to me that she was only human, and that I should be normal and human also, she began to speak, seemingly at random, about her days in the land-gift movement. She told me how she traveled into the villages, with a group of friends, and how they would ask for

land to be given to the landless workers who tilled the soil
that did not belong to them.

'How would you ask them?' I inquired.

'We would walk around singing, in the language of the
village where we happened to be.' She sung a little song, the
words of which I did not understand, and then explained the
meaning, which was approximately, 'We have come to ask
you to give your land to those who need it. We have come to
ask you to share generously.'

'And how did you know where to go next?'

'It would be organized by Vinobaji. He would arrange, and
then tell us where we were to go. Oh, that was something
wonderful,' she continued, 'To see the wife of the wealthy
landowner hand over the title deeds to the wife of the poor
villager. You see, we always wanted to encourage the
women to participate, if possible. Once, one of the women
came forward and said she wanted to give ten thousand
acres. I felt it was too much for me to handle alone. I called
in Vinobaji.'

Despite all the demands on her time she had talked to me
with effort, in order to encourage me to relax in her presence,
but the enormity of her impact upon me meant that I was
rapturously exhilarated, and slightly restless, unable to
concentrate properly or follow a coherent conversation.

'India is at its lowest point. There is so much greed and
corruption. When I came to Mt. Abu it was covered in trees.
Now half the trees have gone. This place has become filthy,
it's overcrowded and full of drunken people.'

'Maybe they do not know why they come,' I said, 'Maybe they come because of the emanations from Vimalaji.'

'No dear,' she answered, 'Some time ago the government of Rajasthan lifted the ban on alcohol and, because Gujarat is a dry State, they all come here to drink, because it's just across the border.'

And so it was, that although she was great, and although she was dwelling in a place beyond words, and was dipped in other dimensions where words were just superfluous labour, she chose to limit herself to a small conversation with a paltry person, who was Christine, because of the love, and compassion which brimmed from her, and which wanted to demonstrate that I need not have fear because she was a human like everyone else.

And even though she had attained a state in which her personality had quite gone and vanished, for the movement of Life conducted all actions, still I noted that she was deeply disturbed about the loss of the trees, and was not hesitant in criticising the behaviour of Indians; she saw and acknowledged the flaws. I felt perplexed to be confronting this inexplicable mixture of divine and human. From her being radiated an effulgence which was all-encompassing, and yet she spoke and behaved like any other person. I remembered that Ouspensky had written somewhere of his Master, Gurjieff, that Gurjieff was actually able to change his appearance and veil the light which beamed from his person so that he looked insignificant and unassuming. I wondered whether Vimalaji was also doing this

After I had said goodbye to her, Kaiser walked with me
down the steps. 'I wonder if I could read the books which
have the letters and articles you put together about
Vimalaji's life,' I asked her.

I was surprised that I had been in contact with Vimalaji for
ten years, and knew only about her Teaching and not at all
about the details of her life.

I went with Kaiser into the office, which was in a separate
building nearer the entrance. A small room on the opposite
side of the hall was lined with bookshelves that held copies
of all the publications. I scanned the titles and purchased
whatever I could.

'How does the publishing work?' I asked Kaiser.

'The talks are recorded if Vimalaji agrees,' Kaiser said,
'Then I transcribe them from the tapes, and when the
material is completed I go to Amedhabad to have them
published. I have worked out a system now, which, although
it involves more work, enables me to get the books published
at a very low cost, and so provide it cheaper to the readers.'

There was a trust which funded publication of the books, but
it seemed that in general Vimalaji was very much against
any kind of structure or establishment, due to the fact that
she believed foundations, societies, schools and centres were
liable to result in crystallisation of ideas, thus leading to
authoritarianism and worship.

Kaiser selected the books that I had requested from the shelf,
and I continued to scrutinise the titles, selecting several
more. After I had paid her and she had written a receipt, she

offered to take me on me motor scooter up the hill to the hotel, but I declined, for I had a ruksack, and did not want to trouble her.

Besides, I was starting to enter that state of ecstasy which I now realised was a characteristic aftermath of any meeting or even phone conversation with Vimalaji.

'I can hardly speak, it happens every time,' I said to Kaiser. 'She gives so much. I go into a swoon for days afterwards.'

....

The next day, I sat again in my room in silence.

My interview with Vimalaji had not really solved any of my questions. Clearly she had thought that I was analysing everything too much, that I had to let go all reasoning and intellectualizing, and go beyond the mind, into that other dimension where time and place did not exist. There, everything would be solved. I suspected also that she thought I had to find the way myself, and that it was not her position to provide easy answers.

'As soon as I think of the Fire, the total Fire comes,' I wrote to myself. 'That holy, sacred pure Fire has descended into this very body. It cannot be denied. I feel it. It is present right here and now. When I feel that Fire all the Energies combine – the sense of being removed, the Fire Itself, and the sacredness. There is only the Fire, in and through everything, and a sense of removal and wonder and miraculous adoration and a flaming head, and abstraction from the outer world. There is only the emptiness of Infinity inside my being, but outside these little things, the personality, like mythical animal shapes on the walls, jumping about in indignity. Today has been a most sacred day for me, perhaps the most sacred ever. Self realisation is seeing that there is only God and nothing else.'

Due to the advent of *Divali*, Mt. Abu was flooded with revelers, who had come, not because of the sacredness of the ancient pilgrimage site, but because there were shops where they could buy alcohol and legally consume it. Horn-blasting yahoos drove round the lake, pushing pedestrians out of the way. At ten pm at night fire crackers were being let off outside my window, and again they began at five in the morning. I could not understand why people would want to fill such a quiet place with so much noise.

It was also the first day when I woke up feeling the One Unicity moving within me.
What was the difference between this new state and the feeling of the One Unicity which I had first noted when I went to the Blue Mountains for retreat, ten years previously? I tried to analyse the strange changes which were taking place in my being. Previously I had not understood the feeling. It had been there, but it had been an uninterpreted stranger. Now something in my understanding had changed, the perceiving unit, the personality, was a shell, it was empty. Before, it had been the experiencer of the One Unicity, but now there was only the emptiness. Before, I could not understand it, but now everything in the world, including myself, seemed to be outside.

I began to read one of Vimalaji's books which I had purchased from Kaiser. It was called *'Message of Chandogra'*. As I read I became enraptured by the profundity of the words. I felt that they had been spoken and recorded for me alone.

> You have to penetrate layers of existence and reach the essence and get rooted there in consciousness and whenever you have to come back to the movement, you bring back the perfume of awareness of that supreme Reality, of that emptiness, of that space – akasha. You bring back that perfume of awareness and you move whenever movement is necessary in relationship [2].

> We are using the term 'empty' but it is not a void, it is not absence of energies, rather it is condensation of all energies possibly imaginable. As the movement of the planets, the stars, the various expressions of life are held together by the Akasha, by the vitality of emptiness, let all our actions and movements be held together by the awareness of the Reality, by the awareness of the Emptiness. To be rooted and grounded in the inner space, in the inner emptiness, to be in the state of meditation will enable all the movements to be held together. Then the movement and impulses of the body will not go in contraction to the thoughts and emotions contained in the psychological structure and the thoughts and knowledge contained in the consciousness will not contradict the energy of love and compassion contained in the Intelligence, in the emptiness ...[3]

> Within you is contained the same reality of Divinity and therefore you are that, I am That, this whole existence is really immortality, eternity and infinity.[4]

In the afternoon I went to the post office. The postman was a person who never smiled. It was my secret goal to make him smile, but even my bad Hindi did not evoke a response. Like

---

[2] Thakar, Vimala, *Message of Chandogra*, Vimala Prakashan Trust, 1991; 158.
[3] *Ibid;* 166.
[4] *Ibid;* 198.

many Indians, it took time to reach behind the façade of
suffering and indifference, the blank inscrutability which
concealed poverty and ennui, a hopeless sense of cornered
inevitability, and a certain jealousy and suspicion of those
who bounced in, rich and blooming, from other, wealthier
continents.

'How long will the Diwali holidays last?' I asked him.

'About ten days,' he answered. I was filled with dread at the
thought of ten days of fireworks, shouting, roaring cars on
narrow roads pushing you into the gutter, and screaming
children kicking balls in the courtyard below. I was filled
with horror at the thought of all the groups of people who
would stand outside my window on the verandah, and,
having examined the view, would then proceed to stare
intently into my room. I had tried all methods of veiling the
windows, but the only satisfactory way to eliminate curious
stares was to close the wooden shutters completely. The
room then became dark, but this was preferable to the stares.
However, even when the shutters were closed, the sound of
people talking and laughing outside was almost unbearable
to me, partly because it seemed so selfish, and partly
because, in my state of heightened sensitivity, ever small
gesture, every movement and sound was doubled and trebled
and multiplied in intensity. I had found my hearing and sense
of smell had considerably sharpened, and that I could detect
hidden meanings and intentions which lurked under surface
gesticulations. I felt I knew about people and that they could
not cover themselves. Furthermore, I noticed that the
appearance of all external objects was beginning to change.
Everything seemed more translucent, less permanent, more
fragile, a drawing made in light, rather than a substantial
presentation of matter.

I considered all sort of options which would lessen the torture of the shouting drunken inmates calling each other over the verandah from outside my room. I thought of offering to pay for the room next door, so that it would remain empty, and the small children would not stand outside my door, crying and banging the railings, but I realised that even if I were to do this, people would still idly walk along the verandah, call to their friends below, and let of fireworks, whilst loudly play their cheap cassettes with distorted, stretched, agonising sounds that rent the air and clashed, one with another.

It seemed that I would have to move, and so I walked down to Kaiser's house early one morning, when she was busy organizing a villager to help her with the gardening. Unphased by my sudden appearance, she asked me into her small house, which was a rather cramped and cold dwelling underneath the offices and meeting room. I was able to see how simply she had chosen to live, when she could have lived a prestigious life, travelling the world with a wealthy husband.

Then she spent a whole day taking me round on her motor scooter to show me various places, none of which were suitable. However, I remembered that she had mentioned a hotel where some of Vimalaji's friends stayed, and going there, I asked the manager, if he would have a room which I could use for two months.

He agreed to show me the house. It belonged to a Maharaja who lived in a distant Rajasthani village, and it was newly painted and furnished. It was not far from Swami Narayan and looked down on the white buildings and temples of the

Brahma Kumari complex. Along the road, visitors from all over the world walked to their quarters, or spilled from buses with suitcases and eager faces.

I was delighted with the new room and its peacefulness. There was a kitchen, and a young man called Arjun was provided to do the cooking and cleaning. Once more I began the process of sitting in silence.

From five thirty when I awoke until late at night I sat locked in the room, exploring, inquiring, trying to maintain the state of silence in which the One Unicity could be felt, trying to rid myself of the idea that I was a person, Christine, who had been born, and who had memories and thoughts, and wants.

I had given up worrying about defining Silence or Wholeness or Intelligence in terms of my Christian and Theosophical background, but I began to understand how Vimalaji's terminology was completely integrated with that of other sources of the ancient wisdom. I realised that the only way to escape identity with the ego, the body/mind complex, was by freedom from thought. When there was freedom from thought, then the activity of the personality ceased, and one was confronted by a huge void. This was the moment of fear, when there was an inner split between the lower being which did not want to let go of all the excitement of daily living, which did not want to let go of the power to decide, to act, to think and to reason. There were no words in the emptiness, there was nothing to plan, nothing to initiate, no action could be undertaken. The ego was helpless, afraid, reluctant to proceed into the unknown emptiness, to forsake the past, the memories, and even the idea that Christine as an entity, existed.

In her commentary on the *Yoga Sutra's of Patanjali*, Vimalaji had discussed:

> unconditional suspension if not abeyance of the whole psychic structure that mankind has built up through centuries...When that gets suspended or goes into complete discontinuity, cessation or abeyance then authentic perception takes place. As long as this man-made psychic structure, the so-called man-made mind moves through the senses and looks at the reality around or at the material objective world around through the senses, it will project its past memory and the choices from the memory on the reality and bring back wrong information. This man-made psychic structure is not capable of authentic perception, or pure perception. When the movement of this psychic structure goes into non-action then the authentic perceiving agent, the pure seeing energy – the *drashtutva* contained in us, the mutational, creative energy contained in us, takes charge of our being [5].

I wrote: 'I am beginning to twig – not only does the soul perceive, but the Whole perceives. What is in me is perceiving through me. The shell is the means by which the Thatness perceives. So really that is all there is to say. It is perceiving. It has used the soul to perceive, or rather, is using. It was always meant to be this way but as V. said the soul got distracted and forgot to be used. All that has happened is that what was always meant to be, is now Being Itself.'

As I read Vimalaji's marvelous words it was as though she had pushed aside a curtain, through which I gained a glimpse of the whole cosmos, of floating planets, and strips of

---

[55] Thakar, Vimala, *Yoga Beyond Meditation,* Vimalaji's Dialogues on "Yoga Sutras", Dalhousie, 1996, Vimal Prakashan Trust, 5, Theosophical Housing Society, Navrangpura, Ahmedabad-380 009, India, 1998; 114.

carpeted sky, and in that cosmos was the dot of Christine which felt the Fire.

There was the *prakriti* which was the created world, including consciousness, and there was the *purusha*, which was the formless Absolute. Inherent in the *prakriti* were all the tendencies of nature and these moved as an inseparable part of the natural world, even for a realised person who was still in a body: 'Even when the ego centre does not work,' Vimalaji explained, 'These three urges (appetite, thirst, sex) will be vibrating in the body of a yogi. For the bliss, for the sense of fulfillment of the seer, the *drishya* (seen energy, *prakriti*) exists'.

Thus there was nothing like an individual Christine who contained a bit of *purusha* and a bit of *prakriti*. It was rather that there was one huge blanket of energy, some of it more rarified, of higher frequency, and thus formless, but all of it interpenetrating, and divided, for the purposes of human understanding, into *purusha* and *prakriti*.

'There is a natural passion in the *drashta*, the seeing energy,' Vimalaji had said, 'In the existential mind-stuff to enjoy the *vastu* (objective reality)., The *chitti shakti* (cosmic intelligence) in a dual expression wants to become one through interaction ...
When the consciousness is merged in the non-duality or *Advaita* or the awareness of the Wholeness of life, then the male and female energies of your body get harmonised and you feel the communion of *purusha* and *prakriti* in your own being. In the unmanifest, in the subtle, at the energy level, in

the relationship, the communion, the sense of fulfillment takes place[6].'

At last I understood about the Fire. It was a total merging of *prakriti* and *purusha*. The energies of spirit and matter had merged in the 'mystic marriage', as the Sufis had called it. Personality, psyche, emotion, A*tma* or spirit, all were felt as one united, unseparated Unicity, as *Advaita*, non-duality.

The Fire felt like cold peppermint. It seemed to be in my jaws and across my shoulders. I tried sitting in different positions in case the sensation might have been caused by tired muscles but whatever my posture, the Fire seemed to persist. That Fire was Love, it was the Love of the Cosmos for the created. It was the love of the Father for the Son. I saw there was nothing else at all except the non-dual love. I saw that I had been incredibly arrogant thinking that I could do anything at all to make anything happen. All humankind was destined to mutate this way. It was not individual. It was like having a baby. Everything happened automatically and miraculously as a part of being human. You didn't believe the baby was in there inside you but it did eventually emerge, because it had to happen as part of the movement of nature, of *prakriti*.

I felt that I had never before truly turned to that which was the origin, the source, never truly got to know Its love, Its closeness. The time has come to humbly enter into communion with It. And so I sat, and it was as though I had fallen in love, and all of the natural world, and all of divinity was united within me in a glorious, triumphant sacredness.

---

[6] Thakar, Vimala, *Message of Chandogra,* Vimal Prakashan Trust, Ahmedabad, India, 1991; 282.

Like a drop in the ocean, the individual consciousness
has merged itself into the Whole, into the cosmic, into
the universal. This is what the Sufis call the mystical
marriage of the individual, and the universal. The I
consciousness is no more active. It is the Other that is
active [7].

But I was still at the stage where I was an individual feeling
the blissful marriage of *prakriti* and *purusha* within myself.

[7] Thakar, Vimala, *Meditation in Daily Life,* Vimala Prakashan Trust,
Ahmedabad, India, 1998; 22.

CHAPTER FIVE

THE STATE OF MEDITATION

Since childhood the whole Cosmos has appeared
to me as a festival of love and compassion. Every
expression of Life has been felt as a communication from the Divine. It is only in the society
created by mankind that the flow of Love and
Intelligence gets arrested and cloaked. Human
relationships are an evidence that we, the human
beings, have alienated ourselves from the fantastic dynamism of the Cosmic Life. Meditation is
nothing but the ending of that alienation. As soon
as the man-made contrivance of the Ego structure
is seen to have no factual substance, then the
arrested flow gets remobilized[1].

I would look down at the activities outside the Universal
Peace Hall, the foreigners clad in the mandatory white
clothing, the guides taking new disciples up the steps of the
Peace Hall into that vast and ugly edifice. The Brahma
Kumaris had purchased many of the surrounding houses
from the Maharaja's ancestors, and built blocks of flats for
the faithful. All these were painted white, and most had solar
heating panels which glittered on their roofs in the sun.
Above the roofs to the right the ancient, rocky mountains
towered. Once they had been forested, but now one could see
distant figures winding their way up the tracks, and returning
with bundles of sticks on their heads. Goats and cows also
availed themselves of the remaining vegetation, and troupes
of monkeys swung and chattered, tumbling and playing in
the few old substantial trees which remained. In the garden

---

[1] Thakar, Vimala, personal correspondence to Christine Townend, July,
1998.

below, a gardener furiously and regularly banged on a wall
with a stout pole, shouting curses to the monkeys, which
threatened to tear the plants asunder.

After some days, I wrote a letter to Vimalaji:

> Dear Vimalaji,
>
> Thanks to the help of Kaiser I am now staying in a very
> lovely place. It is much easier to meditate here. I did not
> realise before how difficult was the atmosphere in the
> other place – like pushing against a curtain.
>
> Since meeting you last Friday, 'I' saw that this whole
> shell contains nothing but the Infinity and is therefore
> very sacred; I mean that, as a point of perception where
> that Love has chosen to express Itself for a reason I do
> not know, in all humanity.
>
> It seems that the job now is to stabilise in this perception,
> uninterrupted by thoughts which at the moment still
> intervene quite a bit.
>
> I hope I could come to see you again in the not too
> distant future.
>
> I am interested that, the whole feeling of empty dazzle is
> similar to that I felt as a very young child of three.
>
> I read your commentary on the *Chandogya* I was amazed
> and transported by the wonder of the visions and the
> concepts which were able to be expressed in words, but
> which are beyond words. I was very grateful to have the
> privilege of reading such a sacred book, which will live
> for all time and which is from another modern Rishi.
>
> Because you are so sacred I am in awe of being in your
> presence.
>
> Yours sincerely,

I left the letter with Kaiser, and after a few days she came to visit me, giving me a time when I could visit Vimalaji. Due to Vimalaji's patience with me on our last meeting, I was not now so nervous, as I walked past the Universal Peace Hall, and the clustered groups of Brahma Kumari students. I walked round the lake, past wandering ponies, my friend the dogs which greeted me with lashing tails, the small image of Hanuman in the wall, and groups of long-tailed monkeys watching me from a wall.

I walked up the stairs.

'Please come', I heard a deep voice call. It was *her* voice, and it did not seem to come from a body at all. I knew that once I was in her presence I would be enveloped by the streaming love, and I knew that after the visit the bursting and blazing would continue to unroll, like billowing sails in wind. But still I was in awe, even panic.

I entered the room and Kaiser came in soon afterwards. Vimalaji was sitting on a divan, her back straight, her legs crossed. She was swathed in white cotton cloth, a white sari with a patterned border, but it was hard to notice anything at all, because all the world receded, as if behind glass. The body reminded me, more than anything of a '*murti*', an image in a Hindu temple, placed on a shelf to represent the Reality behind. The body itself seemed merely a symbol, a point of reference in a conundrum of Vastness, which filled the room and which spoke through that materialized representation.

'And how is Christineji today? She is not looking well,' Vimalaji said. I seemed to be lifted at once into that other dimension of consciousness, where communication with words was only a token of this other awareness, this other exchange, which was taking place between us.

'You can always tell if a person is well or sick,' I said, 'How do you know?'

She said, 'A person looks drawn ...' and did not finish the sentence, because she understood that Kaiser and I knew that she perceived the world through different eyes, different senses.

The phone rang and both she and Kaiser picked up their cordless phones. The two figures, swathed in white, pressing buttons seemed to be so incongruous, for they were embodiments of past traditions, caught in the context of modern technology, a blending of time as the old and new met in that private room, concealed in that historic land. Vimalaji was speaking in Hindi. Suddenly it occurred to me that this wildly contradictory vision of ancient and modern, mixed in one moment, was deeply significant. It seemed so strange to see one who could communicate telepathically talking on the small handpiece. Before I could control my own tongue, words issued forth from my mouth, words which seemed shocking and cheeky, and which had nothing whatsoever to do with my intentional and proposed sentences.

'Even Masters use telephones,' I said and was utterly shocked by my crassness.

I had noticed before this terrible tendency to say things without knowing I was saying them, when I was in the presence of Vimalaji. Words just seemed to form themselves and be spoken, without any permission from the author. I was immediately embarrassed by what had seemed to me to be a tactless remark, but Vimalaji accepted it, and smiled, as though it was normal. The unexpected words, and her acceptance of them, provided a pivotal moment in our relationship, because they put into language a thought which had been lurking, unexpressed, in the back of my mind.

Vimalaji was a Master! She was a hidden Master! She was *Arhat* [2], one who had completely by-passed the use of the consciousness or soul, and, being empty, was merely a form through which Spirit alone was moving. Now I knew why people who knew her whereabouts poured to her door. Although she never advertised herself, indeed, tried to conceal her true identity, she was a central point of hidden spiritual radiance which uplifted and which healed all who came in contact with her. Now I knew why she understood the future and the past, why she was able to interpret the ancient *Vedic* texts with an accuracy seldom, if ever, previously expressed in such elegant words.

As if reading my thoughts, she said, 'You're wearing black.'

I was completely taken aback, that she should refer to my clothing, when she was a being who was connected to the whole of the universe.

---

[2] Master: An Arhat, one who has undergone the fourth initiation, who no longer functions from the plane of consciousness, but whose spirit or atma is directly linked to the personality, which has ceased to function as a separated ego, and the movement of Cosmic Energy through that shell of consciousness, governs every action, every word, every thought. One who has achieved this state does not need to be reborn in the world for further learning or experience, for there is no longer any ego residing in that body. There are only the indivisible, infinite and interpenetrating waves of Life Itself.

'Is it wrong to wear black in India? I'm never quite sure,' I answered, and was equally surprised at my frivolous answer.

'It's fine to wear black, she said. 'I just thought you might be in mourning.'

'No, no. I bought this dress so long ago. I liked the stars and moons which are sort of embedded in the fabric. Now I'm trying to wear it out,' I answered.

She smiled, and I understood she had spoken these words to remind me that the world was normal, and that she was human. And I saw that she did not want to be profound and serious every minute – indeed she would like to laugh. And she had spoken the words because she had perceived my awe, and she wanted to remind me that she was normal, and based in the world, and aware of the world, and all its details.

'And how is Christineji's inquiry progressing?' Vimalaji asked. I squirmed when she attached this honorific addendum to the end of my name.

'After seeing you last time things seemed to fall into place. I read your books again, and I understood that the feeling of the Fire concerns the merging of the individual consciousness and the universal consciousness. But, if the ego is outside, and unreal, why does it need to be involved at all?'

'The ego is an invented and imagined thing, and it has nothing to do with the relationship between the individual consciousness and the universal consciousness, which is a transformation of the psyche, a revolution which takes place in the psyche itself. The ego is right out of the picture, but we cannot separate ourselves from it, as long as we are alive we are connected to it, and our awareness of its existence is related to our awareness of Life and the degree in which we perceive It,' she answered.

I was in a blur of blissful panic as she spoke.

'So is it just their total merging then that one should aim for?'

'Yes,' she said. Then she said, 'I see that a sprout has come up.' I guessed that she was referring to my letter.

'Every time I see you another sprout comes up,' I replied.

She said to Kaiser, 'Christine is looking much more relaxed today.'

Then she said, 'I'll be going to Gujarat on 15th December as my *ayurvedic* doctor has advised me not to keep this body in the cold weather of Mt. Abu over winter.'

'I hope it is a peaceful place where you will be able to relax a bit from all the visitors.'

''Yes, it is peaceful, but not private. Many people still come to visit.'

After a while she asked, 'How long will Christine be staying in Mt. Abu?'

'I will sit in that room until it happens,' I answered. As she did not reply, I asked her, 'Is it wrong to be so determined?'

'You cannot make it happen,' she answered. 'This mind is something on the level of learning and thinking and activity and realisation has nothing to do with thought.'

'Do you mean, I should give up trying? Do you think there is no point in staying here longer?' I asked, feeling very disappointed at the thought of having to return to the outside world before my task was fully finished.

'No, not at all. It is very important to have time alone, to be able to stabilise in that state of meditation, because if you were living an ordinary life you would be interrupted all the time, and the state of meditation would be disturbed. I myself did this, went away.'

'It will probably take a lot of time,' I said, 'As the mind is getting in the way a lot.'

'You *can* stabilise in the state of meditation,' she answered. 'That is the mutational energy.'

For a moment there was silence, and so I said, 'Well, I suppose I should be going now.'

'This is Christine's time. Unless you want to go,' she answered.

I sat down again, shyly. From the room where we sat it was possible to look out through the screen door at the gate below, and Vimalaji caught sight of someone opening the gate, coming through, and beginning to walk up the path towards the office.

'Do you know who it is?' she asked Kaiser

'No,' Kaiser said.

'Then dear, perhaps you could go down to see who it is.'

Kaiser nodded and hurried down the steps. 'Indians are very informal,' Vimalaji said to me. 'They think that a saint should be sitting and waiting for their visit and should be available at all times of day and night, on demand.'

Kaiser returned shortly. She gave the name of the man, and Vimalaji explained to me that he was the leader of a big national movement for secularism in politics. 'He's waiting to know your response,' Kaiser said.

I watched Vimalaji. I was interested to know how she would respond. I thought that if I had been in a similar situation (which often happened at our shelter) I would have been torn as to how to act, whether to agree to see someone who had come from far away without an appointment, or whether to be firm about fulfilling the commitments which were already scheduled for the day. Vimalaji hesitated, but did not seem nonplused. 'He will have to learn that even though he is an important leader, he must wait for an appointment,' she told Kaiser. 'He can come tomorrow at four.'

'Why would he want India to be secular?' I asked Vimalaji. 'It is a country which hides the light of spirituality. Even the travel books recognise the sacredness of India, the holy pilgrimage sites, the beauty of the spiritual journey.'

Vimalaji smiled, but did not answer. 'Why was I torturing her with words?' I thought, and yet, she had said that an hour belonged to Christine. She was giving herself utterly, generously, totally, despite all the others who wanted to see her, and whom she would have to see, and she was doing it solely because she knew that something was developing, there was a relationship slowly budding, and it could only flourish when Christine had learnt to relax in the presence of Vimalaji. This was her gift, her sacrifice, to struggle in conversation with an awkward shy visitor, in order that this Christine being could learn to absorb that incredible force which poured from her being, without being wilted like a flower in hot wind.

I asked her about the animals: it was often said that species of animals shared a group soul, and this was why, for example a flock of birds or herd of deer all turned at the same moment. But it seemed to me that many animals had individual souls. They had individual characters, individual likes and dislikes. Could it be that the animals which lived in close proximity to humans, learnt from the humans in the same was as humans learnt from masters of the wisdom? Could it be that as an animal created its own individual force-field, or soul, it was repulsed from the group soul, and became an individual? This seemed to be the case with dogs. The street dogs were so occupied in struggling to survive, that they did not have the ability to give attention to developing qualities such as loyalty, devotion and sacrifice, but rather were very competitive.

'The animals also are moving onwards and upwards. I do not know about dogs and cats
as I did not grow up with them, but it is certainly true in the case of cattle. I came from a Brahmin family and we were not allowed to keep dogs or cats, but we had cattle and horses. I had a cow, which would stop eating whenever I

went away, but after a while I discovered that if I explained to her, before I left, that I was going, then she would understand, and would eat. This cow never ate on the day when I was fasting. It is undoubted that she was a highly developed being.'

She paused.

I was still in a blur of incomprehensible blissfulness when I took my leave and drifted down the steps, almost unable to open the gate. As I left, I said to Kaiser, 'My mind is blown. You're so lucky to have that all the time.'

Kaiser smiled.

'I'm keeping notes of the whole process,' I answered. 'I feel its scientific. It unfolds. I don't know what is happening. I am watching it happen. It is all curled up in there. It just seems to show itself, to unfurl itself, step by step.'

After I took my leave of Kaiser and walked back to the house through the winding streets of the market, past baskets of vegetables spread on the footpath by villagers eager to sell, past the small sweet-shop with its glass-fronted cabin and dishes of sugary concoctions, and as I stopped at a shop, which was no more than a hole in the wall, cluttered with every assortment of plastic bucket and dipper, and as I examined a small stainless steel container which I thought might be useful for storing biscuits, in that prosaic moment I suddenly realised that Vimalaji was a true Master, a Master of the Wisdom incarnated here on earth.

She did not advertise herself, she did not allow worship of herself, she was able to know the past and the future, and yet

she kept this secret. She would never walk out on a gold
platform, decked with flowers and satin, to cheering mobs of
adoring disciples. On the contrary, she concealed herself in
an old house in a rather dilapidated garden, in a small town
away from large populations. And yet those who knew the
way had beaten a path to her door, coming from all over the
world in their thousands, and her influence extended
throughout India. It was in the small newsletter her trust
published, called the *Invincible*. She did not ever say that her
wisdom was used by those in authority, by those in power,
but if you read carefully, and studied the hints and clues, the
rather haphazard and muddled selection of articles, then it
became obvious that there was something secret and hidden
which was happening and which was concealed.

But more than all of these external things, there was the
amazing information which emerged from her and as I forgot
my interest in the container, and continued on up the hill,
passing a dog which was sleeping on the pavement, curled in
a corner in the sun, I thought; 'Could it be that there is a
similar process available to all human beings, the steps for
which vary in detail depending on the individual, but which
is an inbuilt potential in all of us? Vimalaji's life is a model
for the hidden potential. Every human can attain that
perfection if only they are dedicated. Indeed, even Christine
is destined to attain that perfection. Even if she wished it, she
could not stop, but only delay, the process.'

And as I thought this I was like lost feathers that are
wrenched from birds gone into sky and which rise higher and
higher until they are vanished.

There were geese on the lake, and in the gardens outside the
window of my room I watched the man banging his stick on

the stone wall to scare away the monkeys. Sometimes he picked up a rock and threw it at them, and, calling to each other they fled through the tree-tops, causing the branches to swing and lash as they rose and fell through space, as though they were on secret strings which governed their passage. 'In the arrogance of the intellect and drunken with the power of knowledge,' Vimala had once written, 'The human race feels that this whole kingdom of the universe exists to serve them, as though nature has no justification for existing by itself, but that the purpose of nature is to serve humankind. That seems to be the fundamental mistake that has been committed.'

I still had a notion that it was important to achieve continuity of consciousness through dissolving of the etheric web, that this was the goal for which I was aiming, as it marked a permanent securing of the state of bliss. When this point was achieved, no longer would the state of meditation, the state of Fire, fluctuate from day to day, but it would be forever fixed and definite. The clairvoyance which would accompany the dissolving of the etheric web would be a signal to myself, I thought, not to others, that I had reached the goal; it would remain a secret ability, merely a personal mark that I had reached a particular, consummating point in evolution, that the fire of the body, *shakti*, was finally blended with the fire of spirit, and an irreversible condition had occurred. I wanted it to be irreversible. I wanted to be fixed in the state of bliss, fixed in the state where nothing of the world could ever ruffle me again. And so long as I struggled and fluctuated I had not reached the goal, so it seemed.

I was influenced by information which I had extracted from *A Treatise on Cosmic Fire.*

Continuity of consciousness is achieved when man has mastered the four ethers [3].

The united result of this blending is the destruction of the etheric web and the consequent production of continuity of consciousness and the admission into the personal life of man of 'life more abundant' or the third fire of spirit[4].
The flame of spirit or the fire from the Ego comes more actively downwards [5].
Man has to consciously bring about his own liberation. The results are self-induced by the man himself [6].
By the time the third initiation is reached the man should have continuity of consciousness [7].
Continuity of consciousness is the object of evolution at this time [8].
When a man has reached the point where he can sense and see the fourth ether, he is ready for the burning away of the etheric web .. when this disintegration is completed the man merges with his astral vehicle establishing a consequent continuity of consciousness [9].

The building of the antahkarana on mental levels between the mental unit and manasic permanent atom whereby the path of liberation is traveled and man set free .. the etheric web no longer forms a barrier and the man is fully conscious in the physical brain of what transpires on the astral plane [10].

It was very cold. I sat in bed with four blankets and two jumpers. Outside it was quite dark. I was meditating, looking through the door into the bathroom where I could see the large mirror above the washbasin. A body labeled with the

---

[3] Bailey, Alice A., *A Treatise on Cosmic Fire,* Lucis Publishing Company, New York, 1973; 120.
[4] *Ibid;* 125.
[5] *Ibid;* 125.
[6] *Ibid;* 126.
[7] *Ibid;* 185.
[8] *Ibid;* 810.
[9] *Ibid;* 582.
[10] *Ibid;* 790.

name, Christine, was reflected in the mirror, wrapped in a windcheater and jogging pants. Suddenly, as I sat there, I seemed to actually vanish into the One Unicity. I was absorbed by the Infinity of space, by an all-encompassing vastness. I expanded until I became everything, an everything which was totally separate and apart from anything in the world, and yet was the source of, and sustenance of that very same world. Christine was really not there at all, except as a conveyance, and as the hours passed she vanished more and more totally, until she was nothing, and completely gone.

I sat awake long into the night, but the next morning when I awoke, I found I was again Christine; it was as though the energy which had filled my being was too much for me to hold, and it had receded.

A week passed. I saw from my window that in the Brahma Kumari gardens men were separating all the cacti plants. I went down and looked with avaricious eyes at the pile of gorgeous cacti, of so many species, so many colours, so many shapes, and it seemed they were the only plants which could thrive, for there was the dust, and there were the long months without rain, and there were the monkeys, who ate all the flowers which were tender and delicate. But the cacti had survived and flourished where nothing else could live. I thought they were beautiful.

'Could I please take these ones which you've thrown away?' I asked the man who had once told me he had maintained silence for eight years, and who wrote messages on scraps of paper kept in his pocket.

He nodded happily, and I carried bundles of cacti in my arms
up to the house, where Arjun and I potted them together. At
night, I saw Arjun sitting at the dining room table, struggling
to learn English. I asked him if he wanted a lesson and his
eyes filled with zeal and happiness.

Then again the feeling came. I made notes: 'It is quiet, it is
through the whole body. It is a fire or tingling or streaming, a
flaming might through every nerve, but especially strong up
the back and head. It is like having just had an orgasm and
tingling all over, but it does not stop after a few minutes. It is
the movement of an Energy through the body – not in the
body – only felt by the body. It makes one feel pure, upright,
sacred, holy, blessed, chosen, full of dignity a great being
which is only an empty nothing perceiving this One Unicity
which is in all and through all. The bliss/love is so powerful
that you are removed from the physical plane which seems to
be far away through glass and you don't want to go down
there into that water because the dazzle, the fire, which is
your abode is not down there. Every thought or word is a
sacrifice because it requires stirring from the abode, as if you
had to stand up when someone was massaging you all over
and walk away from the tingling to do a job at your desk.
The fire waited forever to be felt by Christine. The world of
external events now seems the most false dimension where
people have totally lost their understanding of what is
important and are squandering the bliss and violating the
ever-present sacredness. It was December 1998 that I first felt
the Fire. Now, after about one year, I have been able to self-
generate it, and not merely be stimulated by Vimalaji.'

Several days passed. Sometimes the Fire was weak,
sometimes it was strong. I continued to study Vimalaji's
books.

Through the ending of all activity the further exploration takes place, because the further exploration is not going to take place through the movement of the past .. through the gateway of Silence, through the gateway of cessation of the thinking process, one is going to get transported into a different orbit of consciousness, a different dimension of consciousness. Meditation or *Dhyana* is for the transportation of consciousness into thought-free, word-free reality, because after *dhyanam* is *Samadhi*, according to Patanjali it is *dharana-dhyana-samadhi*...You cannot describe *Samadhi*, there is no separation as the cosmic and the individual, there it is all one ocean ...

Dhyanam is the ending of all techniques and methods. *Dyanam* is ending the concept that you can transform further ... Whatever you could do you have done. So meditation is the phase in which the last effort is to be made, and that last effort is to be effortless and to be methodless, to be techniqueless. The last effort is to put your whole being in the lap of the cosmic energy, as it were...

When you go to sleep, you don't make any effort, you relax unconditionally. You have so much faith in sleep ... all the self-consciousness is gone completely, unconditionally gone. The only difference between sleep and *samadhi* is that in sleep there is no awareness except for a Yogi. In meditation there is the same unconditional relaxation, total relaxation, and complete elimination of the centre of the 'Me'. You don't say 'I am going to sleep'. If you try to make an effort to sleep you won't sleep ... so there is a dimension of effortlessness which is also a dimension of Life. Effort in one dimension and effortlessness is another. Is there any effort in love?

....That is why in Silence also there is not effort, not because we do not appreciate the significance of methods and techniques but they have no relevance here. So to relax into an unconditional effortlessness and let the life operate upon you. Your effortlessness does not mean a void or a blankness or a darkness or an inertia. Please do see this: Meditation is not a state of inertia, it is not a

state of passivity, it is not a state of mere void, but when
you thus relax unconditionally, you relax totally, then the
Supreme Intelligence operates. Meditation is the
activisation of the subtle-most energy of Intelligence.
Meditation transports our whole being from the
domination of matter, the domination of instincts and
impulses, from the domination of thoughts into the orbit
of Intelligence and the perfume of Intelligence is the
energy of Awareness [11].

After two days more without feeling the Fire, I realised that
again I was trying, by focusing intently above the head. I had
to remind myself once more that there was absolutely
nothing to be done than to be aware of the movement of the
One Unicity through the shell of Christine. There was
absolutely nothing else to do but to feel the Thatness loving
Itself and to rest in the movement of that limitless love.

Now that One Unicity began to flow down of its own accord,
all that I needed to do was to remember It and It was there. It
seemed extraordinary, unexpected, unplanned. Everything
was happening to me. I had no control, no idea what would
happen next. I was being swept into a great vortex beyond
human understanding. 'It is the communion that breathes
through you. It is the state of communion that sees through
your eyes,' Vimalaji had said. 'You have the protection of
the cosmic energies which nothing can take away from you .
. . spirituality is the awareness of your own abode, awareness
of the relation with that abode and your responsibility
towards it ... We are multidimensional. The dimension of
communion and the dimension of communication and the
interaction between them – you have to live in both the
dimensions simultaneously having your abode in one as you

[11] Thakar, Vimala, *Glimpses of Raja Yoga,* Vimal Prakashan Trust, 1991;
89-91.

have your abode in the self-consciousness, in the thought consciousness. The dimension of self-awareness can be extended to the cosmic awareness and planetary consciousness...The understanding of bondage does liberate. It is not a personal achievement. It is a consummation of human growth applicable to the whole of humanity.'

During this period I underwent several experiences when I would wake soon after midnight in the early morning with a sensation of a Fire being pushed down my back. Filled with bliss, I felt that the *Atma*, was trying to take control, to move into my being. The Thatness was trying to descend, to inhabit the bodies, and it was only a pleat of time, a trick of time that made it appear that the Infinite was not using, controlling, seeing.

During my early morning meditation, while it was still dark, I heard faint singing coming from the Universal Peace Hall. I thought that perhaps the judicious position of the house I rented, with its proximity to the Brahma Kumaris' Universal Peace Hall, had helped by generating a meditative spirit. This was the place I was meant to be. An old pilgrimage destination, now hidden beneath alcoholic tourist invasions, Mt. Abu still harboured a power concealed beneath the smashing of ancient boulders, the clearing of trees, the rising of ugly cement fantasies, the piles of rubbish and the bitumen which engulfed old walking tracks.

I went jogging and conches were sounding as I ran round the lake. But still I had not realised the implications of the Fire. I had not understood what it was, nor how it related to the O.U. No matter how many books I read, no matter how much it was carefully, precisely and profoundly explained by those who had passed through the process, because words

were not sufficient to isolate and identify the different levels
and layers of being, one had to be able to identify them for
oneself. And, without understanding of the meaning of the
various states of consciousness, they remained just feelings,
however blissful, however surprising, however unexpected
they might have been. And, even though the feelings or
states were frequently repeated, as if a higher being were
demonstrating, or revealing Itself to Christine, as if some
great Love were unveiling Itself to her adoring and amazed
consciousness, still, until she could understand, until wisdom
became incorporated in the process, the states were merely
gloriously uplifting experiences. And they needed to become
permanent, and stable, and settled, so that they were normal,
and she lived in that dimension continuously.

Arjun knocked on my door. He was always knocking on my
door, very quietly, and calling, 'Medem, Medem.' I opened
it and asked what it was that he needed.

'Could I have an English lesson,' he asked.

'If you teach me some Hindi words,' I answered.

He smiled and I thought he was beautiful. He had looked
after me conscientiously. Every morning he knocked on my
door to ask me what food I would like him to prepare that
day, and I would give him the money to purchase it. At first
he had kept bills to record the amount of money he spent,
and handed me crushed pieces of scribbled paper, but soon I
said to him that I trusted him, and that he need not worry
with the bills. Over the weeks we had many conversations,
in which he had learnt how to speak Hindi which was
simple enough for me to understand. He had told me that he
lost his father when he was nine years old, and had worked

on the road chipping rocks, then as a driver, before finding the job at the hotel. He told me that he was about eighteen years old, but did not exactly know his age.

So we sat at the dining room table, and Arjun laboriously transcribed English words into Hindi script until it became too much effort and we both gave up.

'I'm worried', he said 'Because the maharaja has not paid me for two months. '

'It seems to me very wrong that he doesn't pay you, and also that he pays you such a small amount,' I said. 'At HIS our most inexperienced staff get 1500 per month, plus four weeks holiday, plus *Diwali* bonus, plus medical assistance, and a supplement for their accommodation.'

In the morning there was no water. It had happened several times, because the monsoon had failed, and the lake and other water sources were almost empty. The huge community of Brahma Kumaris, and the inflow of Indian tourists during *Diwali*, who stayed at luxury hotels, all diminished the water supply even further, as those who needed water simply paid bribes to the officials, so that the water kept flowing in their direction.

There was a cement tank on top of a rock above the house which held the water supply. Arjun was frequently to be seen climbing up this rock, his body clinging to the outcrops, as he peered into the tank to see how much water was remaining.

I had saved a bucket of water from the previous day to meet such contingencies, and heated it in the kitchen. As I stood there waiting for it to boil, I realised something extraordinarily important, which I had never understood before: there were three witnesses, three seers, one after the other being superceded. There was the ego, or personality, which saw the world through its own coloured vision, and then this was superceded by the individual witness, the soul, the consciousness, or psyche, the state of silence, which I first experienced in the Blue Mountains, But behind this there was the universal, unlimited Thatness, the One Unicity, the Absolute Ground of Existence. It was this Witness which was the universal 'I', it was this witness which was eventually revealed in the state of Silence, this Seer which was behind even the conscious witness, so it seemed to me then.

The soul was the first real witness, the witness who made it possible for the real Witness to take control. There was the removed dimension of silence, in which the Wholeness, the One Unicity, could be felt. As its control intensified, it was felt in the bodies as a Fire, and as one became familiar with this Fire, it seemed to take control, to possess the bodies, to descend into one's very being, as though a force-field of electrical energy had completely permeated every control point of the nervous and glandular system. In this state although one was there as a presence, the ego had stepped aside, and this other, greater, effulgent power was in loving governance.

In her commentary on the *Bhagavad Gita*, Vimalaji had described the same process with different words. She had described the trinity as a transcendental principle of life, the Brahman, the indivisible, organic wholeness, secondly as universal matter or *mula prakriti*, of which the human mind and psyche were a part, and thirdly, the individual, individuated consciousness or psyche called *jiva*. The purpose of all yoga was to establish a contact between the individuated consciousness and the non-individuated, transcendental wholeness, she had said. The first step was for the jiva to become one with the *mula prakriti*, or universal matter. I now understood this to mean that when the individual became a soul-infused personality, through direct contact with, or possession by, that soul or psyche separation dissolved, for the soul could not know separation, being part of the universal matter. The final revelation, or mutation, occurred when *mulaprakriti* blended with the transcendental wholeness. This was something beyond the accomplishment of the ego. It happened on a cosmic level between the *mulaprakriti* and the *Brahman*. All the individual human could do was to relax in the communion which was now taking place between these two universal energies, through the medium of this particular ego among the many others.

I returned to my room ecstatic with this discovery. As I sat down on my bed, staring out the window at the man in white with the beard, the man who had undergone eight years of silence, who was now sitting on a seat under a neem tree reading, I felt as though a great wind or enormous pressure swept into my being. Now there was not a Christine who had been possessed by a force-field of Fire which operated and pressed her start and stop buttons, but there was a deeper, inexpressible dimension in which all sense of individuality had vanished, in which all the world seemed to be outside, including the parts and components of Christine's personality. In this remote, vast, spaceless nothing there was only the bliss of emptiness. This then, was what was meant when the sages of *Advaita* said there was no duality. There was no duality because there was nothing but this great force - blowing, electrical, immense, powerful, transforming.

The next day I awoke to human consciousness again. I felt as though a tornado had swept through the room and I was left sitting blown and pummeled by its impact.

Arjun knocked on the door. 'I'm going to see the manager,' he said. He was always going to see the manager, to carry out business to which I was not a party, which had to do with requests for money, with filling of water tanks, with surrender of dirty sheets. Arjun seemed to live in fear of the manager, whom I met once a week when he came to collect my rent. 'The manager said the Maharaja might be coming soon,' Arjun said.

'To stay in this house?'

'In one of the other rooms, only for a day or two, with his wife. He would not make a noise.'

I was enjoying the peace of the house, and was not anxious to have intruders. The Maharaja had become a mythical being. I could not imagine he would ever consolidate and actually materialise. However, I said to Arjun, 'We should make the garden look really nice, and plant it with lots of flowers. Then he'll see how conscientious you are and want to give you your salary.'

'We need wire to cover the flowers so that the monkeys and goats don't destroy them,' Arjun said.

'Could you buy it and you could cover the flowers?' I asked him. He agreed to do this and I gave him some money.

Sometimes, when Arjun was feeling chirpy and full of pride, he wore his tattered, frayed green jacket and cap, the uniform which had been provided to him in his job at the heritage hotel. The pocket was torn, and buttons were missing. His thin, small body looked even more diminished in the strange coat.

He was proud of this uniform, even though it was second-hand. He rushed round the house, frantically sweeping the carpet with a dustpan and broom, while I went down to the garden below, and asked the bearded man who had been in silence for eight years, whether I could take some more cacti cuttings. Again he replied with a written note, scribbled on a pad that he magically produced from folds of white clothing: 'Please take whatever you need.'

I thanked him, and took more bundles of cacti cuttings in my arms. There was a wonderful cactus called 'Rose Cactus'. It had red tintings on its leaves which opened in the shape of a flower, and there were others which sprouted small burgeonings from secret grooves, and others yet again, which stretched and tumbled, and every one of them did something different, and knew exactly what it was meant to do, without receiving any instructions.

So we planted the cacti, and Arjun came with rolls of chicken wire, and he spent many hours collecting oddments of rock and string, and sticks, and creating a strange and exotic design, so that the cacti were almost invisible under the layers of defensive chicken wire, and the garden looked more like a war-zone than a place where plants should grow.

And after Arjun had laboured for the whole day, and watered the cacti too copiously, and after I had explained that cactus liked to be dry sometimes, and after we had stood back and he proudly surveyed his work, I said to him, 'That's really wonderful. The Maharaja will be very, very pleased.'

He looked surprised, and worried.

'What do you mean?'

'I mean, he will be so impressed with all this good work, he will surely pay you.'

Arjun looked devastated. His face crumpled and I thought he was going to cry.

'I didn't do this for the Maharaja,' he said, 'I did it for you. I paid from my own money for that wire, because you didn't give me enough.'

I realised that, due to my bad Hindi, he had misunderstood my reasons for wanting to improve the garden. He thought it was I that had wanted the cactus planted, for my own enjoyment, and he had not at all understood that my plan had been to impress the Maharaja with Arjun's industriousness.

So I said, 'But it's good that he will see it and be impressed.'

'He won't care. Nothing I do would make any difference. He would not give a glance.'

Then I realised that even worse than a lack of payment, even worse than the tattered uniform and the lack of a bathroom, was the fact that he was treated as a non-existent entity whose presence was so insignificant that the product of his labour was not even worth noting. In the eyes of the

Maharaja all of Arjun's loveliness was worthless because of
his position at birth, because he had issued forth from a tribal
woman.

So I said that to Arjun that his work with the garden was not
at all wasted, for now we would have something beautiful to
watch, and when I returned to Jaipur I would take the cactus
with me, as a remembrance of this time we had spent
together in the house in Mt. Abu. And then he was pleased
again, and everything was once more happy, and he said he
also would take some of the cactus to his village.

....

During the following week I was totally unable to repeat the
feeling of being possessed and therefore felt much despair.

It was soon time for my next meeting with Vimalaji. As soon
as I walked in she said, 'You are sick.' So I said, 'A bit'.

'Your face looks pinched,' she added, by way of
explanation, but I knew she had seen on other levels. She
asked Kaiser to prepare tea.

While Kaiser was gone I asked her about the experiences I
had gone through, in which I felt that Infinity actually being
pushed into my back, and then I understood that it was
taking control, but after about twelve hours the feeling faded.
I explained that this had happened several times, and that I
had been quite surprised.

She smiled knowingly. I felt that in our previous meetings
she had chosen not to speak about the process through which
I most likely would pass, in the knowledge that it was

something which I had to discover for myself, and something
which should not be anticipated.

'Yes,' she said, 'At first one can maintain the enormous
velocity of the other dimension for only short periods of
time, partly because the outside vibrations disrupt the inner
state, and partly because the Energy which enters is such a
powerful force that the bodies have to learn to adjust to its
high vibrations. The bodies have to be super-sensitive and
super-refined to be able to absorb that force. At first the
body, the mind, the emotions, they can hardly stand the
power of the Thatness, and they could not remain in that
state continuously, but slowly the periods of time that one
lives in the other dimension will lengthen, until it will
become natural and continuous.'

I was intrigued and fascinated by what she said. She
understood everything that I had experienced, for she herself
had once, long ago, undergone a similar process. I had
needed to give only the briefest of explanations for her to
understand exactly what I was attempting to describe in
clumsy words, and I had an uncanny feeling that she had
known all along, and that the words were completely
superfluous. She was conveying knowledge to me by some
other means. I myself was understanding what she said, not
from the words themselves, but from the meaning behind the
words. We almost seemed to be talking a short-hand, a code
language, like that which the Vedic Sanskrit had used, a
symbolism of sound to describe events which could not be
voiced.

'Ah,' I said, 'I understand, but if that's the case it will take
me a long time.'

Again she smiled, and then she answered. 'I don't know. Christine gave so much of herself for so long in her work ... I'm very optimistic about the outcome of Christine's time here.'

Her words gave me great confidence, as the daily struggle to sit alone, to observe oneself, to keep the mind empty, although not requiring effort, required a certain determination, a certain continual alertness which at times became so wearing, so discouraging, that one felt it was the hardest test ever faced in life.

She said that she and Kaiser had gone for a drive, and that she had asked Kaiser to drive her past the house where I was staying. 'It's a lovely house,' she said. 'It's the first time I have been out of the house for two months.'

Due to a serious skiing accident in her youth she had suffered bad fractures in the legs, and now was losing her ability to walk, although this did not seem to trouble her at all, and she seldom referred to the fact.

Soon Kaiser returned with the tea on a tray which she held out before me. There were only two cups, and Vimalaji said, 'I make tea for myself only once a day in the early morning. I use only a very little tea, just immediately strain it after putting it in the pot.'

It was so simple and ordinary, I was delighted and spellbound.

Then she spoke about how she prepared all her own meals, and how the body needed sleep for only six hours a night.

She slept very profoundly, but sometimes had 'dreams' she added, as an afterthought.

I was consumed with curiosity as to what she meant by 'dreams', because I knew she had said somewhere in one of her books that only a yogi has continuity of consciousness and is aware of events that occurred during sleep as well as during waking. However, I did not like to question her on this topic, as I felt it might be private.

Kaiser had explained to me that every summer Vimalaji went to Dalhousie for four months, where she was available for people to visit. In the coming year again they would be going to Dalhousie round about the end of April. A dear friend would be driving them, and they would be staying one night in Jaipur on the way from Mt. Abu.

I mentioned to Vimalaji that we would be very honoured if she and Kaiser wanted to stay at Help in Suffering en route to Dalhousie. She thanked me, and said that they usually stayed at *Khas Koti*, a hotel run by the Rajasthan Tourist Development Corporation.

'Well, this would probably be better,' I replied, 'Because I think that if you stayed at our shelter some dogs might be barking, and also we don't have air-conditioning. I know that by the end of April it will be very hot.'

Again she smiled. 'You are worried about the dogs disturbing us,' she said, because she was so full of love that she gave credit to other people even if they did not deserve it.

'If Christineji could bring some brown bread, some tomatoes, some fresh boiled milk, we could eat sandwiches together at the hotel,' she added.

I said I would be very happy to do this. There was so much love in the room, so much gentleness, so much peace, and yet still I felt unworthy, undeserving, as though I should not be taking her time. She loved so much that no matter how much you loved her, she always won, and always her love predominated and was over-ruling, and dominant, and could not be beaten or superceded.

Then I asked, 'Vimalaji, what's going to happen to India?'

'India's going through its darkest period,' she answered. The Indian psyche since independence has been obsessed with desire for money, power, and a luxurious life. Casteism and religious fundamentalism, yes, militancy and terrorism prevail. It doesn't seem that there will be any quick solution to all the problems and ills that have accumulated since Independence. But I do think the days of organised religion are numbered, the priests, the rituals must go, in this era of science and technology.'

'So what is the future for India?'

'Don't worry dear about the future. Out of the chaos, violence and bloodshed, I see the emergence of a new culture, a new way of living, a new beauty.'

And if she could say this, then I thought that I did not need to be depressed about the mess and the mayhem, which you could even hear just outside her window, the honking of horns, the shouts and screams of people as the horse owners whipped their beasts into a gallop, the calling of hawkers, and yelling of tourists. And there was no peace left, and everything seemed to be violated, and although she could see the violation, she could see beyond it also, to something more. And because she saw a promise, then I could not be worried.

Then I asked, 'Vimalaji, last time we spoke you told me that you had gone away to sit in silence and solitude. Where was it that you went?'

'I went to many places, dear. I went to Gangotri, which is the source of the Ganges, I went to a cave in Uttar Pradesh when I was about twenty five. After I'd finished my university studies, for about three months. I was very foolish. I did many foolish things in my life. I drunk water from puddles without straining it and I got dysentery. I lived on mangoes and bananas which I collected from the forest. I did not take any food with me. I would dig a hole, and put the fruit in the hole, and cook it. Oh yes, and potatoes too. Finally, I was so weak I lost my footing one day and fell into the river. I thought I was going to drown, but after I lost consciousness, a passing *sadhu* saw the floating body and pulled it out of the water. By chance a friend of my father was visiting, and recognising the body, explained who I was, and took me back to my parents.'

'And when you were a child you were interested in these things?'

'From her earliest years Vimalaji was looking for God.'

Then again a strange thing happened. I lost control of the words which came from my person, for they were being formed in some other place, in some other dimension, and I watched, surprised and shocked as they were emitted from my mouth.

'If it's not impertinent to suggest, it seems to me that you had already realised your true nature at a very young age. If this is the case, it must have happened in another life, because you were born clairvoyant, you were born enlightened.'

I was horrified at the words that seemed intrusive, invasive, impertinent, but she smiled and with great dignity answered, 'That is correct.'

'Then I cannot help thinking that Vimalaji did not need to come back to this world at all. She was reborn only because she had some special purpose to fulfill, something to give, something that was needed.'

Still Vimalaji was not at all offended. Perhaps she realised that the words which were being emitted had nothing to do with Christine, but were coming from some other region, some other dimension.

'Now I am seventy five years old, I can speak of things I have never spoken before,' she answered. Kaiser and I sat in silence, in awe of what was to come. 'I can speak this frankly,' she said, after a pause.

'From earliest childhood I never had any sense of being a person, of wanting anything, of having any desire. There was no sexual urge in me. I felt from the youngest age that my body was there to be used by the divine. Even when Vimala was very young she could not bear to speak a single word wrongly, and if she did she would get very upset, and she would fast and do penance. Still today she is very disappointed when someone in the household does not speak the truth, or only speaks half the truth. This is something which is very painful to Vimalaji.'

'My mother was so worried about my lack of interest in men that she took me to doctors to have me examined but none of them could find anything wrong with me, and all declared that I was perfectly healthy.'

Then she listed the names of five or six realized sages who had visited the household in her youth, and told her parents that she was an enlightened being. 'Once I was called before a shastra of twenty five experts who wished to cross-examine me in order to determine whether I was realised, because a family friend, Dada, had claimed that it was so. They questioned me for several hours. I thought it was quite amusing. They asked me so many questions in great detail, including how did I feel when I had my period, did my desires increase so many days before or afterwards. I explained that I had never had any interest in sex. It wasn't that it was suppressed. It was just not there. They finally agreed that I was what Dada had claimed.'

'What is a *shastra*?'

'It's a committee. Kaiser, I forget that Christine is not an Indian. She seems like an Indian.'

'She loves India so much,' Kaiser replied.

I was overwhelmed by Vimalaji's words. Then I said, 'I have studied the Alice A. Bailey books and the Tibetan Master says that there will be four Masters who will walk the earth by the end of this century, and I believe you to be one of them.'

Again she smiled and was enigmatic.

'But I read in one of your books that you think these books are second-hand?' I asked her. 'It seems to me that the Masters of the Wisdom have tried to convey the truth of the Vedas to Western readers who cannot understand Sanskrit, and the Alice A. Bailey books are the result.'

'The Masters first tried to work with Madam Blavatsky.'

'Yes, and it's only a supposition on my part, but it seems that the Tibetan Master found that there were difficulties and needed to try again with Alice Bailey, because she was a very stable and down-to-earth person.'

'Blavatsky was not a fully stable human being. There were many inconsistencies in her life. This was the case with Krishnamurti too. The things which he spoke were often not duplicated in his life.'

Kaiser and I sat in silence. 'The Energy which pours from Vimalaji overwhelms me,' I said.

Again she smiled. 'There was a Norwegian woman who could not stay in the same room as me,' she said. 'She used to start to tremble and had to leave.'

Again I was learning in her presence. I had heard her make a statement about Krishnamurti that was not complimentary, and yet I knew she loved and revered him. How could it be that she spoke in such a matter-of-fact way, even to the point of telling me that she slept for six hours a night? How could she bother to mention these details to me when she was filled with greatness, when she was carrying the burdens of a thousand people who poured to her doorstep, some of them the highest office bearers of India?

Then I understood that there was simply no personality in her. Whatever words formed were spoken. She had no concept of filtering or choosing, of presenting only those sentences which contributed to her dignity or mystery. She did not care at all what came out of her mouth, nor what image she presented to the world. She spoke the truth, according to the regulation of the force which moved through her, spoke through her, acted through her, and It was shaped by whatever vestiges of the personality, Vimalaji, might have remained.

'Since we will be leaving in mid-December, if Christine wished to come again, she should come on the 7th or 8th December,' Vimalaji said, as I was going.

I walked down the steps with Kaiser. 'Vimalaji has never spoken before of the fact that she was realised as a child,' she said, 'Although once I heard her mutter, 'I'm one of those hidden Masters.'

'Now I understand why she said that Alice A. Bailey books are second-hand,' I said to Kaiser. 'No wonder she's never needed to read any of them, because all that truth is accessible to her.'

Kaiser nodded. Then I continued, 'She didn't say it in a derogatory way – she wasn't critical about the books, but

now I think what she means is this – you see, the Tibetan
Master, we are told, is living in a body somewhere, but he
used another person's mind to take down His words, sent to
her telepathically. In the case of Vimalaji, she doesn't use
any other person. She's already a Master, already in contact
with the truth, which she presents from her own being, and
not through another.'

Kaiser was concurring but did not speak.

It was not until later that I was to find out the full extent of
the truth for Kaiser refrained from disclosing any
information which she deemed to be confidential. And
Christine was just a recorder who was noting and who did
not know anything, and was continually surprised.

CHAPTER SIX

THE MOVEMENT OF INTELLIGENCE

> Those who are awake and aware that they are surrounded
> by infinity and eternity are held by the eternity or the
> infinity of life. But those who are deep in the slumber of
> ignorance that knowledge stimulates, are waited upon by
> that eternity so that they also might wake up some day and
> be helped by life (Sung in Sanskrit by Vimalaji)

My inquiry into human nature now shifted into a new area of
investigation, as I wanted to research and examine
everything which Vimalaji had explained to me. The other
dimension in which a person needed to stabilise absorbed my
attention, and both practically, and through study of
Vimalaji's books, I launched into an intensive period of self-
education. Time was running out. I was half way through my
period of solitude already. Soon I would have to return to the
world, to live in the world.

It was at this time that I sat down one day and read the
collection of letters and talks contained in the two volumes
put together by Kaiser, and called *Vimalaji's Global
Pilgrimage*, and, as an adjunct to these two volumes, I also
re-read Vimalaji's own account of her meetings with J.
Krishnamurti, published in the small book, *On an Eternal
Voyage*. For the first time I began to understand the story of
her friendship with him.

J. Krishnamurti's strange life had been discussed and
analysed in many biographies, and I was familiar with it. He

was born in 1895 and, when a small child, walking on the beach, was intercepted by Charles Leadbeater, one of the leaders of the Theosophical Society, which had its headquarters in Adyar, not far from Madras. Leadbeater, who was clairvoyant, was impressed by the beauty of the aura of the child, and he and his brother were 'adopted', for Leadbeater felt that, in his poverty-stricken village environment he was not receiving either adequate food nor education. In communication with the Masters of the Wisdom, Leadbeater understood that the child was to become a world saviour, to be overshadowed by the Christ himself. The child was soon found to have supernormal abilities and Leadbeater made many claims about 'initiations' and those who were chosen, thus creating an aura of dogmatism which Krishnamurti found stifling.

Krishnamurti underwent what he called 'the process', in which it seemed that his body was forcibly being purified and prepared so that it could withstand the huge voltage of energy which would pass through it should the Great Ones wish to use him as a vehicle to give their Teaching to the world. However, because of the separativeness and dogmatism of groups within the Theosophical Society, the Masters of the Wisdom apparently decided to discontinue the experiment. Krishnamurti, disappointed and disgusted by the narrow-mindedness of his mentors, dissolved the Order of the Star, of which they had appointed him leader, and began to teach in his own style as an individual.

By the time Vimalaji met him, in 1956, he was already known as the 'World Teacher', and his message of freedom from authority had been widely disseminated. Vimalaji described the circumstances under which her first meeting took place:

I found myself in Rajghat, Kashi. I was touring United
Provinces of India in connection with the Bhoodan
Movement (the Land Gift Movement of Vinoba Bhave).
I was staying with Mr. A. He was working with the
'Foundation for New Education.' I did not know
anything about the foundation; nor did I know anything
about J. Krishnamurti, who founded that institution. Mr.
A. asked me whether I would like to see Krishnamurti,
who happened to be at Rajghat then. He was giving
discourses as usual. I had no desire for a personal
interview with Krishnamurti. I was happy, however, to
get an opportunity to attending his talks. Next morning I
attended the first talk. For the first time in my life I saw
Krishnamurti. The morning was bright. The cool winter
breeze was soaked in sunshine. There were students with
their youthful eagerness; there were teachers with their
cultivated restraint, and there were elderly men and
women sitting serenely. The big hall was full of silent
life!
At 8.30 Krishnamurti entered the hall. A gentle slim
figure walked briskly and sat cross-legged on the
specially designed platform. He had remarkable eyes –
deep, expressive and eloquent. His clothes were simple
and elegant. He had such peace about him that suddenly
the hall was filled with it [1].

Krishnamurti requested Mr. A. to introduce him to the young
woman whom he had noticed sitting at the back of the room.
Vimalaji was reluctant, but when again approached, finally
agreed. From the time of their first meeting they were
kindred spirits.

After Vimalaji had met Krishnamurti in Varanasi, she
continued her work for the Land Gift Movement, and met
with a serious car accident in the hills of Assam.
Miraculously her life was saved as she was thrown from the

---

[1] Thakar, Vimala, *On an Eternal Voyage,* Vimal Prakashan Trust, 1989; 9.

jeep, and hurtled down a cliff, for she fell against a tree, smashing the side of her head, and developing an ear infection which was painful and did not heal, despite visits to the best doctors, both in India and abroad. It was Krishnamurti who made the suggestion to her that he could perhaps try to heal the ear, and it was Vimalaji who rejected this offer, for she had held a strong belief, from earliest childhood, taught to her by her father, that autonomy of thought was an indispensable component of living, and to be beholden to anybody, no matter how great, was a distortion of personal integrity.

However, Vinobaji and others had persuaded Vimalaji that when a realised being offered to do something such as this, it was not right to resist. Thus she underwent several healing sessions with Krishnaji, and the ear was restored to normal functioning. It was at this time also that the seed which was already within her began to unfurl and flourish. As she traveled in Europe, she made friends with many of the people who went and listened to Krishnamurti's talks. These people, recognising the strange, peaceful, Buddha-like appearance of the young woman, began to ask her questions about Krishnamurti's teachings, to which she would respond.

Soon she was mixing with the rich and famous of Europe. She was encouraged by Krishnamurti to start speaking, despite her reticence, and thus she spoke to those who had requested it, about the total transformation which was possible in human life, for now she was a yogi; she was a teacher, although deploring any overtones of glamour, she would not allow herself to be called one.

It was her attention to integrity that was to cause the rift, apparently generated by those around Krishnamurti. When

Vimalaji was invited to speak in Europe, she felt it
necessary, for the sake of clarification, to explain to people
that she was not speaking on behalf of Krishnamurti, she was
speaking on behalf of herself. There were certain points in
her own understanding of Life, which did not exactly co-
incide with those of Krishnaji. She had seen the huge crowds
which gathered to ogle at him, rather than to listen to the
words he had to speak, and she had resolved that she did not
want publicity, did not want fame, did not want large
audiences, but wanted to teach in the tradition of the Vedas,
with small groups of friends, with whom an intimate
exchange could take place, and real spiritual upliftment
could occur, rather than with halls of individuals, gathered as
much out of emotionalism and curiosity as out of a real spirit
of inquiry.

Vimalaji had mentioned in one of her books that she saw the
truth differently from Krishnaji in one small aspect:

> We have in the world two categories – those who convert
> the techniques and methods into rituals and make them
> empty repetition and those who throw away the
> conditions or the methods and techniques without
> having touched the truth, the essence as fact in their life.
> You can either throw away the disciplines or you can
> understand the importance of it.

> J. Krishnamurti has tried to take the humanity to the level
> of: Listen, understand, act instantaneously and be
> transformed. And I find that transformation cannot take
> place unless the biological system is cleansed. So sitting
> in silence is for purification, for cleansing, for merging
> oneself into the ocean of silence, of non-motion. But a
> person who reads Krishnamurti's books would say:
> 'Why should you sit in silence day after day? If you sit
> day after day it's a discipline, it's repeating.' You take
> meals every day, does that become repetitive? You also
> sleep every night, is sleeping a repetitive, mechanistic

activity? Is your breathing a repetitive thing for you? Why should plunging into the state of non-action, non-motion, plunging into the state of thought-free consciousness, become a repetitive or mechanistic thing? Unless you merge your psychological system also into the state of non-action and non-movement you cannot be back in the wholeness of your being.[2]

This is how Vimalaji described the events:

...I travelled through Holland, England, France and Switzerland (in 1964). The talks I gave in these countries were received with great interest. Meetings were organized by humble individuals in their homes and the average attendance used to be ·50. The affection and friendship of young and old in those countries nearly overwhelmed me.

I went back to India in December 1964 and spent ten months there. Between January 1965 and October 1965 I traveled through Bihar, United Provinces, Kashmir, Rajasthan, Gujarat and Bombay. It was a strenuous job...

Not that everything has been smooth. The publication of *The Flame of Life*, and *The Eloquence of Ecstasy*, had been widely criticized...Some accused me of repeating Krishnamurti's verses. The word, plagiarism, was used later on in connection with talks given in Holland in 1964. Publication of those talks ... seems to have disturbed many a person. Some of those who knew my intimate association with J. Krishnamurti felt hurt that I never mentioned his contribution to my life in mmy talks. Some felt hurt that instead of propagating Krishnamurti's teachings, I dared to give independent talks. Some felt annoyed that I dared to print those talks. This made my heart rather sad. In great agony I wrote to one of my friends on the 18th February, 1966:

....I have never claimed to be Krishnamurti's disciple I am an insignificant human being – one of the billions

---

[2] Thakar, Vimala, *Glimpses of Ishavasya*, Vimal Prakashan Trust, 1991; page 138.

living on this globe. But I have my life to live. I am
contented in living it. I have no time for carrying on
anybody else's mission. And who says Krishnamurti has
a mission independent of, and different from living? ...[3]

Sadly, although Vimalaji wrote to Krishnamurti several
times, asking if she could meet him, and although they had
been such close friends, he did not answer her letters, so was
never able to hear the truth from Vimalaji herself. She was
never to meet him again in the flesh.

I began to understand more when I read something that
Vimalaji had once said:

The extraordinary quality of transcendence takes place if
there is *mrdu. Mrdu* – the world is tenderness. And
another word, *Madhya*, is moderation. There is
tenderness, and, due to tenderness there is moderation. In
the feel of the person living in *samadhi* everything is in
moderation. ... Otherwise, even after *samadhi* the
aggressiveness of the ego can come back and you may
communicate the purest possible knowledge with the
impure-most aggressiveness. But there can be ..
tenderness and moderation even in the state of
transformation and transcendence.[4]

In other words, if there was an intensive focus on the raising
of *kundalini*, without a concurrent development of love, the
undivided connection of the individual with *mula prakriti*,
universal matter, then even after enlightenment vestiges of
the 'I' consciousness could remain.

---

[3] Thakar, Vimala, *On an Eternal Voyayge*, Vimal Prakashan Trust, 1989;
67-8.
[4] Thakar, Vimala, *Yoga Beyond Meditation*, Vimal Prakashan Trust, 1998;
107.

It was not only the sadness of Vimalaji's rejection by
Krishnamurti which moved me. In the letters and notes
published in *Global Pilgrimage*, despite all the unrecorded
gaps, despite the difficulty of connecting long and seemingly
irrelevant letters with travels across the globe, there was a
story which shone forth, a story of great beauty and sadness,
a story of such a trusting, idealistic person, giving so much,
with so little return, that I found myself crying as I finished
reading. Here was someone so fresh and innocent, so
sensitive to everything, always rejoicing in life, always
giving, everybody asking, everybody requesting, a person so
much alone, despite all those who loved her, misunderstood
except by the very few, because her consciousness was so
high it could not be cognised by normal humans. For such a
person even living in the world must have been a sacrifice
because she suffered as she saw the beauty of creation
constantly violated and abused. It was painful to her to see
trees being cut, to see animals abused, to see India torn by
strife.

The book showed that Vimalaji was a person who could not
avoid speaking the truth, even if it offended, a person who
was so open and so lacking in any sense of being a
personality, that she did not even mind people reading her
private letters which talked about matters such as when she
went to bed and when she bathed. There was simply no
desire in her to present an image of a guru or Teacher. The
intimacies about the details of her life were almost shocking
because they were so prosaic, and profoundly human, thus
highlighting even more the enormity of the life due to the
dramatic contrast between the person and the God.

I had been like all the other seekers, taking whatever
understanding of the truth that I could extract, never thinking

how it was for the source of the truth, but just assuming that the source was inexhaustible.

I was also overcome by a sense of injustice – a messenger of God had been sent and the world had failed to recognise her, the world had not been ready for her Teaching and all that she had given was locked away on the shelves of two rooms in Mt. Abu and Ahmedabad. Although there were many who had recognised her true identity, for the large part her life had passed unheralded and unnoticed by the world. And I wanted everyone to know about her so that the most could be gained from what she had given to the world.

....

I was now finding it relatively easy to remain in a totally neutral, empty Silence. In this Silence there was, to a greater or lesser degree, a perception that something had taken over and was using the vehicles of Christine. I called this state BUD (the 'being-used' dimension), but Vimalaji described it differently:

> Being in silence is being in the wholeness of your being. From the fragmentary you have moved into the wholeness, the totality ... once you find that out, then at every moment of leisure you will go back to that state of relaxation and that will become you abode. The energy of wholeness activised through relaxation begins to function .. the silence will become your normal dimension of living. You live in the emptiness. You are always relaxed. When it is necessary to move into relationships you move out of that wholeness ... if you make silence – that inner, unconditioned relaxation – your abode, and if the consciousness is there in the

emptiness and responds whenever necessary ... then
there is nothing left to be reborn [5].

And again:

> We stop moving consciously through thought. We stay at
> the centre totally relaxed. In that relaxation all the ideas
> and concepts, symbols and measurements stop moving. It
> is Silence. Emptiness. It is not death .... It is non-action
> of all conditioned energy. That relaxation is a psycho-
> physical fact ... Silence is Time-free consciousness.
> Thought-free consciousness. As soon as the separative,
> divisive centre stops moving, the universal starts
> operating ... the universal, unconditioned energy can be
> called the energy of Silence. Let us call it Intelligence.
> As it has no centre, it is an awareness of the wholeness of
> life, of the inter-relatedness of life. Perception through
> awareness results in a sense of non-duality [6]

The 'BUD' was beyond, or uninvolved in, or behind, all
movement. It was the Absolute Ground of Existence. It was
almost too much to endure, due to its effulgent intensity.
Every struggling moment, every waiting minute, every hour,
every confused year of life had been worth it, to taste this,
however momentarily. Christine wanted to freak out, and yet
there was nothing to freak. There was only an unlimited,
endless, watching blankness which contained everything
within it., and yet at the same time, everything was outside.
There was nothing inside. It was nothing. It was utterly
unmoving. The whole wonder of creation moved upon it, and
yet again, none of this seemed right when I tried to describe
it in words. Bodies were bubbles just floating round
somewhere outside this utterly profound, vast, sacred,

---

[5] Thakar, Vimala, *Through Silence to Meditation,* Vimal Prakashan Trust,
Ahmedabad, 1998; 32.

[6] Irani, Kaiser (ed), *Vimalaji's Global Pilgrimage,* Vol. II, Vimal Prakashan
Trust, Ahmedabad, 1998; 196.

adoring black. One could even experiment, first feeling the Wholeness move through one, and then receding again, so that the movement was gone and you were left in the black emptiness. It was so surprising and not at all what I had expected. The more one receded into it the more everything became outside and far away. It was not the dazzle of things, it was behind the dazzle. It was just empty space like floating in the galaxies with planets and stars rushing past. It was total power. It was synthesis because of its potentiality in every stretch of space, because it was the point at which all was synthesised, without duality. And yet it was not a point but all of space.

The soul was merely an empty eye, a clear lens for the issuing forth of the nothing which exhaled this moving love. The material world was so far away, so ephemeral, so fragile. This was indeed the thunder of silence.

The process through which I had passed was now beginning to become clearer.

First one began by observing thoughts. This involved watching from a position above the head. This was hard and took a long time to learn.

After perseverance, the state of thought observation suddenly transformed automatically into a state of freedom from all thoughts, which could be maintained for periods of hours at a time if external conditions were amenable.

In this state, when all thought was suspended, one suddenly entered another dimension, called Silence, when the soul or consciousness awoke to the fact that it was not identified with the ego, but was indeed the Son of the Father. In its initial stages this state was felt as a removed, abstracted dimension, as though the world was far away. It seemed to subside with time as the bodies adjusted to its vibratory field.

The One Unicity, Intelligence, was almost immediately felt in this removed dimension of Silence, and filled the void with the movement of love. This was what Vimalaji called the movement of Life. According to Theosophical terminology it was the layer or level of *Buddhi* which was being perceived through the *chakras* or energy centres of the bodies. *Buddhic* consciousness could also be called as Gurjieff had done, 'the fourth dimension'.

The human then needed to adjust the miniature human force-field so that it vibrated synchronously with the vast electrical force-field of this *Buddhic* energy, which was in fact the etheric body of the Logos or Absolute, or Spirit, in which we lived and moved and had our being, as the bible had explained. And this Etheric body of the Absolute, the Father, was the Son, the Universal Consciousness, Paramatma. Once a human learnt to adjust to this undivided, all-permeating, eternal and infinite energy force-field, duality could not be felt.

At first the Wholeness, the movement of Intelligence or Spirit, was felt weakly, but after repeated practice once again the dimension changed and the Wholeness, instead of being perceived by the ego, descended into that complex and took control. It came down of its own accord and could not be manipulated. It generated a feeling of intimate communion between the material bodies and the possessing, operating Energy, resulting in bliss, elevation, freedom and a sense of triumph and completion. This state was called *bijsamadhi*, meditation with seed, because there was still the sense that the individual was there, being possessed and used by the greater Energy. It was called by the Sufis, 'the mystical marriage', or, by the Theosophists, 'the soul-infused personality.'

When this state seemed to fade, it could be evoked again by entering Silence through focusing above the head.

However, I remained perplexed as to the next step along the way. I had no idea as to what would happen next, or what I should do. I still believed that there was something which I, as a human, could do, and this was a great mistake. I was absorbed in the wonder of the occurrences, which I had not expected, and which had happened to me without warning. I failed to heed Vimalaji's warnings that all these experiences were simply impressions which occurred on the psychic level. They were no more than aids in learning. They were not in and of themselves of any importance except inasmuch as they taught new truths about the nature of the cosmos.

My next meeting with Vimalaji had been planned through Kaiser. As usual we sat in the front room. Vimalaji asked me to sit close to her so that she could hear what I was saying, as I spoke softly.

'Some visitors from Chile are arriving in Mt. Abu at six pm tonight,' she said, 'And if Christine wishes she could go with Kaiser to meet them after we've finished this talk. They had invited Vimalaji to Chile to speak many years ago. Susan said to me today that I had told her ten years ago that we would meet again, and she said at that time she thought it would be impossible, but if the cosmic moves, nothing can stop it.'

'Vimalaji, when I first met you ten years ago you told me I would return to India, and that also seemed impossible at the time,' I said.

There was silence, and then Vimalaji looked at me as if to ask how I would like to spend the time with her. I suggested that since it was our last time together for a while, maybe we could sit in silence. She did not hear this properly and answered quite firmly, 'We will be meeting in April'. So Kaiser explained to her in Gujarati that I had meant, we would not be meeting for a while.

Kaiser and Vimalaji spoke to each other as to how long the meditation should last and it was decided we sit in silence for twenty five minutes, after which time Kaiser would sound the *Om* three times.

Kaiser and I sat on the floor, and Vimala sat in a chair, her eyes slightly open, a seraphic expression on her face. After the period of silence was finished, I found it extremely hard to speak, and I noticed that Vimalaji had even more of a problem. She was aware of something so enormous that her eyes were wide with amazement. They were huge, as though the cosmos was pouring through them, as though she was seeing angels and gods which were invisible to us. Whilst she still seemed to be in this other miraculous dimension, she began to speak with a deep, melodious voice which appeared to come from far away.

'You see,' she began, 'We have not come here as Kaiser, and Christine and Vimala. It is the movement of the Cosmos which has brought us together. It is in the expression of relationship that the Cosmic is fulfilled. The three of us have been brought together from different parts of the world. Dear

Kaiser came all the way from Canada.' She stopped, and I said, 'Without her your words would not be available in books.'

'She has given her life for this,' Vimalaji answered.

'And Christine has come all the way from Australia to do her work in India,' she continued. 'We have all been moved together to fulfill the expression of Intelligence.'

Then again she was silent, and, after a while she said, 'It is hard to return to this room after being in silence. Kaiser, how many people have ever asked if they could sit in silence with Vimalaji?'

'None, well, maybe one or two,' she answered.

'It is what I like to do most of all,' Vimalaji said, 'But I find it hard to wake up afterwards. Once, at a camp, we sat in silence, and when I woke I found that everyone had left the room and that I had been sitting alone there for two hours!'

We laughed, and then, because there was a pause, I said, 'Well, maybe I should go.'

'There is no need dear,' she answered, 'Unless you want to go. We have another quarter hour remaining before you need to leave with Kaiser.' Turning to Kaiser, she said to her, 'Maybe you could make us some tea?'

Kaiser nodded and left the room. I began to try to thank her for all she had done to push me on my way, but she interrupted and said, 'You see, its not a matter of thanking. I too have been fulfilled by your inquiry and by our being brought together.'

While Kaiser was out of the room, I asked Vimalaji about the strange experiences I was undergoing, when it seemed as though there was a sort of black stillness behind the movement of the love, a universal Seer, a powerful velocity which seemed to have its own volition and to descend at its own choosing, not that of Christine.

'It has its own vibration,' Vimalaji answered me. 'One has to adjust oneself to It to be able to perceive It.'

She still seemed to be very far away, in a very ecstatic state, and she said, 'It is not only global but it is universal. It extends beyond this globe.'

I began to panic that I was alone with her. I wondered what I could say to fill the silence. But again the strange phenomenon of words issuing forth uncontrolled and unplanned, from my own disobedient mouth, began to occur.

'I have read the two volumes of *Global Pilgrimage*,' I said.

'Have you?', she answered. 'I have not read it myself. Kaiser asked if she could put together the material and I gave my consent to it.'

'It moved me to tears,' I replied. 'Even though there were so many people surrounding Vimalaji she was still very much alone due to her state of consciousness.'

She nodded at this, and I said that the book showed how she could have had fame and fortune if she had chosen it, but she turned away from the offers of positions and posts, and determined instead to hold small group meetings.

'Ah, yes, this was the important thing,' she replied, 'To relate fully, not to attract crowds or publicity, but to build a network of global friends.'

'It became apparent from the book – there were even small details about Vimalaji's life – what you ate – there was a total lack of any sense of personality.'

'This is the case,' she answered. 'It is very hard not to be worshipped. Indians love to worship people.'

Then there was another silence, and the words proceeded apace and unchecked from my mouth: 'Has anyone ever written your biography?'

At this point Kaiser came back with the tea, three teacups on a tray, which she held out to me, and I took one, anticipating the creamy sweet taste. I was furious with myself that I had asked such a stupid question, because Kaiser had already told me that people had wanted to write Vimalaji's biography, but that Vimalaji had always refused. This made my stupidity all the more exasperating, and I was disgusted with myself that I was speaking in such a provocative manner.

'Kaiser has written the book, nothing more is needed,' Vimalaji replied. 'You see, a biography would be just about the personality, the external. Such a thing is not needed.'

'No - but something is needed for the internal,' the uncontrolled words replied, 'Something is needed as an inspiration for the general pubic to fill in the gaps, because *Global Pilgrimage* is more for serious researchers and friends. Its too long for people to just pick off the shelf for a light read.'

I was now feeling even more furious and humiliated. I was presenting a point of view which had nothing to do with the way I felt, and which was actually in contradiction to Vimalaji's words.

'What are the gaps which need to be filled?' Vimalaji asked me.

'It would not be about the external. Rather – what was it that moved the beautiful little girl to go and sit in a cave? What was it that made a human so imbued with a sense of divinity? We're all human, and this life shows that out of humanity can come a new race, a new evolution, that there is a miracle in our own bodies, our shells are so built that we cannot help becoming divine. It's inevitable. At a certain stage of my life I wanted to read books which would inspire and uplift, which would be for the heart, which would give the promise that it was in all of us to reach our divine potential.'

'Such a book would be helpful,' Kaiser said. Then there was silence. I was no longer shocked. I was clearly not responsible for the conversation which had been emitted from Christine's speaking apparatus.

'Very well then,' Vimalaji replied. 'If I am still here and if Christine still has the wish, then let her write the book.'

I felt amazed and in awe, but still the persistent words went on presenting themselves.

'Such a book would need to be written very carefully. I would need to ask you questions.'

'You can ask me whatever you need to ask and I will be available to answer,' she replied.

We sat in silence, and then Vimalaji spoke again, as if to explain what had happened, as if to persuade me not to feel uneasy. 'Our words are not the words of Kaiser, or Christine, or Vimala. Our words are not from individual people. The Cosmic Intelligence has brought us together, and the words have come from the movement of the Cosmic, not from our minds. It is expressing Itself through the words.'

It was time for Kaiser and myself to leave. As we walked down the steps, Kaiser said, 'It's very wonderful that you'll be able to do this. Such a book is really needed.'

It was cold and Kaiser lent me a woollen shawl. I sat behind her on her motor scooter, and she roared up the narrow roads, wending her way through crowds of people who were walking in the streets, and bargaining in the small tourist shops. She had booked the visitors a room at Swami Narayan Mandir, and I felt uneasy returning there after my hasty and peremptory departure.

Anita and the manager smiled at me, and told Kaiser in Gujarati that they would like me to return to the hotel after the crowd had departed. Kaiser and I sat and waited in the dark for the Chilean visitors to arrive.

'I had written a letter of thanks to Vimalaji which I had not been brave enough to give her,' I said to Kaiser, 'So maybe you could read it and if you think it's alright you could give it to her.'

I handed it to her and she read it to herself. It said:

Dear Vimalaji,

At first I thought I would like to thank you for all you have given over the years to this one personally, from your books and your Being because without you this one would probably still be wandering in the mire and mud of confusion. But somehow I cannot thank you – I can only rejoice that out of the Ocean of Being you came and gave and shone with that Love which is in the whole dazzling movement of the earth and focused it and expressed it and even managed to catch it in words so people could understand. So this letter is one of humble rejoicing in this Sacredness which is embodied in you and which you have shown to me and the miracle that humanity is made in such a way that it is eventually inevitable for us to become the God which we are. So humbly do I kneel at your feet rejoicing.'

'That letter's fine,' Kaiser said. 'Shall I keep it and give it to Vimalaji?'

'Yes, thank you,' I answered.

Anita, the cook, came out and gave us two plastic chairs on which to sit. The cemented courtyard was still warm from the vanished sun. Below we could see the lights of Mt. Abu.

'People say that for centuries many saints came and sat and meditated in all the caves dotted through the forest,' I said to Kaiser. 'They must have left something behind, some radiation.'

We sat some more in silence.

'Maybe I could ask the questions when you and Vimalaji are in Dalhousie next April.' I answered, explaining that I did not even want to think about it while I was still in retreat, and that as soon as I left Mt. Abu we would be going to Australia for two months.

'I think that would fit well,' Kaiser replied. 'I'll asked Didi if it suits.'

Kaiser also advised me to ensure that I researched the questions thoroughly so as not to waste any of Vimalaji's time.

Then I said to Kaiser, 'She must have been a very revolutionary person – her teachings are revolutionary, and she is a feminist, and Gandhian socialist, and she does not accept authority, but believes everyone must have total freedom, both politically and personally. And she gave so much of her life working for India, in the Land Gift Movement, and later when she undertook the *Satsang yatra*. Walking all round India, speaking at the request of others, a pilgrimage for freedom and democracy. Were you with her then?'

'I edited the book, *Eloquence of Action*, which contains some information about those years 1978-88,' she replied.

'After Vimalaji came back from abroad and settled in Mt. Abu, a number of religious inquirers started to live with her, or near her. Many lived in other States as well and they decided to travel through India meeting people through personal contact, to encourage them to wake up, to stop being so passive, and to take control of their lives.'

'The village people?'

'She wanted to reach any people so that they could recognize their rights as voters, and their responsibility to keep democracy alive in India. So she led this pilgrimage in order to awaken the awareness.'

'And you went also?'

'I was there.'

'It must have been a bit uncomfortable when you travelled for weeks at a time, a whole group of you, camping at night....'

Kaiser shrugged. I knew that she felt that nothing was difficult so long as she was with Vimalaji.

. . . .

Christmas was coming, and the new century. I felt very much alone shut in the small room all day. However, the regular interruptions of Arjun provided me with some company and our friendship deepened. In Jaipur at Help in Suffering Jeremy had been doing all my work during my absence. Although he was busy he took the night bus to Mt. Abu and we spent three very happy days together over Christmas. Arjun went into service mode - a frantic rush of continued, excited activity, whipping from the kitchen with steaming dishes of fragrant curries, producing the best china from a locked cupboard, exuberantly washing cutlery and saucepans, and industriously chopping vegetables, and insisting on photographs being taken of himself in his uniform serving us meals on a tray. It was a time of great happiness.

The other person who gave me much support was Kaiser. We had now grown close, and kept in contact. The day before she and Vimalaji were to leave Mt. Abu for the warmth of Gujarat, she called to see me.

'How is your *Sadhana* going?' she asked me.

'Dreadful,' I answered. 'I don't think I'll ever get there. Sometimes it happens, and then it just goes.'

She gave me a letter from Vimalaji, which I opened and read out loud to her also.

Dear Christine,

Many thanks for yours of 7.12.99. Your visit to Abu this time seems to have caused an inner revolution in you. The preparation might have been going on in the subconscious.

When the perspective of life goes through a change the attitude towards all relationship changes radically. Your sensitivity towards the animal kingdom – our non-human fellow beings – has been extraordinary. It bring about an ecological awareness.

May the Divine Energy of the Cosmic Consciousness take charge of your Being and your Life.

Let us hope that we will meet at Jaipur in the last week of April, 2000.

With deep love,
Vimala.

'What a wonderful letter,' I said to Kaiser. 'She is saying that to comfort me and encourage me because she knew I'm feeling depressed and not succeeding.'

'Oh, and she asked me to give you this too. It's a copy of a letter she wrote to a friend.'

I briefly glanced at the letter. In the first paragraph it said, 'Many thanks for your (letter). We are physically far away from each other! Psychically we are in communion with each other! Space and Time cannot create distance in the dimension of Consciousness. That is how I live with the ancient *Vedic* Sages as well as those who have lived on this planet in different continents.'

'Have you read it?' I asked Kaiser, incredulous.

'Yes', she said.

'She is in communication with the Masters of the Wisdom.'

Kaiser smiled. She must have already known this, but had not spoken of it, as was her responsibility.

'There's a tape which was recorded when she was speaking to a small group of friends. I could lend you it,' Kaiser said. 'I'm transcribing it for publication.'

The next day she brought me the tape, and when I was alone in my room, I turned it on. I listened to the calm, measured voice of Vimalaji speaking. She was talking about the forest culture of the Upanishads, at a time which she put at about ten thousand years ago.

....Bliss and joy were incorporated into their way of
living. I know it is not possible but some time, were we
to spend together a full year then I could tell you all
about the ancient culture and way of living which I have
seen and lived.

'What did she mean?' I wondered. I continued to listen and
soon heard her say to the small group to whom she had been
speaking, 'My friends, We the Seers of ancient India, do not
recognize anything as matter. For Us life is divine and it is a
dance of divinity.....' There was a long pause, as if she was
speaking from far, far away, and then returned again into the
room, became conscious again of her listeners, and said, '
...so!...'

Had Vimalaji given me the letter as a confirmation of my
questioning when I had last met her? I could only conclude
that she had admitted me into this knowledge because she
knew I had already sensed it for myself.

Over the following days, I visited Kaiser several times. She
asked me round to her small flat, and cooked for me Parsi
food, steaming, aromatic, full of new tastes and flavours. She
would not allow me to return her hospitality, as she said that
I should not be distracted from my period of silence and
solitude.

She, like Vimalaji, loved the natural landscape, and she took
me walking in the hills one afternoon. We wound our way
round bush paths, over stones, past rocks, and tawny,
scrubby bush. All the great trees had long since been cleared.

'When Vimalaji first came to Mt. Abu she climbed every
peak,' Kaiser said, 'She wanted to see everything that
surrounded her.' It was hard for me to imagine her as a

young woman, enthusiastic, curious, brushing the hair back from her face, climbing the rocks, staring into the wind, towards the distant haze, towards the plains of Gujarat, shimmering in the heat below.

CHAPTER SEVEN

THE OTHER DIMENSION

> When there is a radical, a comprehensive, a total change at
> the centre of the being, at the source of your perception, at
> the source of your responses – such a radical,
> comprehensive or total change is called revolution. It is
> called mutation. From the science of physics you can use
> this term 'mutation'. Mutation is a radical, comprehensive,
> total, qualitative change in the mutant [1].

After the New Year, and the start of the new millenium, I
moved back to my room in Swami Narayan Mandir, and
Arjun went back to his village. He was going to resign from
his work for the Maharaja, and come to work at Help in
Suffering.

The last three weeks of my three months seemed to pass all
too quickly, although I missed my friends and family and
sometimes felt lonely. But I reminded myself how fortunate I
was to have this gift of time which I could spend alone and
in silence, without any external work commitments, time in
which I could continue this sacred investigation.

Gradually, as the 'Other Dimension' became more familiar I
found it could be realised quite quickly, almost automatically
when you were in the state of Silence. The division between
the Silence and this deeper dimension began to blur, and I
was finding it difficult to tell which was the dimension of

---

[1] Thakar, Vimala, *The Invincible,* Vol. XI, No. 1, Jan-March, 1995.

Silence and which was the even deeper dimension of the 'Being Possessed Dimension'.

Then within the last few days before I left Mt. Abu, I was sitting on the bed one evening when it seemed as though I was suddenly given an explanation of the relationship of human consciousness to space and time. This was a question which had often puzzled me, and I had never been able to understand how consciousness could be everywhere and yet also in one place. As though a whole three-dimensional screen was placed before my eyes, while I sat in a darkened theatre, I saw the image of my own consciousness, a contrived, constructed ball of fuzz, which had condensed from the space of the cosmos into a collection of matter. I saw this ball of fuzz suspended in the void of timeless space, and within this condensed ball, space and time became trapped by the perception of the ball. For outside the ball of consciousness there was only a void, in which space and time were unknown. It was only while I, Christine, was enmeshed in the ball, that I remained unable to extend everywhere. If somehow I could realise the limitations of the ball of fuzz, not only would be everywhere throughout the void of blackness, but I would also be in an eternal suspension, in which only the present moment existed.

In this manner other profound insights, which language could not express, were also answered for me. For example, on another occasion I understood suddenly that Christine definitely could not exist. This happened when again I seemed to be looking at a three-dimensional screen in which a gate was represented in the void of space. There was a tiny figure at the gate which was this object called Christine. But all viewing of the gate and of the small figure came from behind, not from any particular point, but from the whole black void of space which looked through and around everything.

At the same time as seeing the image, an explanation was presented to my mind which clarified beyond any question the fact that Christine was not the one who was the Perceiver. The Perceiver was this Universal Energy of Awareness which was unlimited, all-pervading. It was simply an indisputable, verifiable fact that Christine could not at all be there, because she was not the one who perceived, she was not the Presence.

This momentary insight had a profound effect. Although I had known it before, it suddenly became a factual facet of my conscious existence. I, or Christine as I became, for this ego was now objectified, was overwhelmingly disoriented. There seemed to no longer be a point of reference. I was in no place, for 'I' was not in existence at all. Thus I felt profoundly free, whilst at the same time suspended in limbo, sort of swinging in the black void. I did not feel I belonged anywhere. I was not in the world, and yet I was not out of the world.

One of the characteristics of these experiences was that of the surprise and unexpectedness which accompanied them. They were not something that one could have caused to have happened by means of anticipation or imagination, for they were events which solved problems, about which I had no concept of a solution, no means of even expressing or conceptualising the question. And for this reason I believed that what I had seen were presentations of universal truth which somehow had manifested as symbolic pictures with full explanations attached.

It suddenly occurred to me that because I was no longer
seeing the world from the viewpoint of Christine, that
somehow my soul must have been universalised. The false
division between myself as an entity as separate from the
surrounding space, had dissolved. Now it seemed that there
was only the Awareness being Aware of Itself. I understood
suddenly and with amazement how Vimalaji had described
this condition as 'communion and communication' as multidimensional beings, on the outside level of the personality,
communicating with the world, whilst simultaneously, on the
'inside' in communion with the One Unicity.

There was one other thing which I noted, which had
irrevocably changed my life. For most of the three months,
when I sat in silence, there was an effort, however subtle in
which the consciousness, or psyche was focusing on
maintaining the silence. This in itself constituted an effort,
even though it was effortless! The very act of focusing in the
centre above the head, although one seemed to rest there
with great peacefulness, constituted a positive maintenance
of position, in contradistinction to a negative and receptive
position.

If, on the other hand, a totally receptive, non-active
awareness was maintained, and I did not even try to stay in
the state of silence, then, *of its own accord and without any
effort,* the Energy started to pour down. It was the most
amazing, most miraculous incredible bliss that absolutely
without any attempt to be in any state, but just with
acknowledgement of, or a thought of It, It descended. And
yet it was almost impossible to define, let alone describe in
words, this crucial difference between positively attracting,
and negatively being aware and open to its descent. It was in
fact a reversal of everything. Instead of the Silence trying to

attract the Energy downwards, the Energy was waiting to come down all the time, and only seemed to want the acknowledgement in order to flood and possess the bodies. This new state brought with it an extraordinarily intoxicatingly delirious and miraculous wonder, which later was to settle into a continuous and ordinary background of 'Presence'.

When it was time for my departure I took a taxi, because of the thirty cacti. I sat on the back seat and felt confused. The driver stopped at a midway point where we ate all the wondrous foods of India, seemingly so easily produced from out of a simple kitchen, on a rather greasy plastic tray, but tasting of heaven, fragrant, hot with chili and spices, rich with *ghee* and *panir*. And into this delicious dream of vegetables we dipped the hot, flat bread, which had been cooked in the wood-fired oven, and my being rejoiced in the details of *Rajasthani* culture. And when we had washed the oil and vegetables and spices from our hands, and when the driver had rinsed out his mouth and spat down the basin, we climbed back into the hot Ambassador, with the cacti still looking contented on the back seat, and we continued our journey until we came to Jaipur.

There was Jeremy to greet me, and there was a pile of papers on my desk, and there were the people I loved, as they had always been, and yet I was in hell because the impact of demands meant that the Awareness was not looking through me.

I went and sat on the bed. I saw that this return was also a 'test'. Was the Silence more sacred and important to me than all the colour and beauty and excitement of the outside life? Could Christine continue to keep herself empty so that the

Awareness could operate, come what may? Could she recognise and devote her life and her attention to the Reality, rather than to the beautiful external phenomenal world?

I wrote to Vimalaji and explained to her some of the experiences through which I had passed since last meeting her. I also asked her whether she thought it would be necessary for me to go away again in order to complete the process.

Vimalaji's reply came shortly afterwards:

'Dear Christine,

Many thanks for your detailed letter .. You can arrive at Dalhousie as per your desire and convenience. ...

The temptation to verbalise the events that take place when Silence dawns upon the heart, is common among all the enquirers. Intellect wants to identify, recognize, define or describe whatever happens in the waking consciousness. Hence the first encounter with the nothingness of Silence and its effect in arousing neuro-chemical upsurges, is also interpreted...

Individual consciousness which is addressed by the names like Christine or Kaiser is the conditioned part of the Universal consciousness. When it relaxes into its source or matrix of existence, it ceases to function as Christine or Kaiser. In that dimension of unconditional awareness, the impersonal operates through the person. In the beginning this state of personality lasts for some time and the pull of the past inter-woven with the flesh and blood, drags one back into the individuated unit of consciousness. When the inquirer persists in dwelling in silence, the frequency of the grip of impersonal Universal consciousness gets stronger and stronger. Gradually it becomes the normal dimension and the individuated personal consciousness gets reduced to a useful tool for inter-action with the world.

It seems to me that we better discuss your questions when we meet personally. Otherwise my letter will get enlarged into a discourse on silence and meditation. Let us wait until the month of May.

With deep love and blessings,
Vimala.

....

It was a very hot April in Jaipur. The temperature had already climbed over forty degrees Celsius, and would continue to rise until the monsoon was due to break at the beginning of July. But on the day which Vimalaji was to pass through Jaipur on her way to Dalhousie, 21 April, 2000, the skies suddenly clouded, and the afternoon was cool. The sky was luminous, surreal, hanging like a faded pink silk canopy in a raja's tent.

I asked the receptionist to give me the keys for the rooms that I had booked for Vimalaji, Kaiser, and Raju, a friend who was driving them, so that I could turn on the air-conditioning before the travelers arrived. Vimalaji and Kaiser were to share a room. It was a humble room, with worn carpet and faded paint. However, the sheets and pillow-slips looked white and crisp. I wondered that she would stay in such a simple room, but Kaiser had said it was where they usually stayed.

I sat in the room, and surveyed the dishes of food which I had cooked in consultation with Kaiser. There was a hot, spicy potato called *aloo dum,* sliced tomatoes, fresh wholemeal bread, butter, and a stainless steel tiffin containing fresh milk that I had boiled and cooled. The milk had been given by Babu, one of our senior staff, and it had come from his jersey cow, which he had rescued abandoned on the road, a few years previously.

I wondered whether Vimalaji would know that I had sat on her bed, and whether she could feel the other people who had previously used the room. The room was stuffy and the old air-conditioner shook and roared, its noise emanations far exceeding its ability to cool the room.

As the sun began to vanish, I went outside and sat in a frayed wicker chair on the verandah. Soon I saw a new Tata Sumo jeep coming up the driveway, in which was sitting Vimalaji in the front passenger seat, with Kaiser behind.

Everything began to happen fast. Kaiser alighted from the jeep, looking concerned.

'Should we drive further up the drive towards the rooms?' she asked me. She seemed concerned about Vimalaji's ability to walk the distance from the driveway across the wide stretch of lawn.

'The rooms are up there, so you could drive a bit further forwards,' I answered.

Kaiser asked Vimalaji whether they should drive forwards, and she answered that this was not necessary. She slid herself down from the rather high seat of the jeep, and, having given me a brilliant smile and greeting, hobbled towards the room. She moved so rapidly that Kaiser had to run to catch her up.

I helped Ajay to unload the luggage. 'I'm Christine,' I explained. 'I hope its alright if I come along with you.'

'That's fine by me,' he said, smiling. 'I'm only the driver.'

'Its your jeep?'

'No, it's a new jeep. It's belongs to the trust. Vimalaji was having much discomfort when travelling,' he said, 'But when she travelled to Gujarat last year, she travelled in one of these, and found she could sit for a longer period.'

'So, you're a friend of Vimalaji?'

'Our family has been friends with her for many years. I live in Delhi, and came down to Mt. Abu to collect Kaiser and Vimalaji.'

'It's a lot of time when you must be busy with your work.'

'I don't mind at all. It's a great honour to be requested to drive her.'

He was a strong young modern Indian, dressed in casual Western clothes, the jeans, the cotton polo shirt, the broad chest and healthy, fair skin, fresh from the city, from the world of commerce and email. It seemed to be miraculous, that from that mayhem of economics and profits and board-rooms, there were still those who recognised the things which had no monetary value, no means of being priced.

Kaiser, Ajay and I ate our food in a separate room from Vimalaji. Kaiser explained that Vimalaji was resting, and thus I did not see her again that evening. I returned to the

shelter at about nine p.m. and finished my packing for the
next day's journey.

Babu drove me the next morning in to the hotel. It was still
too early to be hot. Bullock carts, camel carts, scooters,
buses and cars had already started moving on the roads. I felt
strangely sad to be leaving our small cottage, the dogs,
horses, cattle that lived in the grounds with us. But my body
was becoming more and more sensitive to the heat, and I
found it more and more difficult to survive the incendiary
Jaipur summer. I sat beside Babulal and watched his dear
face. He had been at the shelter long before the day I had
arrived, and worked stolidly and conscientiously ever since.
It was Manju, his wife, who did all the cooking for the
volunteers and patients, and between them they had
produced two children, who left for school each day with
slicked hair and polished shoes.

When we arrived at the hotel, Ajay was already packing the
car, and Vimalaji was sitting on a cane chair outside her
room. I did not know if she could see me. She was at a
distance of about 30 metres. I had determined that I would
not say anything, nor interrupt in any way, but instead I
would use this occasion, this incredible opportunity of being
in her presence for the six hours of the journey, to try to
intercept and perceive the Energy which was emanating from
her. Hence I did not go over to greet her, but stood at the
jeep with Ajay, until Vimalaji came across the lawn, stood
on a small wooden step, and clambered up into the front seat.

I sat in the back, behind Vimalaji, with Kaiser beside me,
and Ajay had some brief words with Babulal who had agreed
to show us the way through the Pink City onto the Delhi
road. Even though I knew it well, Kaiser was worried that I

might lose the way. Babulal thought it was strange that I should want him to lead us through the city. No doubt he was looking forward to returning to his breakfast, but he politely agreed.

As Ajay started the engine. Vimalaji turned to Kaiser and said, 'Is Christine with us?'

Perhaps she had not seen me when she sat outside on the verandah, and, when she had walked over to the jeep, I had hidden behind it, as I had not wanted to impose myself upon her. This was partially due to the fact that I was still feeling anxious about having written to Kaiser and asking if I could accompany them, even though I had explained to her that I felt I could ask this because I knew them well enough, and I understood Vimalaji would be completely frank about it. Kaiser had written back and said I could accompany them as far as Delhi, as, after this, Vimalaji had private arrangements. I accepted the offer gratefully, but nonetheless felt deeply uneasy about the fact that I had invited myself, and, several times in the intervening period had considered postponing my journey with them. It was only because I was greedy about such an exposure to Vimalaji's Energy, that I persuaded myself, however hesitantly, that it was suitable to accompany them.

'Hun, ji,' Kaiser answered.

Right from that first moment of our journey together, the tremendous power that swelled from Vimalaji's being and filled the car, was palpable. It was so present, and so insistent and so obvious, that I felt the vehicle would burst into flames. I felt that every place we passed was illuminated, and irradiated, and blessed, and changed. And, because I was in the back seat, so close to her being, so blissfully exposed to her emanation, I entered immediately that other dimension where there is no separation. I was aware of being unified with Vimalaji, I know of no other way to describe it. At the same time I was skeptical about the ecstatic experience I was undergoing. I wondered whether it was not just a healthy imagination that transported me into this extraordinary state.

As we left the hotel, Vimalaji chanted a small sanskrit song. I thought it sounded very beautiful. We drove through the streets of Jaipur, and she did not speak at all. I held my mind effortlessly in that removed dimension.

But eventually, perhaps sensing that I felt uneasy about thrusting myself upon them, Vimalaji broke her silence and spoke. She said, 'We are very grateful to Christine for making all the arrangements for us, for finding us such clean rooms, and for preparing the food.'

I replied that it was I who had been honoured to be able to do so.

'It is we who had the honour,' she answered, 'And we are also very honoured that you have decided to come with us on this journey to Delhi.'

When she said this, with such genuine love and humility she dissolved all my anxiety. Again I wondered if she had read my thoughts, had sensed my discomfort at imposing myself upon them.

In front of us the shelter ambulance, with its blue writing, and the Help in Suffering telephone number, drove boldly leading the way. In this vehicle we had rescued so many animals, caught so many street dogs for our animal birth control programme. It was dear and familiar to me, and I was pleased that Vimalaji could see it.

As I thought this, Vimalaji asked Ajay, 'Are we following this vehicle in front?'

'That's the ambulance from Christine's shelter,' Ajay replied. 'Babulal's leading the way for us.'

'It's Babulal's cow which gave the milk for you,' I said. She raised her hands in a namaste of thanks to the cow, and, perhaps to all the creatures.

Vimalaji then seemed to enter Silence, and did not speak at all for perhaps half an hour. Exhilarated by my 'communion' with her, feeling as though I had been drawn into her very being, I felt a certain sense of superiority. Neither Ajay nor Kaiser could have known what was happening. Kaiser, from time to time, spoke to me in a soft voice, so as not to disturb Vimalaji's meditative state. She asked me about the programme which our shelter was conducting, and I explained that the purpose was to control the spread of rabies and stabilise the street dog population by catching, vaccinating and neutering the street dogs. After a full recovery they were returned to the place on the street where they had been caught. So far, over 15,000 dogs had passed through our programme. Kaiser wanted to know if I was in charge. I explained that I was the Managing Trustee, so technically I was responsible for everything that happened.

After Babulal had departed, and we had left the Old City, we passed through the hills, covered with dry scrub, as the road wound upwards towards Amber Palace, the ancient seat of the first rulers of this area. We passed many elephants, slowly walking along the side of the road, many painted and decorated with embroidered, mirrored cloths.

'Where are they going?' Kaiser asked me in a soft voice so as not to disturb Vimalaji.

'To Amber, to give the tourists rides,' I answered. 'Someone did a scientific study and found that most of them walk too far each day, with a result that the pads of their feet are injured on the hot roads, and they are not fed well either.'

Even while speaking to her the wondrous communion continued. I was so full of bliss that I could hardly open my mouth to articulate the words, I could scarcely hide my feelings. I was full of triumph and self-satisfaction that I was able to prove to Vimalaji that my three months of seclusion had produced this result.

We arrived at Midway, a hotel owned by the Rajasthan Tourist Development Corporation, designed to provide feeding and toilets for people traveling the highway. Three hours, half of the journey time, had already passed, and yet I felt that the journey had just begun.

Ajay pulled up right outside the door, and Vimalaji, having slid off the front seat, walked with a swaying gait, into the restaurant. There were busloads of people arriving, eating a quick snack, and then departing again. None of them recognised or knew who was among them. I had stopped at Midway so many times, eaten soggy idli, and drunk sugary watery tea, but never had it looked so glorious as it looked now. The people seemed to be moving round as though they were lighted figures in a dream.

Vimalaji did not drink anything. She said she would take some of the cow's milk later, which was in a thermos in the jeep. She said, 'You go to the bathroom first. You're quicker than me.'

When we were ready to leave, she, Kaiser and I sat together on a vinyl-padded bench. I wished that we could sit there forever. She sat with her distant, deep gaze, completely still. Even to a passing stranger she must have looked an outstanding figure.

'This whole Midway place is transformed by your Energy,' I said to her. 'It's completely different from normal.'

Even as I spoke, I felt that I was being precocious, that I was again boasting, in front of Kaiser, about my ability to perceive the huge Presence which filled the restaurant. Vimalaji did not answer. She smiled and put her hand on Kaiser's knee.

Still in communication with her at that other level, I understood immediately that she was telling me that one's ability to perceive the Otherness had nothing whatsoever to do with one's worth as a human being. Indeed, Kaiser had given far more than I could ever dream of giving. I was only interested in understanding Vimalaji's vibration. I began to feel ashamed.

As if to comfort me, Vimalaji spoke. She said that my Australian accent reminded her of a dear friend she had known in Perth, who was a Quaker, and who had arranged for her to speak at Quaker's groups in several different countries.

'It is good that the Quakers were interested to hear you speak,' I said, 'Because sometimes the orthodox religions can be very narrow-minded.'

Then Vimalaji answered in such a way that I knew there was another meaning to the words which she spoke. She said that she never made a judgment about anything. If she made any judgment, even about the clothes that the people were wearing in the room, then the Silence would be interrupted.

I had judged. I had thought that somehow I was superior, more 'advanced' because of my ability to be absorbed into Vimalaji. I had even spoken of it, in front of others, boasted about it. How much more preferable was Kaiser's gentle, unassuming, attentive love, which asked nothing other than to be a servant of Vimalaji, in comparison to my demanding, inquiring, restless invasion of Vimalaji's most inner being.

Despite this reprimand, the rest of the journey continued as a smear of joy, passed in a moment. Vimalaji was no longer in silence, as she had been for the first part of the journey, but spoke to Ajay about the situation in Pakistan. It was hard to hear what she was saying, but at one point she turned round and spoke to Kaiser. She mentioned a number of names, then said that these were receptive minds. 'You and I have a lot of work to do in Dalhousie,' she said, to Kaiser.

'What does she mean?' I asked Kaiser, who was sitting beside me in the back seat. The engine was roaring so loudly that I did not think I could pursue this question with

Vimalaji. Even though I could see the back of her head, the black hair, the upright shoulders, she was far away.

Kaiser did not answer, and I was left to puzzle as to the nature of the work.

We passed an elephant, and Vimalaji said to me, 'Those elephants which we saw this morning, they were unhappy.'

'How do you know that?' I asked her, leaning over the seat and screaming.

'The look in their eye,' she said. 'Their whole demeanor.' I wanted to know more about how she understood elephants, but did not like to ask.

Then she said, 'When I was working for the Bhoodan Movement, the Land Gift Movement, I rode an elephant. I rode a camel, I rode horses. I travelled in jeeps, in trucks. I walked eight thousand miles in nine years.'

'You must have had a very strong body,' I said.

'It was strong, now it is not so strong, but it still gets me where I need to go.'

'When you rode the camel, did you ride it alone?'

She could not hear what I was saying, so I said, 'I'll ask you later.'

We lapsed into silence.

Ajay phoned his family on his mobile to let them know that we were running slightly late. 'If Christine has no other urgent engagements, maybe she would like to take lunch with us,' Vimalaji said.

Naturally I did not refuse.

Ajay lived with his family in a smart apartment on the outskirts of New Delhi. Vimalaji ate her lunch in a room, which only Kaiser and Ajay's wife entered, in order to take her food. After Vimalaji had finished, we ourselves also ate a delicious lunch. Ajay and his wife both invited me to stay the night with them, but I felt it would not be considerate to Vimalaji.

'Didi once said to me,' Ajay said, 'That this is her house and that we are the guests in it. Our mother, Sangeetaji, whom you will meet in Dalhousie, has also been her friend for many years. I feel that it is such an honour to know her.'

It was time for me to leave, and I asked Kaiser if I should say goodbye to Vimalaji. She said I should not disturb her. Ajay took me to an auto-rickshaw stand, where he not only arranged for my safe delivery at the Blue Triangle, but also paid my fare.

....

From Delhi I journeyed to Patankot in Punjab by overnight train, and took a taxi up the foothills of the Himalayas to Dalhousie. As the van began to climb I could see the snow-clad Himalayas in the distance. We left behind the dust and noise of the town. The air became cool, and when we reached Dalhousie, we wound through narrow roads until we reached Gandhi Chowk, a small group of shops, from where we drove up a lane with broken surface which climbed the mountain.

Due to Kaiser's recommendation I had rented a wooden cottage in the grounds of a beautiful old house, owned by a Mr. Verma, with spectacular views of the mountains. In the cottage there was a small kitchen, bathroom, living room and two bedrooms. I stood on the verandah and looked at the valleys, the slopes of the mountains covered in pine and fir forests, and the distant mountains, brilliantly white in the sun. Jeremy had declined to come with me. He said he would be bored, because I would be meditating. He said he had to stay and do my work at Help in Suffering. I was both disappointed, and filled with a sense of guilt.

'Come and have some lunch,' Mr. Verma. said, and took me into the large house where laid on the table was butter, wholemeal bread, jam and peanut butter, and tea.

'This first meal is free,' he said. 'If you want other meals prepared for you, my servant can bring them at a small cost.'

'It's alright,' I said. 'I like to do my own cooking. I don't eat much.'

'We make the bread,' he said. 'We order the flour specially from outside, grind it ourselves. We've worked out a system. It's very easy. The butter, the jam, they're also home-made.'

It was a spacious wooden house, settled into the earth, with windows and verandah which looked over the Himalayas, spread before us, snow-clad, dazzling in the sun. He led me through the sitting room, through a small office in which was spread a meditation cushion and mat.

'You're Buddhist?' I asked him.

'Zen Buddhist,' he replied. 'I'm connected to the email,' he said. 'If you want to use it to communicate, please feel free to do so.'

'That would be great,' I answered, 'I was going to try to find a place in the market, because I'll need to be in touch with our shelter every day.'

After unpacking and cleaning the cabin, I walked down to the shops, and bought provisions. I did not know when Kaiser and Vimalaji would be arriving and decided not to bother them, but to wait until Kaiser contacted me.

I looked at the library and read the small notice which explained why Dalhousie was established. The hill station in the Chamba Hills was built by the British as a sanitarium so that those who were ill could leave the heat of the plains and recuperate in the cool, fresh climate of the mountains. The idea originated with Lt.. Colonel Napier, then Chief Engineer of the Punjab. In 1851 an appropriate area was selected for the project, and boundaries determined by a committee which was specially appointed to oversee the establishment of the town. An arrangement was made with His Highness, the Raja of Chamba, by which the English agreed to pay him an annual tribute for the right to lease his lands, and the proposed site for the Hill Station was then sanctioned by the Government of India, marked into sites, and development began.

I walked back up the hill with my ruksak full of vegetables and fruit. From the window of my wooden cabin I could see below and across the valley to a patch of trees, the canopy of which I knew covered the roof of the house where Vimalaji stayed. I stared at the trees, and remembered how I had looked from the window at Mt. Abu towards Shiv Kuti.

As night came I sat alone in the room looking out at the black ridges dotted with yellow and white lights. The sky was lit with thunder and was yellow, like stained cloth with grey watermarks as the evening descended. The sun was hidden by strips of clouds which seemed to thread the world together. The slow movement of thunder rumbled the earth as though it was stirring, and occasionally patches of brilliant orange sun emerged to hover over the black ridge, with its human lights utterly meager in comparison to that wild, eerie glowing majesty of sky. I was deeply, richly joyful.

After a few days I decided to ring Kaiser, and, after some deliberation, I asked Mr. Verma if he had Kaiser's number. He was, as ever, helpful, rummaging in a small book to find the appropriate reference.

When he read it out to me, I said to him, 'Oh that's the number I've got. That's the *Shiv Kul* number, the number for Vimalaji's residence. I didn't want to speak to Vimalaji, just Kaiser.'

'There's only one number,' he said. 'Kaiser's house doesn't have a phone and she's always at *Shiv Kul*.'

'But if I ring there Vimalaji might answer the phone.'

'Why don't you want to speak to her?' he asked.

'I don't like troubling her. I'm afraid also,' I added.

'Oh, pfff,' he said. 'What's there to be afraid of? I know them all well. I used to go to all her meetings, but I never found anyone that it helped. It's all vague and nebulous, just watching yourself. I found in Zen Buddhism all the answers I needed. I don't go down there anymore now.'

He took the phone and dialed. 'I wondered if I could speak to Kaiser,' he said into the mouthpiece. Then he turned to me and said, 'It was a man who answered the phone, and he's gone to look for Kaiser.' He handed the phone to me.

I waited for a while and soon a deep voice was there, and speaking into my ear, and it was the voice of Vimalaji, saying, 'I'm sorry, Kaiser's not here right now.'

'Oh Vimalaji,' I said, 'It's Christine. I asked Mr. Verma to ring because I was afraid to disturb you.'

She was silent, and then she said, 'We were about to ring you, dear. The telegraph wires are working well. We wanted to ask if you wished to come to *Satsang*, which will begin tomorrow at four p.m.'

'Oh, yes, thank you very much,' I said.

'I hope your journey went well,' she said.

'Yes, it was good,' I answered.

'Until tomorrow,' she said.

'Thank you,' I said.

As I hung up a stream of love seemed to pour into me and through me. It was so tangible it was like standing under a waterfall, a physical experience. I stood in front of Mr. Verma, unable to speak, unable to move, transfixed by the sudden torrent. He watched me curiously.

After a while, I said, by way of explanation, 'It always happens. Whenever I see her, or speak to her, or even get a letter from her. She sent that Energy down the line.'

He could see that something had happened, but remained silent, and I felt he thought that I was foolish and emotional to be carried away in such a fashion.

'Lots of Italians used to come, lots of students,' he said. 'They used to stay here. They used to sit in this room. They used to say they didn't understand what she taught, and they used to discuss it between themselves.'

And I thought that so many students had come and gone over the years, and she had touched so many lives and yet, even for those who were close to her, her life remained a mystery.

Vimalaji's house was below *Thanda Sarak*, which meant cool road, because it faced northwards towards the mountains and did not get the morning sun. I went through a gate and followed a path which wound steeply downwards. I was confronted by an open door, which led into a room, a whole wall of which was windowed. On the opposite side of the room there was a divan, an *asana*, on which Vimalaji was sitting, her eyes closed, apparently already in deep *samadhi*. Facing her, cross-legged on the floor, sat about six or seven women, sari-clad, graceful, gentle and lithe, their backs straight, their necks long, their hands resting in their laps.

Kaiser came forward to meet me, and I gave her a loaf of bread baked by Mr. Verma. Vimalaji smiled and said, 'Ah, the cosmic telegraphy is working overtime. We were wondering where we could find some good bread.'

As I sat on the floor, before starting, I felt a moment of pride that I was again able to enter her mind, or become at-one with her. Then I thought, Christine, whatever you have is because of Vimalaji, and I sent her a great thought of love. At that exact moment she turned towards me and gave me the most brilliant smile. It was the only time she had smiled at any one since I had entered, and I knew that it was a response to my thought.

Soon the small group of women started chanting to the haunting sounds of a harmonium, played by one of Vimalaji's friends. The outside world of cars, of laughing people, of news of wars, and financial collapses, ceased to exist, and we were caught in suspended time, like cable-cars that float in space between the cliffs, and I thought that I had always meant to be here, and it was simply a mistake that I had been somewhere else, because this was the true India, the hidden India.

I was filled with a conviction that there was a great Presence in the room with Vimalaji. The potency, the portent, the fulsome atmosphere seemed to be almost overwhelming. It was as though there was a Being, or Beings, standing beside her, floating above her, somewhere in attendance, pouring Their love and compassion into that room, which sung and throbbed with the intensity of the moment. I felt that whatever Presence it might have been, it filled the whole earth with the enormous magnitude of its attendance.

After the singing had finished, and we had sat in silence for about twenty minutes, Vimalaji began to speak.

'It's for more than fifty years that I have been visiting the Himalayas whenever I could get an opportunity to do so. If I remember correctly, I was in Kalimpong in 1946, and then Gangtok and Sikkim and Darjeeling, etc. Himalayas are my abode though the destiny keeps me with the people and among the people in the plains of India as well as the whole world. There is hardly any Himalayan resort which I have not visited and lived there.

'Sometimes in the forest rest house of Gangotri, then the source of the Ganges, sometimes Amanath sometimes Kedanath, sometimes Narayan Ashram in the Eastern most parts and the Indo-China border. One has climbed the Himalayans from Simla right up to Tibet and visited Tibetan villages so my love affair with the Himalayas is perhaps more than 60 years young. It is the urge to taste the flavour of silence that one visits the Himalayas. The towns and the cities that the stupid Indians have built-up in places like Dalhousie or Simla or Manali or Nanital etc. - somehow they are not in my cognisance. So I come here; I live with the Himalayas, and listening to the sound of silence in the deep nights of Himalayan summers, enjoying the music of the mountain breeze and the chirping of birds at dawn and dusk. Its like paradise on earth.

'People come here to escape the summer heat of the plains. And they bring with them all the desires of worldly life, eat, drink and be merry, so they go back empty-handed. Except the pleasure of escaping the heat, their hands and hearts are empty. So one should come to the Himalayas if there is an urge to taste Silence, to taste intimate company of both nature which is manifested divinity, and Silence which is unmanifested divinity.

'Unless one can shed all the identifications with worldly responsibilities commitments and relationships its no use coming up to the Himalayas. You have to denude the consciousness as you denude the body by bathing, you denude the consciousness of all sense of belonging to the world, and come here to explore in the intimacy of sacred nature what is there more to human life than the physical body and the psychological thought structure built up by mankind.

'These words are addressed to the persons who have come here because they want to be with or around Vimala for a couple of months. It is their responsibility to live the aloneness though they are with one another, minimising verbalisation, and whenever they indulge in verbalisation, not to indulge in shop talk or cheap talk. Let them verbalise if they want to exchange their understandings, their experiences, sharing, because opportunities are never repeated. You get them once in your life-time. This is the place where you can wash out all the toxins - psychological toxins of memories. Wash yourself completely of them, detoxification of consciousness.

'Out of hundred crore the population of India it is only a handful, privileged ones, who are economically, financially capable of coming up here. They are very fortunate.

'I do not know how many of you are aware that the *Vedas*, the *Vedanta* and the *Upanishads*, the six systems of Indian philosophy, all these have been written in the Himalayan region. This is the fountain of ancient Indian wisdom which has now become a global heritage. 'Life is divine'. proclaimed the *Vedas*. 'The cosmos is the cathedral, the abode of the divinity. Respect life'. The great mantra of the *Rig Ved*. Reverence for life. Respect life. Love every expression of life. Be friendly with every expression, whether it is the mountains, the rivers, the trees, the birds, the animals, the lions, the tigers. Respect and love confer sanctity, sacredness on life. Life is One, it cannot be divided. You cannot create compartments in life proclaim the Vedas. The non-human the human species are creations of the same divinity. They are inter-related. If they isolate themselves from one another it will lead to the extinction.

'The Rishis, the ancient sages, lived in the forest and Indian culture was called Forest Culture. The *Upanishads* are called, the wisdom emerging from the forests, emerging in the forests. The manifest and the unmanifest are one, proclaim the *Vedas*. In a small seed is contained the whole tree with its trunk and branches, leaves and flowers. So there is nothing like matter separated from the spirit.

'Birth is one door, to emerge into the manifest, and death is another door out of which you go back to the unmanifest. Life knows no birth and death. It's just a circular movement of emergence and merging back. I should not bother you with more, but these are a few pourings of my heart. And there was a special urge to share in English language as our dear friend Christine has come.'

When the Satsang had finished, Vimalaji introduced me to those present, by saying that I had spent three months in silence and solitude in Mt. Abu, and was now writing a book, for which Vimalaji was answering questions. I could come and meet her on Wednesday, if that suited me. I happily consented.

....

Right from the start it was a meeting with Vimalaji in which I had no control whatsoever over the words which expelled themselves from my body. Vimalaji was sitting cross-legged on a divan in an inner room. Many people seemed to hurry through the room. There was a phone on the table which constantly rang, and was answered either by Kaiser or someone else who would appear out of the depths of the house. To one side of the room there seemed to be a large kitchen area, and outside on the cemented patio area, I saw several young men chopping, preparing and cooking food. It seemed as though this was an ashram, and yet I knew Vimalaji would not allow the use of such a word or such a concept, for in modern terminology the word often indicated a compound established by a guru, in which his or her followers could congregate, living and studying the teachings of the guru, abiding by rules laid down by the guru, and contributing to the maintenance and running of the ashram. To Vimalaji the people who came to learn from her were 'friends', and these friends came, not to learn, but to 'share.'

'So, do we wish to begin?' Vimalaji asked.

'I have questions about Vimalaji's life which I would like to ask, if this is alright,' I began. 'I think it's important that I am accurate, and maybe I could begin by asking for some clarification on a few terms.'

So far, so good! Christine seemed to be behaving herself and obeying the instructions she had been given so carefully and thoroughly, in the preparations she had revised over and over again, both with herself, and with Kaiser, who had made many suggestions as to what should be asked, and as to how it should be asked. By now I knew Kaiser well enough to understand what she was thinking. She knew that Vimalaji was scrupulous in her attention to detail and to terminology and was deeply concerned that I would ask stupid things which would cause Vimalaji to think the questions were unproductive, and therefore to terminate the interview.

'I told Christine,' Kaiser said, 'That I could answer many of the questions about the events, but Christine would have to ask Vimalaji any of the spiritual questions.'

Vimalaji nodded.

'Well, first I would like to ask you about the word 'Teacher', I said. Already I could tell that the situation was beyond my control. That same sense of being far removed from the world, of being an observer, while the play took part on another level of existence, took charge. Kaiser had already told me that Vimalaji did not like being called a Teacher, and I knew it from all my reading of her books, letters and articles. Indeed, she had written to one of her friends, that 'there are no supports and crutches in the dimension of Silence. In fact, every assertion of the 'I' consciousness is an obstruction and a hindrance. .. 'I do not allow anyone to develop a personal relationship of a Master/disciple with me.'

'I know that Vimalaji does not like this word, Teacher,' I continued, 'But it seems to be the only word which I can find to explain the body of knowledge and understanding which has existed for all time, but which has been expressed through the being of Vimalaji in a particular individualised mode.'

Vimalaji smiled. 'Christine could use the word Teacher,' she said, 'It seems preferable to the word Master.'

'Would this be because the word Master had been glamourised and emotionalised by the Theosophical Society.'

Vimalaji nodded. "But how then does one refer to those great Beings, those Rishis?

Vimalaji said that she referred to Them with a capital 'T' for Teacher. 'You could use the word Master, with Teacher in brackets', she added. 'Vimala, Master, Teacher to describe Vimala.'

Kaiser and I were furiously scribbling. I felt that Christine was totally absent and therefore was not sure that I would remember anything if it was not recorded as it was spoken. This was not difficult because Vimalaji spoke slowly and deeply, often with pauses, as though she was waiting for words to project through herself from some other source.

Having grown bolder, the being which was in control took even greater liberties. 'I know Vimalaji does not like the word 'disciple," I said, 'But I feel that I *am* Vimalaji's disciple in the Vedic sense of the term, in the sense that

Vimalaji had caused the awakening of the awareness in a hastened process due to her interaction with Christine.'

How could I have said it! She had constantly refused to accept the word (not the fact) of discipleship, because it led to a sense of dependency and worship. She knew that an important pre-condition of liberation was total freedom from all dogma, from all concepts, from all claims of special relationships.

But with great love and compassion which seemed to stream from her being, so that it was all I could do not to allow myself to fall at her feet, Vimalaji answered that Christine could use the word Teacher with 'Master' in brackets, or vice a versa and similarly the word disciple with 'student' in brackets. The word guru had been spoilt by its misuse by all the people who claimed to be gurus and it could no longer be used due to its connotations. Then Vimalaji turned to Kaiser and said, 'Look, Christine is writing the book out of her understanding, in Australia, it is Christine's book and she should use whatever words are correct in the flowering of her understanding. In the book she should say in the introduction how she came to know Vimalaji, her own background, how she found a Master, and how she looked upon herself as developing, then if given in practical terms, this would sustain the development of the book.'

In this way she had written the book, and presented a completed synopsis to me, but Kaiser and I had already conceived of the book as being a biography of her life, and I was therefore, at that time, too stupid to fully absorb the gift she had given.

'Vimala is now seventy-five, and every year is a bonus year in India at this age, so she is now ready to discuss things she had never talked about before about her life. At the age of 3 she had started to look for God, and it was that which had led her wandering off into the forest, where she thought she could find God. From the age of seven she had trained herself to sit for fourteen hours at a time, and at the age of fourteen she sat for seventy-two hours at a stretch. She had gone into *samadhi* during one of these sittings, and her parents had needed to call a yogi known to the family in order to bring her back to body consciousness.'

I was fascinated. 'How was this accomplished?' I asked.

She looked disappointed that I was asking about unnecessary details. 'There are some traditional practices - the yogi accomplished this by carrying out the traditional practice of rubbing butter into the body. There was a small hole at the top of the head through which the psyche could pass, and the butter created a heat. I don't know, dear, how it worked, only that it was an ancient practice.'

'When she was about seven or eight,' she continued, 'A yogi visited the family and said to my parents, 'Don't look upon her as a person belonging to you.''

'You were already realised when you were born into the world?'

'Look, the seed was there, the seed sprouted and blossomed. Vimala's life is a mystery to her. She does not know what she is.'

The atmosphere in the room was deep and profound, despite the noises which were coming from other sections of the house, dishes rattling, and doors sliding. Kaiser, Vimalaji and myself seemed encapsulated in an energy of love, in a vortex of purity. And in this state I continued to question Vimalaji and she continued to answer.

'But you have not actually confirmed my question that you were already realised when born.'

'That is what many saints and sages said to my family when they saw me as a child. What takes place is an unfolding, uncovering of the seed. From the age of three, I was aware of another presence, of some power behind this material man-made world. I saw this world as a shadow, with the reality behind. That is what made me run to the forest. I thought, 'I'll go and meet God.' I walked five to eight miles and felt nearer to the invisible impersonal force that was running the world. God never appeared to me as a personal attraction. I never felt any desire to have personal interaction. I never felt a sense of belonging to the world, or of belonging to a body, never felt lonely, I did not miss my parents if they went away.'

'I remember when I was a child,' I said, 'That I saw the whole of matter as being insubstantial, translucent, as though there was nothing inside, it was just masses of moving dots. Did you feel this?'

'I felt this but I do not have the words to express it as you have just done.'

'Vimalaji is always surrounded by people. Is it difficult for her to have so many demands?', I asked. 'Does she want to be alone more often?'

'Until 1962 I was always wanting to be alone but from 1962 onwards the solitude became so intact, so deep within, that I did not feel the need to be alone any longer,' she answered.

'Was that when you achieved *mukti*, liberation? I don't know of the right word to use. I am struggling for words. Was that when the final descent of that spirit occurred, when you became enlightened?'

There was a long silence and then Vimalaji said, 'I have never spoken of these things before. Ten year back, five years back if anyone had asked me I would have refused to speak. Kaiser used to beg me in tears to tell her what had happened. I never accepted authority. Not of Krishnamurti, nor of any other teacher. The seed was already deep within. It only needed to flower, to open out.'

'When did that moment occur? There must be a culminating moment, when that spirit fixes the state, when the soul is crystallised?'

'The psyche cannot be crystallised. It has fluidity and the capacity to change and develop. There was no feeling of having arrived, only an energy of dynamism unconditioned by anything - all the conditioning of the human race flowing through the being.'

I was enraptured by the words, by the intensity of the discussion, by the immensity of her sharing.

'Is that the first time a person knows *samadhi*, at the moment of liberation?' I asked.

'It has never appeared to me as a fixed location to be obtained. I felt it rather like a river in which you were slowly submerged. When we go through the process of self-education there is a period when you are studying, when you are learning to be in Silence. After that there comes a moment when *Samadhi* is known, at first it seems to be rather touch and go, it comes for an hour, it fades but every time it goes on increasing in intensity and depth and if the daily lifestyle is a supportive factor then *Samadhi* crystallises into the ordinary dimension of consciousness. Perhaps you could call that moment the last flimsy curtain being removed, the last influence of personality ceased, and it was as if a curtain was drawn – is this the word I am looking for? I mean, moved aside. The last sense of duality was gone. That was in July, 1962 when I was in Saanen - 16th July 1962.'

'Under what conditions did it occur? Were you sitting in your room, in meditation?'

'I was sitting in the garden alone. It was a bright and sunny day. One sees things dimly and one goes nearer and nearer.'

She was far away, and then returned, with effort, it seemed. 'Right from the beginning of my life, the cerebral movement was a minor instrument of action. It never governed the consciousness, call it the feel of some Energy, neither psychic nor cerebral, which is used to perceive and understand, without the need for words. There was never any need to try and control the thoughts, and when I discovered that it was not so with other members of the family or with my teachers I was baffled. I could never understand any thought coming up. I could not understand how it could be that people had to battle with their thoughts, that the thoughts were governing their lives. People talk about it. I have never experienced it. It seemed as though my being was a cave in which I lived in Silence, I was a being in the silent cave, and that Silence of being, the cave was my abode. Body was merely the means of expression. One did not have the feeling of the body belonging to you. One never became obsessed about it, nor was it ever something to be transcended, so when I listened to Krishnamurti's first talk, and he said afterwards, could you understand, I said of course, because it was what I had always known and experienced.'

'When one is in the state of *dhyan*, that is the bliss and the ecstasy – is that state of *samadhi* what is behind – when everything is empty, when it seems as though the world is behind glass. There is the sense of a vast Presence? I am struggling for words here, to put into words something which is inexpressible.'

Vimalaji was hard of hearing, my voice was soft, and we were struggling to hear each other, so she turned to Kaiser and said, 'I couldn't get it, Kaiser?'

Kaiser summarised my question rather skillfully. I felt she must have had a lot of experience in this regard over the years. 'Christine asked: is *Samadhi* the pulsation of some Presence which one feels?'

'He is in that pulsation. There is no duality to feel the pulsation. There are various stages of samadhi. There is *bij samadhi* where there a very delicate sense of duality is still felt. In the beginning this is felt as an overwhelming presence. That is in the beginning. You are admitted into that dimension. Then comes *nirbij* in which you become a part of that pulsation. Then the pulsation is the movement, the breathing ...'

For the first time I was able to understand what I had read about meditation with or without seed. *'bij'* (pronounced 'beej') was the Hindi Sanskrit word for 'seed', and *'nir'* I realised, meant 'without' in Sanskrit. So there was meditation with a seed of awareness of the presence of the ego, and meditation without any awareness at all of the individual ego.

'Vimalaji said that the inside adjusts to the outside. Is this the same as the Theosophical or Buddhist terminology in which it has been described as the jewel in the lotus, that jewel being the point of individualised spirit which is contained within the psyche, and when the psyche opens up, that spirit, that Transcendental is revealed? This is why it would be difficult to separate *Purusha* from *prakriti*, because the psyche contains the Transcendental, yet the psyche is in the *Prakriti*?' It was a complex question and I did not express it well. My voice was too soft, and Vimalaji's hearing was not keen enough.

'What did she say, dear?' she asked Kaiser

'Is this what would be called the jewel in the lotus?'

'I do not know the Theosophical terms. There are many ways to describe it. I can only talk about what Vimalaji has experienced.'

'When you said before, 'the inside adjusting to the outside', what did this mean?'

' The inside adjusting to the outside.' She repeated the phrase as if pondering upon it and then continued, 'I use different terms when I speak to different people. I do not know in what context I would have used 'the inside adjusting to the outside'. *Purusha* is the Transcendental, it is called the inner, the heart, *Atman,* spirit.'

So I asked her, 'Is the *Atman* − is it the individuated Transcendental? And *Paramatman* is the all-pervading, universal, Unicity?'

And she replied: '*Atman* is the invisible all-permeating within us and *Paramatman* is the objective Unmanifest.'

Again I felt liberated by the clarity of her responses in such simple words.

For a moment she hesitated, and then asked Kaiser the time.

'It's four p.m.,' Kaiser replied.

'Christine had left her room at two thirty and she is thirsty and should be offered tea.'

'No, really, I don't want Kaiser to bother about the tea, because she might miss out on what you're saying, and I would rather drink Vimalaji's words than worry about tea. I don't need tea.'

I was afraid the magic, the spell of mystery which filled the room, which united us as one, would be broken by the intrusion of tea-cups and trays.

'Christine is apt to forget about the body, but the body should also be cared for,' Vimalaji answered. 'Christine needs tea.'

After she had said this I realised she was correct, for I noticed that I did feel a bit dehydrated. Vimalaji said it would not require Kaiser to be absent, because someone else could prepare the tea. She would take half a tea. She said I had been talking since three p.m. and did I feel tired? I said I could go on asking questions forever, and she should tell me when she was ready to stop. She said she had nothing else to do. She said we could relax for a little while and then continue after the tea.

She spoke to me about her friend, Dr. R.P. Kaushik, who had been born in a small village near Delhi, became a medical doctor, and then, having an understanding of the truth, gave talks by invitation overseas and in India. In 1977 he had bought a house, called 'Dakhshinamurti' in Dalnousie, with the view to making it into a place where people could stay with him and hear him talk during the summer months. He had died in 1981, and now a dear friend, Sangeeta, looked after the house. Sangeeta was Ajay's mother.

She also spoke about one of her American friends, Barbara, who had come to Dalhousie every year for six years, and from her the books, *Himalayan Pearls* and *Being and Becoming* had resulted. 'The integrity of the questions is similar to that of Barbara's questions,' Vimalaji said.

'Christine reminds one of Barbara. Since Barbara, there has been no-one to ask such questions.'

I felt a great sense of thankfulness that she spoke these words, because I was feeling very uncertain as to the intensity and intimacy with which I had probed.

After tea, the level of the exchange became even deeper. I cannot describe the incredible energy which existed between the three of us, the extraordinary magnetic rapport in which I was held.

I began by saying, 'Returning to the analysis of the word, 'disciple', the disciple feels that the easiest way is through the Energy of the Teacher. Is this the right path? I am struggling for words here. The disciple actually feels that it only because of the aura of the teacher that the state of bliss and ecstasy is known. Is this correct?'

With great, great love which radiated from her being, Vimalaji answered: 'The light of love and understanding – they accompany the disciple. The light of love helps you warm and does not allow any sense of being isolated or lonely, gives a sense of being grounded in truth so fearlessly the disciple moves forwards.'

Kaiser sighed audibly, with a gasp that contained both wonder and awe.

'Love is the fragrance of Truth, and Vimala gets that Truth as the river flows. It is for you to enter the river too. The river is there. It is the receptivity of the Truth which leads to the understanding.'

'But you are not actually confirming, you are not actually admitting that – I'm being personal now – Kaiser has lived with you, and has known what it is like to be with you, but I feel that it is only through you, because you have actually lifted me into your aura, you have actually uplifted Christine so that she can adjust, or tune into that vibration, that Energy which comes from Vimalaji – it is only because of Vimalaji and only through Vimalaji that Christine's realisation is possible. The small cloud of Christine has been absorbed into the vast cloud of Vimalaji. The only words I can find to describe it are profundity and vastness.'

Vimalaji nodded and smiled. 'Infinity is in one and It gets expressed by consciously sharing. Wherever I find a listener, the truth behind the sharing gets revealed by itself. Vimala has not spoken like this before.'

'And neither have I,' I answered. It was a declaration of love on my part. I could love her and not be ashamed of loving her. This was a love beyond sex, beyond any human attachment, beyond any attempt at possession or identification. It was simply something that existed. It was there. I felt it, and it could not be denied. And she too had felt the connection. Could it be, in all her greatness, that she was actually also rejoicing in the relationship? Her words seemed to indicate that this was so, but her rejoicing was nothing to do with one ego meeting another – it related instead to the invisible connection on higher levels, where there was no division, no separation, and yet where there was 'individuated, condensed cosmos', as she had described it, that 'condensed cosmos' representing an individuated spark within the homogenous, undivided infinite whole.

For a while there was silence, and then I asked her about another word, 'technique' – I asked whether it was correct to use the term 'technique' when it related to the body/mind, as there were certain practices, such as those that Vimalaji taught, which could hasten the process of inner revolution.

'The term, 'technique' is not a good one,' Vimalaji answered. 'Self-education depends on the sensitivity of the organism. Where revelation of truth has to take place, learning to put one's body and mind into a state of self observation is not a technique, it is an inquiry. If you use the word technique, it sounds as though a result will follow, but Silence is not a result, it's a state which has always been, but just needs to be recognised.'

'The word 'technique' is too authoritarian?'

'It has a rigidity, there had to be fluidity which every person can shape.'

Then I said, 'The ancient body of wisdom has always existed and from time to time people have come to express and reveal that wisdom in new ways. It seems to me that Vimalaji's Teaching is a re-presentation of the Vedic truths, essentially *Raja Yoga*, modernised for the Western world.'

Vimalaji smiled in confirmation. 'I use the psychological terms that the western world understands. Essentially *Raja Yoga* is an ancient teaching, and such hints and clues as would be helpful can be given in a friendly way.'

I felt that I had no more to ask. I was full, and thanked Vimalaji for giving her time.

As I was going she asked, 'Why is Kaiser also taking notes? This is Christine's book!'

'She's helping,' I answered. 'Without her I couldn't do it.'

But I should have been aware of the reason behind her question, for it would have saved me from proceeding in the wrong direction.

I walked back along the road, past some laughing Indian tourists trotting on small ponies shepherded by owners who walked alongside with whips, past a group of stray dogs sleeping in the sun, past the traffic jam of cars in *Gandhi Chowk*, past the row of wooden stalls selling baskets of vegetables, past the hazardous shed which was called the Tibetan market, crammed with tiny shops illuminated faulty electrical systems, and selling assortments of kitch from China, up the hill through the patches of forest, of moss and flowers, to the small wooden cabin where I stayed.

I had entered a new phase of my relationship to Vimalaji. I had become a *Bhakti*, a follower of *Bhakti Yoga*, in which union is sought with the divine through love and faith and trust and adoration, in which *gyan*, or the enquiry into self-understanding, is abandoned and in an utter surrender of all effort, one rests in the love of one's Teacher.

CHAPTER EIGHT

QUESTIONS ABOUT SAMADHI

Those of us who are born in India are born in an ancient
country where the pursuit of truth, the quest of Reality has
been the primary concern of our ancestors. They had
converted their lives, their bodies, their brains, into
laboratories, and the exploration, experimentation and
verification have been verbalized and put into the form of
books, etc. [1]

I was soon to have my next meeting with Vimalaji. There
was a sense of unpredictability about it. I did not know what
could happen. I felt that events were unrolling themselves
without my being able to command them, nor to govern
them. I was being pushed and pulled by the manipulations of
fate, to which I had resignedly surrendered myself.

I had talked with Kaiser who had said that Vimalaji had been
asking her exactly how I planned to write the book. I realised
that I had never spoken about myself to Vimalaji, as I had
always assumed she knew about me, and that it would be
only courteous to explain how I had arrived at the position in
which I now found myself. Thus I sat down and wrote her a
letter in which I explained that I had been a writer, had five
books, articles and short stories published, that after my first
visit to India in 1976 in which I had met Diana, I formed
Animal Liberation, for which I had worked until 1990,
leaving after I had met Vimalaji.

---

[1] Thakar, Vimala, *The Invincible*, Vol. XI, No. 4, Oct-Dec, 1995; 15.

The next part of the letter was more difficult to write. It involved exposing beliefs about which even I myself felt vaguely suspect. Perhaps she would think I was stupid or fanciful, or, at the very least, egotistical. Then I recalled how she was brave enough to speak about her innermost spiritual revelations to small groups of friends, and afterwards to allow them to be published, and I thought that this inner exposure must have been even more difficult for Vimalaji as it involved a disclosure of the deepest and most private inner spiritual divulgements.

So I said that I now believed that it was destiny that had led me to work in Jaipur, which was only a few hours' distance from Mt. Abu, instead of tens of thousands of kilometers, as was Sydney, and that I thought I may have future work to do with her. I printed out the letter on Mr.Verma's computer, re-read it several times, and finally put it in an envelope. As I was too apprehensive to personally give it to Vimalaji, I left it at the house with one of her friends and helpers, after much hesitation.

When I met her for the interview, however, my anxiety about the contents of the letter wilted and vanished. Her face was so serene, she was so distant and so far away, and yet so present, and so intimately attentive, so penetrating and understanding, like an oracle so that one was able to totally trust and abandon all petty worries.

It was as though she already understood my concern about the letter, because she began by thanking me for it, and then said, 'Vimalaji has not spoken about her inner life until now, but as she has come to the last phase of her life, the time has come to speak about it.' She sat so straight, and the voice was so deep, and it came slowly, and continuously and melodiously, and was beautiful and measured.

'It is very significant and mystically important that someone from Australia comes and has an urge to understand all the ins and outs of Vimalaji's life,' she said, with much compassion. 'It's a manifestation of human relations. If any Indian had asked I would not have spoken.'

Then I was reassured and all the faith and the trust which was already in me was added and packed and stacked even higher like rooms piled with books, where there is no empty hole.

'If any Indian had asked to write this book, I would not have agreed,' Vimalaji continued. 'When Krishnaji spoke about himself it was to people who had been his followers and lived with him for 30 or 40 years. Something in Christine, a seed, which was the dormant relationship, got activised, and caused this project to happen.'

And in these words she had validated and endorsed the letter which it had been so hard for me to write to her. And then I did not feel ashamed of it anymore, but, due to her love, I felt glorified that life had moved in this way.

Vimalaji then asked if she could see the questions, and took the paper with them printed on it, and began answering them one by one. In this way I lost control and could not probe, as I had not expected her to take the questions, and did not have a copy.

She read out the first question: 'If Vimalaji went into *samadhi* at the age of fourteen it means that the *brahmarandra*[2] must have been open at this time, and she would have been clairvoyant. Would this be correct?'

'Yes, I don't know if it was open or not but the child was clairvoyant and clairaudient. This started when I was ten years old.'

I was writing furiously and not speaking, but I felt that the harmony which had prevailed at the beginning of our meeting had mysteriously vanished. She was perhaps displeased with the questions. Something was askew.

She read out the second question: 'Christine read in Vimalaji's books that a yogi is conscious when asleep. Could Vimalaji comment on this, and has this state remained permanent or does it change with time?'

'The dimension of sleep is the dimension when the thought structure and its movement go completely into abeyance,' she answered. 'So, from the dimension in which one is focused during the action of the day, the person then moves to that level or dimension of consciousness when in profound sleep. The principle of inertia allows us to have sleep, and that is the time when the body and mind gets relaxed completely. In waking hours the chemical and emotional activities of the body and the thought system are never relaxed, but in sleep all is relaxed and goes into passivity. When a person lives in the state of *yoga* there is no pressure or tension in the waking hours, because in the state of *samadhi*, the brain moves only when movement is warranted. Emotions and feelings get activised only when

---

[2] The *brahmarandra* is the name sometimes given to the 'hole' in the etheric web at the top of the head through which a yogi can pass, thus attaining continuity of consciousness.

their response is required, but that activisation do not leave any trace - no memory - so does not leave any residue behind. Thus the sub-conscious, conscious - all the layers of the mind - are relaxed, and therefore unconscious sleep (in which the mind can relax) is not needed in the life of a yogi – the yogi does not need to become immersed in the inertia, as he or she lives in a constant state of profound relaxation. There's no qualitative difference between the waking state and state of sleeping in the life of a yogi.'

I felt she was not giving a direct answer, because she was depersonalising the question which became a discussion of theory rather than a reference to her own life. I said I did not quite understand, so she elucidated further by saying: 'When you sit down for self-education you are conscious that you are in Silence. But once you have grown into that dimension, you are there. It is natural and not an effort. The vibrant energy maintains itself. The awareness is there. It permeates. Education and awareness are states through which you must pass, but then awareness becomes natural. If you live in a particular room of a house, you leave the house through the door of that room.'

I understood this to mean that, if one was living at a level of awareness which enabled one to be submerged in the universal consciousness during the day, then that level of awareness would persist during sleep as well. One would walk out of that room, in effect, as one fell asleep, into the same dimensional room of awareness during sleep. One would no longer be an unconscious, snoring, breathing slumberer but, leaving behind that resting form, one would travel in the light body, healing and helping wherever one could, bringing back the awareness of the night's activities upon awakening.

In order to further divert my questioning, she asked me if I had read a particular book, to which I replied, 'No', and she suggested that Kaiser would find it and lend it to me. Thus my probing as to what happened to Vimalaji's consciousness at night, was peremptorily ended.

She read the next question: 'What did the parents feel when the saint told them that Vimala did not belong to them?'

It was clear that she felt uneasy about this question, but she answered stiffly. 'My mother's father knew Swami Vivekananda and four months before Vimala was born my grandfather travelled a long distance to that place where the mother was living when he knew that the child was coming. He spoke to my mother and told her then, the child which is coming does not belong to us. He used to spend every leisure hour with her, talking to her about the divinisation of her being. As regards Vimala's father, before he got married he had spent two to three years in the Himalayas studying the basics of all religions – Jainism, Buddhism, Hinduism, and the twelve chief *Upanishads*. His Teacher was Swami Ramtirth, an exponent of Advaita from Punjab. So both my mother and father were very happy when they heard what my grandfather had to say. Other yogis told them later, after they saw the child, from seven or eight years of age onwards.'

Then she read out the next question, which made me squirm. 'Did V. meet the Masters in her childhood?'

She seemed to hesitate for a long time, to start to speak, and then stopped again. Then she answered, 'Not that she remembers.'

She read out the next question: 'What was V's first conscious memory on earth?'

I could feel her palpably bristling with disappointment and frustration, but she answered with much patience, 'I never had a feeling of belonging to a house, to a society, to a country, but I always felt I belonged somewhere else. It is a feeling similar to that of arriving in a strange land, a feeling that you don't belong to the place where you have to live.'

I knew she meant that, as one detached from the material world of events and thoughts, the 'psychological and biological inheritance', as she had called it, then one had a continuous awareness of watching events that were happening as though in a strange land which one was temporarily visiting.

Then she read out the next question: 'Is *bij samadhi* when the psyche merges with *atma,* and is *nirbij* when *atma* merges with *paramatma*?' It was a short-hand in which I had used her own terms, which had become also my own – words as symbols of states of consciousness which were beyond description. Somehow the Sanskrit seemed most apt as a spiritual terminology, because the terms were untainted, uncoloured, free from the distortions and connotations associated with so many words describing spiritual states, words that had been hijacked by religion, by dogmas, and by gurus.

By *atma,* I meant the point of conscious light which was embedded within the human forms, and *paramatma* – the unlimited light which spreads through everything, which underlies all life, which is undivided and undifferentiated. I had begun to detect something which was hidden in, or describable only as a technical point, which sounded like a quibbling detail of terminology, but which to me represented a massive new opening in understanding. I badly wanted Vimalaji's confirmation as to the correctness of this unfurling discovery.

I wanted again to clarify my understanding of *nirbij samadhi*. For the first time it had occurred to me that 'meditation with seed', as I had often seen it translated from the Sanskrit, was equivalent to *dhyan*, or that state of meditation in which one felt 'possessed', in which one felt that the personality was occupied and controlled and used by an unlimited, all-permeating Energy which moved through everything. Because there was still a sense of Christine-being-moved-through, there was the 'seed' or sense, however faint, of still being Christine.

But when that individual light within oneself, that *atma*, fused and united with the universal light, *paramatma*, then the state of *bij samadhi* became the state of *nirbij samadhi*. This surely was the ultimate moment, the moment of self-realisation, when all sense of being human, of being individual was finally and irreversibly eradicated, and the person became an empty vessel with the universal, unlimited consciousness, the only Self.

After reading my question slowly and pointedly, she was silent for a moment, as she let the paper rest on my lap. Had I understood it as it was? I remained incredulous that such momentous facts were the underlining of life. I somehow needed someone else, someone who knew, to confirm this extraordinary truth.

Finally she responded with one word. 'Yes,' she answered, and then once more fell silence. Yet I believed that she knew that this answer was a tremendously elucidating and liberating confirmation, a validation of the miraculous human construction.

She then read out the next question: 'Is *bij samadhi* the state which Vimalaji was in when she wrote in her book *Eternal Voyage* that 'A tremendous tempest has swept me away?'

'I don't think Vimalaji was in *bij samadhi* or any other *samadhi*,' she answered, 'when I wrote *Eternal Voyage*. It was a kind of intoxicating joy of discovery. You see, Vimala was born in a small town and she comes across J. Krishnamurti called 'World Teacher' who had his psychic empire, all over the world, so the dialogues had kind of overwhelmed Vimala. He invited her to Switzerland so she felt it was a responsibility to put down the facts, to do justice to the sacred relationship that had come up, not as a disciple, not as a worker, just sheer, pure nectrous love and respect of each other. She was persuaded by Dada Dharma to put down the facts, just a record of what had happened. He told Vimala that it would be useful for other people to know what she had spoken about with Krishnaji. The 'tempest' was a dropping away of all sense of belonging, of all sense of personality. She had worked for 9 years in the Bhoodan (land-gift) Movement, and she used to speak like an Indian, with a sense of belonging to India. All that went. She no longer felt she belonged anywhere. She had a sense of being in a void.

'I remember a day in Banares in October or November, 1962. I walked up to see Krishnaji who was at his residence in Benares and said, 'Krishnaji, what has happened that I am so denuded? I don't have a sense of belonging.'

'He took my hand and he led me up a path along the verandah to a rose which was half-opened and he asked me, 'Where does this flower belong?' Then he continued, 'It belongs to the space, and space carries the flowering. Why must you belong anywhere?' So it was like this.'

She paused for a moment, and then proceeded to read out the next question: 'Is *bij samadhi* the feeling that the Cosmic has taken control, even possessed, the whole being, and looks through it, so there is no personality left to look? Would it have been for her this feeling? And this feeling brings with it a great sense of bliss and ecstasy?'

She asked, 'How does Christine know about this *bij samadhi*?' in a sort of playful, teasing way. I did not answer, but just smiled, so she continued, 'That's what it is, what you have described, and for some years it was so - Vimala lived in it from 1962 until 1968. All the talks given, wherever I travelled in that time – Europe, Canada, and back in India, came from that dimension. I would not know what I was going to speak, even one minute before I climbed the dias. After I did not remember a word I had said, so sometimes when people said to me it was a wonderful speech, I asked them to play back the tape, and when they played it I would get stunned, and said, 'How lucky you are to be with such a person!' When you are possessed, there is a kind of intensity. Later, this intensity subsides and becomes mellowed into a continuous state of bliss. Then you don't lose the balance. This is the difference between ecstasy and intoxication. Intoxication is the state in which one is still new to the *samadhi*. Later, it becomes apparent that there is a situation where it is simply that the consciousness is different from that of the consciousness of the people you see around you.

At this stage the ecstasy assumes a soothing quality, not an exciting quality.'

Again this seemed to me to be a very important statement. I understood her to mean that the tremendous velocity, the blissfully overwhelming ecstasy, which she called 'intoxication', became a permanent, low-level, all-permeating state of consciousness, which was forever present, forever renewing itself, but which became an indivisible part of life, rather than a crashing wave of total drenching drunkenness.

'What happened after 1968?' I asked.

She answered that she didn't know. 'I just remember these years. After that the intensity settled, it became quiet.'

She read out the next question: 'Would the final moment of the mutation process be when *nir-bij* descends, when *atma* merges with *paramatma*?'

By this I meant that I suspected the moment of enlightenment, that irreversible moment of understanding, occurred when the electrical force-field, the 'net' or 'web' or energy which separated the individual consciousness from the universal consciousness, was dissolved or torn, thus resulting in a merging of the universal and individual lights, a total blending.

She paused, and then said, 'I don't know. There's no final moment. Even today I don't feel I've arrived – the nuances and shades of reality go on opening up every moment so mutation is a dynamic, infinite process which would go on until the cosmic evolution exhausts all the potential contained in its Wholeness. The final word in spirituality, if there can be any final moment of spiritual growth and maturity has not yet occurred. That's why when I first heard Krishnaji speak, I heard him speak of my own experience, an experience verified and confirmed by him. I had not even wanted to hear Krishnamurti speak, but I was staying with someone who was close to Krishnaji. I was in Benares as part of my work for the Bhoodan Movement. It was A. who asked me to meet Krishnaji and I said, why is this necessary? I know the truth already. Krishnaji had seen me at the back of the hall, and said to A. that he wanted to meet me. A. and Krishnaji were walking across the bridge over the Ganges, in Benares. It's about a kilometer long, and they saw me boating on the river beneath. I loved boating and Krishnaji again said to A., 'That's the one I want to meet.'

She paused, and then continued, 'When I first met him, I asked him, where do you stay?
And he answered, 'Ah, you don't know anything about me, so you don't know any of the nonsense.' I knew nothing about him whatsoever. I had not even heard his name before, and so he spent 20 minutes telling me how Leadbeater had found him, how he had no childhood, how they chose the clothes for him, they chose what he would eat, how he had no youth. He talked about this to me on many subsequent occasions also.'

Kaiser and I were listening intently. 'I didn't think', she continued, 'That I would meet him again, but he asked me, before I left Benares, where are you going now? I said, my work will be taking me to Madras, so Krishnaji said, 'Oh, I'll be giving talks in Madras', as a hint that I should attend.'

I would have loved to have asked her more on this subject, for there were many questions in my mind as to the tragic events which were to transpire between her and Krishnamurti, but she ended her reminiscences at this point, and read out the next question, which somehow did not seem to follow at all from what we had been discussing.

'Would that be the final moment of the mutation process when *nir bij* descends?'

She seemed to consider the question, and then answered carefully and precisely. I had noticed she was always very careful with the language and words she used. 'The total mutation for humanity has yet to take place,' she said. 'The humans are the expression of divinity, - how can we assert the final mutation has taken place? Life is infinite and so is truth infinite.' Then she paused, and said, as if surprised, 'I have written for you, as it happens, which addresses this issue, something about this, which I'll give you. She unfolded a piece of paper which was on the divan beside her, and read it out to Kaiser and to me.

'The Homo-Universalis,' she began. 'The human race is a product of dual evolution. The human body is a product of millions of years of cosmic biological evolution. We belong to the animal species – perhaps the most evolved and complex physical structure up till today. The human brain-mind complex is the product of thousands of years of collective psychological effort by the Homo-sapiens.

'Biologically we are rational animals. Psychologically we are social animals. Biologically we are organically related to all the Non-Human species, existing on the planet. The Minerals, the Vegetable-plants, the birds and the animals are all our Fellow-Beings. Psychologically all the communities living in different parts of the Globe are members of one Global Human Community.

'The human race has to learn to share the natural resources with all the human communities as well as non-human fellow beings. All the socio-economic and political systems and structures will have to be refashioned and re-patterned to meet this spiritual challenge of sharing life.

'Further phase of cosmic evolution depends to a very great extent on whether the Humans realise their responsibility and play the role of Partners with Divinity or remain prisoners of their collective-ego and the illusion of being a super-race! Up until now the egoistic self-centred activities of the human race have resulted in plundering the planet and upsetting the Rhythm of complex cosmic life. It has also brought about misery and suffering, exploitation, confrontation and violence among the human communities living in various parts of the globe.

'Life is one indivisible wholeness. Every expression of Life – right from a blade of grass – to the mighty emperor of an empire, are Inter-Related. Their survival and prosperity are dependent on their reciprocity and mutual co-operation.

'Let the species of Rational-Social Human Animals recognise this fundamental fact and co-operate with the Divine Forces of Supreme consciousness for the sake of themselves as well as for the sake of further Evolution.'

I felt frustrated. I wanted to know about Vimalaji, about a particular point, about the *brahmarandra* opening to the gush of the infinite. And she was trying to convey to me with her answers the fact that the physical, psychic events which may occur at any moment of human development, were merely phenomenal events in the material world, merely results or expressions of something which was happening independently in the greatness of space, in the movement of cosmic energies. Whatever small event such as self-realisation was nothing more than one tiny dot in the endlessness, suddenly becoming a bit more of a spark.

She handed me the article she had written, and then again picked up the sheet of paper that contained the questions I had prepared.

'In this state of *nirbij* would the pulsation of bliss be felt?' she read.

She thought for a long time, and said, 'I am trying to feel this. I am trying to analyse,' and then she answered, 'No. The emptiness cannot feel itself as emptiness. The bliss cannot feel itself as bliss.'

She groped for words. I said, 'We, in our limited consciousness, cannot understand.'

She said, 'I have to focus and see what happens.' She was silent. 'I don't think there's any registration of bliss. No more a pulsation, no more an ecstasy.'

I felt it was so fundamental, so amazing, that this type of consciousness was there, contained in this human being who spoke with me, and who sat facing me, a body and a translucent face which covered and reduced to detectable levels the fire of the universe. And yet, because her state of consciousness was indescribable, because there was no human word which could define its dimension or awareness, and because I had not yet known that emptiness, I could not understand it. For the energies which she could perceive were so rarified, due to the tuning of her bodies, that I could not as yet hope to touch them.

She looked at the next page, and saw there were more questions. She seemed to hesitate, and then said, 'I'll answer the rest of the questions on Wednesday. I'll keep them to look at and think about.'

'Don't do that,' I thought to myself. 'I might want to change them.'

She handed the questions back to me. 'It's better to answer them spontaneously,' she said, by way of explanation for her change of mind.

It was quite a cold day, and I had worn sandals, which I had left at the door. I had forgotten to bring a jumper and was wearing light cotton clothes. 'These Australians are hardy people,' she said to Kaiser, smiling. 'Once I was invited to speak to a group gathering there. Poor Kaiser and I, we had to camp, using trenches for latrines and so on.'

Then she said, 'Yes, it was a cosmic plot that brought together Christine and Vimala.'

. . . .

The next day I had arranged to meet Kaiser at her house to ask her questions about Vimalaji's life. Kaiser had purchased a small dwelling almost next door to Vimalaji's house. She had prepared a delicious breakfast of *dal* and *aloo paratha*, an unleavened bread made in the shape of a pancake with wholemeal flour, stuffed with potato and spices, and fried in *ghee*. As we were eating, Sangeeta, to whom Kaiser had previously introduced me at *Satsang*, pushed open the door, calling gently, and, kicking off her shoes at the entrance, padded into the room.

She was a small, large-eyed, grey-haired woman, slim and lithe, swathed in a sari, carrying with her that air of humility which Indian women can accumulate after a life-time of servitude to men. Kaiser by comparison was vigorous and organising, always working and planning to ensure that people behaved as they were meant to behave. She had long ago discarded any inhibitions about male dominance, and was complete in herself, lacking the soft self-apology and humility that accompanied Sangeeta.

After Sangeeta had produced tiffins containing *dal* and sweets which she had prepared, and after we had eaten too much, and after Kaiser had made us tea, I asked Kaiser to sit down so I could ask her questions.

We sat on the divan together, with a view of the mountains visible through the windows, and I held a small microphone under her chin, so I could record what she said. For some reason I felt very guilty while doing this, although I dismissed these emotions, and concentrated intently on extracting from Kaiser every single detail which I could think to ask.

I began with the *Bhoodan* movement and asked the circumstances under which Vimalaji had joined.

'After Vimalaji finished her university studies, she was sent to Switzerland, America, and Yugoslavia as a representative of the Asian Women's Association. So when she was there she got a letter from Dada Dharmadikhari a friend of the family, he was also from Maharashtra, as is Vimalaji.'

Kaiser stopped, and looked at Sangeeta. 'You're not bored?' she asked.

'No, It's interesting,' Sangeeta answered, forever pliable.

'What's interesting is that you're putting it in context,' I said to Kaiser, 'But you shouldn't feel anxious about telling me anything different, because these things are already known. They're scattered around in books and so on.'

'Yes,' she said, but I sensed that she too felt anxious.

'So it was when Vimalaji was in Europe that she heard about the *Bhoodan* Movement – the Land Gift Movement - for the first time?' I asked.

'Vimalaji was there in Europe when she got a letter from Dada. He said, "You have always been interested in social work and now see - someone in India is beginning social work with spiritual basis. If you want come and see it, and participate, why don't you do so?"

'So Vimalaji left everything and she went back to India and she met Vinobaji and at the same time Jaiprakash Narayan was interested in this so they both joined together at the same time for one year, and she spent one year finding out what it was all about because the amazing thing about Vinobaji was that he wanted a revolution but he didn't want to do it like the communists and Maoists. He wanted to appeal to the goodness of the peoples' hearts, so they marched throughout India appealing to the goodness of the people. They said, now come on, you have this land and five sons. Take this labourer as your sixth son and share a part of your land. So that way they revolutionised the land ownership - it's a fantastic thing they did. Her inspirational speeches caused people to hand over thousands of acres of land.'

'Who exactly was Dada?' I asked.

Sangeeta was sitting like a small, patient doll on the chair which she had been allotted. Again we asked her if she was bored, and again she said she was interested, and so we continued.

'Dada was a family friend and also was friend of Vinobaji, so Vimalaji travelled with Dada as an assistant to Dada in land-gift movement. From her college days she used to know Dada because Dada was considered as one of family He used to take them all together to educate them. When the Constitution of India was being made, he used to take them all to Delhi to listen to the debates in parliament.'

'She had told me something about this,' I replied, 'And I also read it in different places.'

I thought back to her descriptions which had been given in interviews. When Vimalaji had finished her final exams, at the age of about nineteen, she went immediately to the Himalayas. With what joy and wonder she must have looked upon the turquoise blue water of the Ganges.

She spent about three months in a cave where Swami
Ramtirth, one of the great Vedantins of India, had lived.
Totally alone, eating mangoes, and potatoes which she
roasted in a small fire, drinking the water of the Ganges,
sometimes sitting in the forest, she grew weak and feverish.
Vimalaji was later to emphasize that she should have looked
after her health with greater diligence.

In the cave, alone in the forest, with no sounds of traffic,
with only the call of birds and the cries of monkeys and other
wild animals, something extraordinarily important was
happening in the silence of the cave, in the depths of the
forest. Privately, secretly, intensely, she realized was able to
attain that state of meditation.

She did not then fully comprehend the dimensional change
which was taking place in the consciousness. She saw lights
in the cave, and at times heard sounds. Fearless, alone,
curious, amazed, she must have been totally lost in the
passion of her quest, soaring to heights of bliss and ecstasy,
loosing an interest in eating, loosing all concerns for any
material aspect of life.

As the Ganges flows through Rishikesh its waters are wide
and still. Unpolluted and pure, they appear to be of turquoise
colour, and small beaches, stretches of river stone, and great
rocks, together with tangled vegetation, ashrams and assorted
buildings, line the banks. From central points along the river,
small trails lead into the forest up into the hills.

Bathing one morning in the Ganges on its rocky shores,
treading among the slippery river stones, each one coloured
and shaded and shaped by the flow of water and wind over
the eons, the young woman, slipping, fell into the river. The

current was strong and rapid. Unable to swim she struggled frantically to reach the shore but was soon exhausted. Her fasting and her immobile life in the cave had weakened her body and she thought she would die, so offered her body to the river and then lost consciousness.

Further down the river there was the Ashram of Swami Sivananda at Rishikesh. He was a doctor and homeopath and seeing the body floating down the river, he hauled it from the water. Noticing that she was still breathing, he took Vimalaji to his ashram, where she was nursed, and on the eighth day after the accident, she regained consciousness. On that very day it happened that a friend of her father's was visiting Swamiji's ashram and said, 'Oh this is Vimala! This is my friend's daughter!'

'And Swamiji was very happy to know that this was not an orphan but someone who was taken care of properly, so he handed over that wretched, miserable, weak body to my father's friend, and that is how I was brought back. All my efforts at self-realisation were over,' Vimalaji was to say many years later when reflecting on the experience.

'I went back to my parents place and the experience of that deep silence and the other mystical experiences; the memory was very fresh with me. But the desire to isolate myself from daily life had gone and the search began in daily life,' Vimalaji was to explain in 1972 in an interview with 'Mr. Frederic'[3].

'It seems that the main thing about the *Bhoodan* Movement was this idea of sharing the land with the landless tiller and appealing to goodness of human heart to give out of kindness

---

[3] Irani, Kaiser, *Vimalaji's Global Pilgrimage, Vol. I.*

and compassion?' I said to Kaiser. 'And she didn't worry
about the discomfort or hardship, it seems. During the long
walks she would only eat the food which the village people
could also afford to eat.'

Kaiser nodded.

'In her book, *On An Eternal Voyage*, she mentioned that the
Bhoodan Movement was badly reported in Western
newspapers.'

'The West did not catch what a huge revolution was taking
place – there was the French Revolution, the Russian, the
Chinese – all with so much bloodshed. Yet there was no
bloodshed in India.'

'It must have been landmark decision which she made, after
she had met Krishnamurti and become enlightened, to
disassociate herself from the Land Gift Movement,' I
commented. I thought of Vimalaji's published letter to her
friends in the *Bhoodan* Movement, in which she had
announced her withdrawal.

> I am writing this letter after a great hesitation. Hesitation
> because I wonder if I could succeed in putting into words
> what I really want to communicate to you. But write I
> must. The compulsive urge to share the utterly new
> experience obliges me to write. You know my life
> history and the history of my inner voyage too well to
> need any mention .... let me tell you that I have
> undergone tremendous upheavals, tempests and volcanic
> upsurges, inside me, within the last eight months.
> No words could describe the intensity and depth of the
> experience through which I am passing. Everything is
> changed. I am born anew. This is neither wishful
> thinking nor is it a sentimental reaction to the healing (of
> the ear which she injured in a car accident, which was

healed by Krishnamurti: ed). It is an astounding
phenomenon.

…After spending a few months in the West and studying
books on science and philosophy, after contemplating on
the problem of fundamental revolution, I have arrived at
a conclusion that liberty is the criterion of evolution. The
development of human personality consists in liberating
it from all bondages. Thus for me, freedom is the only
way of collaborating with this universal phenomenon of
evolution.

No more peace and contentment. But a profound
revolution. A human revolution which consists in freeing
oneself from every kind of personal, national, racial and
ideological preoccupation. At the source of all evil is the
very substance of our consciousness, we will have to
deal with it. Everything that has been transmitted to our
mind through centuries will have to be completely
discarded. We will have to deal with it in a total way. I
have dealt with it. It has dropped away. I have discarded
it.[4]

I looked out the window at the Himalayas, a string of white-
capped mountains dividing heaven from earth. They came
from the left and exited at the right, and you could not see
their beginning nor their ending, for they crossed the horizon
from unknown sources, to unknown ends. And perhaps it
was also like this with Vimalaji, that the sequence of events
in her life were just a small stretch within my horizon, and
there was no beginning, and no ending, for she had emerged,
and would merge back, and all the antecedents and prefixes
and propositions were additional notes to the small page
which I had opened.

'There's one thing about her life which must have been
heart-breaking,' I said. 'I read, in Vimalaji's book, *Eternal*

---

[4] Thakar, Vimala, *On an Eternal Voyage,* Vimal Prakashan Trust, India,
1989; 50.

Voyage, that the one she so respected and revered, her close friend, Krishnamurti, who taught spiritual truths throughout the world, that he rejected her. I opened the book and read out: 'Some of those who knew my intimate association with J. Krishnamurti felt hurt that I never mentioned his contribution to my life in my talks. Some felt hurt that instead of propagating Krishnamurti's teachings, I dared give independent talks. Some felt annoyed that I dared print those talks. This made my heart rather sad.'

Kaiser said nothing.

'How incredible,' I continued, 'That he listened to people gossiping around him, people who said Vimalaji had 'plaguarised' his words, when in reality she had repeatedly explained to people in Europe, when they asked her to speak, that she was speaking as herself, and not as a follower of Krishnamurti. And then his rejection of her – she wrote letters to him, and he never answered them, never even gave her an opportunity to explain, to talk it over.'

We looked across at Sangeeta. She was still sitting eagerly and obediently, like a well-trained dog, hoping for us to finish, but much too polite and self-effacing to ever hint that perhaps we had talked enough. I turned off the recorder, and we sat in silence, and even though the Himalayas were out the window, and in the sky, and distant, their immense presence bore down on us, and humbled us, and made everything be nothing.

....

The following day at *Satsang* there was a mist. The view from the house was obscured by veils of white, shifting clouds.

After the *Satsang* Kaiser handed at letter to me. It was hand-written by Vimalaji, and it said:

Dear Christine,

I looked upon you as an inquirer of spiritual Truth. Your experiment in living in silence and solitude in Abu was proof for me of your concern for Transformation in Consciousness through Meditation.

I gladly agreed to have personal dialogues with you at Dalhousie on the basis of that understanding.

The questions that you had brought in a written form surprised me as they were about Vimala's personal life. They had biographical quality about them. Surely you cannot write Vimala's biography as you have not lived with her! Even Kaiser cannot do so as she has come to V. only in 1978.

I am not interested in biographical sketches or narrations. If you are interested in the phenomenon of dimensional transformation and how it is lived in the movement of relationships let us continue our bi-weekly dialogue sessions. Otherwise it is better to wind them up tomorrow.

With deep love,
Vimala.

For a moment I was ashamed, and then I realised, with a rush of gratitude that she was shaping the book for me, that she was giving me guidance as to the direction it should take. And, as I thought about her letter, and the fact that the questions I had asked her at the last interview had not really been biographical, I suspected that she had seen, through her supernormal abilities, that I had pinned Kaiser behind a microphone on a couch and questioned her intensely for an hour. It was too much of a co-incidence that yesterday I had been interviewing Kaiser about Vimalaji's life, and that today Vimalaji had given me the letter. Clearly she had been able to know what I had been doing, and was putting a stop to it. I wondered how I could have done something so stupid. I did not even want to write a biography. It was far more interesting to be given the opportunity to investigate the topic which Vimalaji had suggested, the phenomenon of dimensional transformation and how it was lived in the movement of relationships!

As Vimalaji had already left the room, I knew that I would have to wait until the following day before I could apologise to her. The next day, as I walked down path, I felt so much love brimming from that house. I felt incredibly close to her, and extraordinarily grateful that she should waste so much time on me.

As I opened the door to the meditation room I saw that she was already sitting in a chair against the wall. She looked at me intently, saw that I was smiling, and projected in response a tremendous radiant beam of dazzle towards me. I could hardly walk. I felt I needed to grab hold of a wall so that I would not be lifted into the sky, so that I could cling to earth through the touch of the world.

I gave her a letter which I had written which started with an apology. 'It is not my calling to write Vimalaji's biography,' I had written, and had then outlined my proposal for the book, which she studied carefully. As she read it to herself I thought, 'Well I don't care what happens. I trust her, and that's all there is to it. Whatever she says, I trust her totally. If she is angry with me, I will be happy for whatever comes from her is always right.'

The love was pouring from her. 'What beautiful handwriting,' she said.

Then she said, 'Yes, dear, you're right. It's not the role of Christine to write the biography of Vimalaji; it would only delay or interrupt the transformation which is occurring. Why write about Vimalaji? What is there of interest in Vimalaji's life when Christine's own book on self-transformation will be so much more useful?'

I nodded dumbly. I was sitting on a low stool, facing her, so that I could be near enough for her to hear what I said. 'Write about the role of Vimalaji in your life,' she said. 'Her only role has been to lend a helping hand.'

Such was her great modesty and self-effacement, despite the mightiness of her realisation, that she could make another person feel wanted and worth-while, and however much I might love her, it seemed that the love which emanated from her being was more powerful and overwhelming than anything which was generated from me, so that I was always the one who was the receiver, and never able to equal the volume and velocity of her giving.

Then she read on and said, 'The purpose of Vimala's life (which she was quoting) – there's no purpose, dear. You see we are like the river, you could say the hidden purpose of Life is expressed through Vimala – that's all.'

Then she read some more and said, 'We're not
'programmed' for self-transformation: on the biological level
the organs are programmed to function in certain way but
consciousness or free will do come into it, the consciousness
has to decide whether it will open up to divinity or not open
up. That is the choice. Each human is cosmically predestined
and there is the eventual certainty of self-realisation – this is
the claim of the *Vedas*, that human race as a result of
uncovering of the destiny, is destined to get rooted in that
destiny. The 21st century is going to be a century of many
people attaining that predestined heritage of the human race.
On the one hand, natural science and technology and
spirituality or science of consciousness on the other hand. So
it seems the whole planet is like a cradle in which the whole
human is being born.'

Then she said she didn't get what I meant when I said,
'Transformation happens because of living in the
phenomenal world'. She said, 'It occurs in spite of living in
the phenomenal world.'

I said that for example, peoples' involvement in the *Bhoodan*
movement had assisted in their inner spiritual development,
but it seemed to me more than that also. It seemed important
to prevent communism coming to India because then the
ancient wisdom might be lost.

She said it was very important to keep India as a democracy
and the *Bhoodan* movement, Vinoba, Gandhi, Narayan had
provided an alternative to communism, although
communism had done a lot of good for the human race, in as
much as it said that poverty is man-made, not human-made,
and it asked for a more equal distribution of wealth, but
where it went wrong was that it became a path of violence,

using jealousy and hatred which were actually contrary to its very philosophy – and this is where the contribution of Gandhi came in.

'Vinoba was manifesting to the world that there was an alternative, Democracy could not survive with millions of suffering people in India,' Vimalaji said. 'Vinoba had believed that the means and the instrument of production should belong to the worker.'

'Yes,' she said, after falling silent for a while. 'The vested interests opposed the path of Vinoba, Narayan and others. They did not want the tiller of the land to have the land – the landowners wanted to keep the land, and to keep the poor suppressed

'When we were at a village, we used to go round to each house and beg for a little food. Vinoba was resting in a hammock. One of my brothers (not a real brother, but one who had said to Vimala, 'I want to die,' and Vimala had answered, 'If you really want to die, my brother, join Vinoba!') - Vinoba was a god-intoxicated person. Well, after we had been round collecting the food from the villagers, we went to the hammock where he was lying, to bring him the food, and we saw a big knife lying underneath. At first we looked at the knife and did not understand. He saw us looking and said, 'The Lord had just come to fetch me but I was not ready.' We were puzzled for a moment and then we realised what had happened. Someone had been going to kill him with the knife while he lay asleep, and just at that moment when the murderer lifted the knife to stab him, Vinoba opened his eyes, looked at the man and said 'The Lord has come to fetch me.' As he said this the person was so afraid, he dropped the knife and ran away. The landlords had arranged for him to murder Vinoba, but he couldn't do it.'

'So there was a lot of danger, a lot of resistance from the wealthy people?' I asked.

'The Indian government pretended to support our movement. They put garlands round our necks and so on, but in fact they would not co-operate. Vimala personally collected over 200,000 acres of land. Once it had been collected, in order to be redistributed, the name on the title deed needed to be changed. For this we needed the help of the government, but they had instructions from Congress to keep postponing it.'

Is it correct then, that some of the land is still in possession of the government?'

'Yes, some land is still undistributed [5]'

As she talked, it was as though she was conveying to me a whole landscape of history, a massive ribbon of endless pictures which stretched through time, and which were imprinted in space. I saw the ancient golden age, in which there was no desire for wealth, in which great beings sat in the forest, their group of disciples clustered round them, the farmer tending his cattle, the king dispensing financial allocations to the schools of the gurus. I saw the spreading of this culture based on spirituality and ethics, its interconnection with other points of light throughout the globe, its later distortion, the melting of the ice, the great floods submerging the corrupted knowledge which prevailed. And I saw the retreat of the Rishis into the Himalayas where no waters could reach, where no greedy humans could grab

---

[5] See appendix for Vimala Thakar's comments on the true social activist.

and pollute the knowledge which could never be destroyed, which had always existed and of which they remained the repositories.

I saw how the Aryans flowed into, and possessed the rich plains of the Indus and how once more the Rishis appeared to them, to reveal the truth that had never been lost, but which had become hidden. And I saw how they listened breathlessly to their teachings, remembering, recording, passing from generation to generation. And I saw India flooded with invaders, who came from across the lands, and I saw her changing peoples, her changing cultures, the armies, the elephants, the slaughter of humans and horses, and tribes. And I saw that the ancient truth once more became hidden in the cry of the battle, in the blood of the sword. I saw the Hindu priests, corrupt and greedy, being forced to eat cow meat by the Muslim invaders, and again it seemed the truth was suppressed by the ambition of humans

And Vimalaji was a part of this never-ending cycle of receding and advancing, of revelation and concealment, of exposure and containment. India in the nineteen fifties was a young democracy with a new Constitution, freed from the rule of the British, a sub-continent with hundreds of languages, with multifarious cultures, customs, costumes, religions, castes and creeds. It was a fantastically diverse and secretive country, with the vast inheritance of the *Vedas*, the gift of India to the world, and the heaviness of tradition choking the new adaptations and developments which began to emerge as the new India formed to fit a modern world.

The twentieth century was one in which numerous great souls incarnated in India with the purpose of lifting and guiding her through the transition from the past to the future.

Those great souls, such as Gandhi, Tukraji, Vinobaji and Vimalaji, Swami Vivekananda, Sri Aurobindo, and Jaya Prakash Narayan, were moved by the same philosophy, the same grounding. It was as if there was one great sweeping ray which washed across the land, and in that colour, that vibration, these numerous individuals appeared as lights as they touched the soil of India, to fade again and be replaced by another growing flare.

These people knew each other, were connected by thought and by deed, together or separately faced danger so that the India which they loved could maintain the beauty of the past, together with the democracy of the future. 'Even if I die,' Vinobaji once said to Vimala Thakar, 'The soil of India will produce another one hundred to replace me.'

The communist movement was spreading across many countries of the world. Vimalaji believed that communism, of itself, was a necessary step in breaking the religious hold of the past, the traditions of caste, of an elite who ruled, but that the very message of communism, which was freedom for the oppressed, became distorted by its own leaders. There was concern that India would fall to communism, as had China and other Asian nations. If this were to be the case the irreplaceable spiritual inheritance could have been crushed and destroyed, as was to happen in Tibet. India's spiritual heritage needed to remain protected, her ancient pilgrimage sites preserved, and, because of this, there was an uprising of people inspired by spiritual principles, both erudite and passionate, intellectual and fervent, determined to see India's hidden light secured for the benefit of future humanity. For even if it was only sensed rather than voiced, the leaders of twentieth century India must have known at some unconscious level, that India, despite all the difficulties

through which she was to pass, was yet to be a beacon, a
centre in the world to which those who wanted to know the
truth, could undertake the pilgrimage. And all the crassness,
and all the greed, and all the commercialism which was to
come when the doors of India were opened to the world, all
the ugliness, the cement, the highways crashing through
villages, the glittering cars pushing the camel carts into the
gutters, all the destruction of the ancient dignity and rhythm,
all the misunderstanding and spurning of the past, none of
this could smash nor demolish the eternal living truth which
was concealed beneath the growing chaos.

Vimalaji had once written that Indian civilisation had only
one aim which was to ensure that human beings should
arrive at the consummation of their holistic growth in the
state of Yoga, which was, she explained, equanimity inside,
and balance at the sensual level.

'Every imbalance is called impurity by Indian heritage,' she
explained. 'The science of yoga helps us to learn how to
balance the biological energies, how to purify them, how to
harmonise them. This is part of self-education. No individual
can contribute to the social welfare, to the ascendance of
society, the cultural growth of prosperity of society unless
within himself or herself the person arrives at this state of
equanimity, equipoise, equibalance.'

> A new economic morality has to be spelt out for the
> world, in which human beings look upon the non-human
> species and non-human expressions as partners of Life,
> partners in production, partners in consumption of the
> produce. This man/nature partnership is one way
> towards finding a solution, if it could be called a
> solution. The other is looking upon the whole global

human community as one family for sharing the
resources of the planet.[6]

The Land Gift Movement in India, of which Vimalaji was
one of the leaders, was a part of the great saga, the great
journey of India, in which the hidden light had to be
protected from being crushed and extinguished. The Land
Gift Movement was a part of the great wave of social
revolution that swept India after independence. It was
instrumental in preventing an uprising of the proletariat, in
its place to encouraging a democratic and voluntary
redistribution of land from the rich landowners to the
landless villagers.

For the social leaders of India in the twentieth century, it was
freedom from authority, re-distribution of wealth,
particularly land, and the right to self-determination in
government, which was important if India was to retain her
culture and yet adjust to the modern world in which she
found herself. In the parliament there was heated debate as to
the decentralization of power. Some believed, as did
Vimalaji, Vinobaji and Narayan, that the village people
themselves could govern and determine their own lives,
through a system of decentralised village governments,
called *panchayats*. But first, before any real democracy
could be implemented, the poor in the villages needed their
own land. So long as they were working the rich landlord's
properties, they were basically bonded labourers, without
any resources of their own, dependant on whatever small
handout the landlords might deign to offer.

---

[6] Thakar, Vimala, *The Invincible,* Vol. XI, No. 2, April-June, 1995; 11-12,
28.

The 'external events' which had brought Vimalaji in contact with these great leaders, of whom she was one, were indeed only outer expressions, as I now clearly saw, as I sat before her, and listened to her speaking. Her life had nothing to do with external events, but was concerned with the inner recognition of That which she had always been. These Indian campaigners had emerged from the darkness, into a collection of light, travelling, meeting, parting again, blown seemingly by the waves of propulsion which originated in the vibration of infinity itself. And for one who had been born with a desire to help humanity it seemed it was a natural response for Vimalaji to immediately return to India to take part in the new movement, the news of which had so greatly inspired her.

'The important thing,' Vimalaji said, 'Is that there were so many people in the last century who appeared in India to work for it to retain democracy. 50,000 villages in India have a system where the land is owned by a *gram seva*, now called *panchayat*. This is not communism, where the state owns the communes, nor capitalism where the land is privately owned, nor even a co-operative. The land belongs to the tiller, but if his son does not want to till the soil, then the land is given back to the village council. This was enacted under Rajiv Gandhi's rule. Up until 1990, there were 50,000 villages running this way. The village committee owned the land, the cattle, the water resources, and if they wanted a tractor for the village, they would buy it.'

She said India has the responsibility to give guidelines on spiritual development. The whole of Asia could provide a different model. India has the responsibility to show the synthesis of social action and religion to the world.

She said, yes, you could say it was a divine strategy that caused so many people to be crowded into one century – the emergence of Marx, Lenin, she would even say Trotsky was a necessity for Europe as guild socialism, etc. had not succeeded.

'It was a divine dispensation that provided so many God-intoxicated. people like Gandhi, Vinoba, Naryan - Vinoba said, even if I die, the soil of India will produce 100 more Vinoba's! Narayan said, in 1974-5, just before he was arrested, so what if I die. Suppose I die tomorrow, you have to take up the torch. Don't let the flame die?

'These great leaders were worried about Indira Gandhi's dictatorial tendencies, and Narayan declared, India cannot rot. They were worried that the texture of India was becoming very authoritarian, very detrimental to democracy. It was important that it did not follow the trend of China or Russia. However, India could not become communist, for the life of so many sages and Rishis have gone into the soil, protect the very earth of India.'

Awed, I sat in silence before her. She had seated me very close to her so that she could hear me, but by now she understood that I felt more comfortable if my head was at a lower level than her own.

Then she returned to my letter. 'What is the hidden purpose of Vimala's life?' she read out. 'What do you mean by this?' she asked me.

"It seems to me that, first, Vimalaji has given the Teaching, which is a modern presentation of the ancient wisdom for this generation and for centuries to come.'

She nodded at this. Then I said, 'There's also this other
phenomena which I feel. It doesn't really seem to matter
what Vimalaji's doing, she's radiating Energy; she's
bringing that Energy down to earth wherever she is.'

She smiled and spoke. 'This is done,' she answered, in her
measured, deep voice, 'By becoming a small instrument. It's
very necessary to empty yourself so you don't have any
purpose and then, when the Cosmic works through you, the
Cosmic gets fulfilled. It does require to be totally empty in
order to be filled with the Cosmic. The event of Vimala's life
is like a flute being played by Krishna. The divinity plays its
own music. It's just staggering what is happening in the life
of a person called Vimala.'

Then she talked about the two people from Calcutta. They
were from a homeopathy business which earned massive
amounts of crores of rupees every year, and something had
happened absolutely incredible. 'One feels staggered by the
speed and force with which the divinity is working,' she
said. I wanted to know more, but knew it was something
about which she could not talk, and so I did not question her
further.

Then she said again, 'I have never talked of these things
before.'

'There are probably hundreds of people in very high
positions, or positions of great influence who are somehow
led to you, and through you great miracles occur,' I said.

'Do you direct it?' I asked. I meant by this to inquire as to
whether she needed to work these miracles by the power of

thought. Even though I expressed myself badly she understood what I meant.

'You mentioned in the car to Delhi you had work to do about Kashmir,' I said.

'It is there. It has taken charge of the being. This has become the abode for That Energy to be on the planet and express Itself. While I was in movement and conducting camps there was a conscious effort to channelise energies of human species towards dimensional transformation but since 1997 when I discontinued the camps there is no effort.'

'The solution to Kashmir is on the way to getting solved. Congress, BJP, socialist parties, etc. peace activists and so called militants all of them are preparing themselves for peace.
There were seven delegates from Pakistan who came to see me when we were in Delhi on night of 21st and that same night seven delegates from India also came. On 23rd when we were passing through Patankot again we attended a meeting. I have helped to prepare the agenda, themes to be taken up. I communicated very clearly how I saw it. If you empty your consciousness as a person and have the humility without knowing what is going to happen, it happens, there is no knowing, there is an unpredictability, and there must be a fearlessness. Fearlessness is very important.'

'Not to worry when people might think you are mad, running away to be on retreats, to sit in a room alone? Not to worry when they think it's rude when you turn down offers of dinner parties and entertainment?'

'Yes, not to worry what the people around you say. But it is important that you're conscious of the health of the body so that it remains in a proper state, to be used by the divine. But mainly what is needed is a completely impersonal person in which there's no giving, there's no making effort - the container of that Supreme Energy has been emptied of a personality.'

I thought she had described her state of being with such elegance. I was overwhelmed at the vista of life which appeared to me as she spoke.

She said, 'The important thing is the human pilgrimage to total transformation – how it takes place, how it gets adjusted in personal life. Then she spoke about my future, and the words were a prediction. It seemed as though she spoke the words without intending to do so. Deeply moved by their content, I remained silent.

Then I said, 'I know it's time for me to go, but would you mind if I asked you one more question?'

'Not at all dear,' she answered.

'To eat animals destroys the human/animal relationship?' I asked.

'Definitely', she answered. 'To eat the animals violates the law of life – we have to share this planet on the basis of ecology – the human race has got to put aside their greed. Why make your stomach a graveyard?'

'Do you think it is wrong to give a mercy killing to an animal if it's suffering? Some people say we should not kill an animal as it would interfere with their karma.'

'I had not thought about this,' she said. 'Let me think.' Then she continued, 'You see, even Gandhiji asked some people to put down a calf which was suffering. If the animal is suffering, then I would say it is not killing at all, but mercifully delivering it.'

She thought some more. 'Mass killing by councils and so on, mass killing of healthy animals, this is not the right way, but when it is done by people who love the animals, for the animals, this is merciful.'

I had wondered what I would have done if she had said she opposed euthanasia of suffering animals, for I believed that if an animal was in pain, and its prognosis was poor, that it was a human responsibility to intervene on behalf of the one who had been given into our care. Vimalaji's answer was totally free from any cultural conditionings, for most Brahmins would have considered it against the precepts of Hinduism to kill an animal, no matter how greatly it was suffering.

'When I first met you, in that first interview, you said you had campaigned against the slaughterhouse? Do you remember?' I asked her.

'No, I'm so sorry, I don't remember,' she answered.

I had wanted once more to ask her about the killing of the animals. The mass slaughter of millions of animals all over the world for food, every day, was something that was forever with me, and although it was not a conscious thought, nor a conscious remembrance, the scenes of slaughter which I had witnessed, both in India and in Australia, were a deep pain that I carried with me, and whenever I allowed myself to think of the creatures, I thought of this, and I was burdened and did not think I would ever escape the horror of their suffering, nor of the human callousness that permitted and executed such violence.

It was time for me to go, but I asked one more question.

'I won't be able to write the book without saying something about the events in your life,' I said.

'Of course not, dear,' she answered. 'It doesn't matter if you put three of four pages in each chapter about the 'external events' of Vimala's life. There are no watertight compartments and you could not separate external from internal. These are only terms reflecting our limited way of dividing life into compartments.'

By now there seemed to be nothing but love which filled the room. Although there was a Vimala and a Christine somewhere within that love, it was not a personal love, but was one sheet of flame, in which we seemed to be submerged.

Trying to rouse myself, I stood up and said, 'Well, I'd better stop.'

'I'm sorry I'm a little deaf,' she said, 'Because it makes it so difficult for the person who's trying to speak to me, when they have to shout.'

'I don't mind shouting at all, but I don't like the idea of shouting at Vimalaji,' I answered.

Again I said, 'Well, I should finish,' and she said, 'Could you call Bhavna for me as she's leaving tomorrow, and I want to say goodbye to her.'

'Of course,' I answered.

Then she said, 'Did you see the storm last night?'

'How beautiful it was,' I answered. It had been very violent and the sky had been rent by lightening. Thunder had seemed to split the earth, the make it shake with its force.

'One was amazed and transported by the beauty,' she said, 'The lightening made the sky so bright. And the thunder . . .'

Again, I had the feeling I had entered her mind, or rather, we were sharing the one mind. She showed me the vastness of Life, and all the little questions which I had thought about so much seemed so petty.

Then with so much love, she held out her hands to me, as an invitation, and, responding to that great gesture of complete openness, I put my hands in her hands. Holding my hands, and looking into my eyes, with so much compassion and understanding, she said, almost as if it was someone else saying it, and she was a by-stander to the utterance, 'You will ....' And again she spoke of the future, a glorious future.

I was so moved that I knelt on the ground before her and touched her feet with my forehead. Never had I done such a thing in my life before, but it happened naturally, as though executed by some other, remote director. And as I knelt before her with my head on her feet, she touched my head in blessing. And I wanted to lie with my forehead on her toes forever, and to never leave her.

CHAPTER NINE

SATSANG

Spirituality is a science of life: they call it physics of consciousness. As physics tries to explore the nature of Reality through analyzing matter and energy, spirituality explores the nature of Ultimate Reality by analyzing the nature of consciousness. Let us be very clear that spirituality is a science of life, it is not related to any beliefs, traditions or dogmas. So you have come to a friend who has dedicated her life to spirituality as a science and to finding out ways of relating the discovery of this science to daily living, to individual life and to social life [1]

Vimalaji held *satsang* three days a week, on Mondays, Wednesdays and Fridays. I would walk down the hill from the log cabin.

One day, I was the first to arrive and Vimalaji was already sitting on the *asana*, in deep meditation. She did not seem to notice my entrance. Soon other women filled the room. I felt strangely out of place, dressed in my *salwar kamiz* which I had found was the most practical clothing to wear because it was loose, pure cotton, cool and easy to sit cross-legged without revealing any portions of body. I was feeling lonely and I thought I should not have been wearing Indian clothes, for I could never be Indian.

Even though I knew a smattering of Hindi, and even though Vimalaji spoke Hindi so slowly and clearly when she addressed the people who came to *satsang,* I was unable to understand most of it, due to the fact that my vocabulary was

---

[1] Thakar, Vimala, *The Invincible*, Vol. XI, No. 2, April-June, 1995; 1-2.

limited to issues which concerned rescuing animals, complaints about sick cows on the roads, and operating on body parts of dogs. Vimalaji had sometimes followed her Hindi talks with an English interpretation, but I had said that she did not need to do this, as I felt uncomfortable that nearly everyone else in the room had to sit patiently while she repeated the talk in English, just for my own benefit.

As I tried to meditate, to tune into her emanation, I could not help wondering what I was doing here, and why I had come, and whether I should have come at all. Vimalaji was so full of love that she would have accepted whatever I did, but perhaps I was just wasting time that could have been used better in some other capacity. Maybe I should not have left Jeremy and Nirmal struggling away at the shelter in Jaipur. Maybe I was just a foolish foreigner imposing herself on people too courteous to turn me away.

After the chanting and singing, Vimalaji began to speak. I was surprised and delighted to note that she was using English, and that I would be able to understand. She had developed bronchitis, and was speaking with difficulty, so she asked Kaiser for a microphone in order for her voice to be heard, even though it was not a particularly large room. Kaiser handed her the microphone and then went to turn on the tape recorder, but Vimalaji indicated that she did not want her talk to be recorded.

'Yesterday,' she began, 'Was the birthday of Krishnaprem, previously called Austin Nixon. He had been flying a war plane to bomb Germany in World War One when two strong pale brown hands and arms had seized his hands, and taken control of the wheel. Try as he might, he could not get the plane to fly onwards towards Germany. The hands forced the plane to return all the way back to the British airbase. He was taken into a room, and questioned as to why he had returned. 'Were you afraid?' he was asked. 'No,' he answered, and explained about the pale brown hands and arms. Just then the news came through that his colleagues, the other pilots in the two other planes which had been flying with him, had both been shot down and killed. He decided to go to India and find out what were these hands and arms which had saved his life. A post came up at Lucknow University for Professor of English. He applied for it and was appointed to the position. He learnt Hindi and Sanskrit and studied all the scriptures. His guru was a very strict Teacher. She made him put on robes and go round begging. All his English friends laughed at him, as did his Indian friends. But he underwent the total transformation. Austin Nixon vanished and in his place Krishnaprem appeared. He never left India again.

'So many of the English have come to India and undergone a total transformation, whereas the Indians who live here don't have that inquiring spirit, don't have the commitment and determination to do it. They're still tied up in the words. But the foreigners came – Maurice Freidman, Bede Griffith, Paul Brunton, and they recognized what was here. And so Vimalaji is grateful to them all, and would like to thank them all on her behalf and on your behalf.'

As she spoke I began to cry. The image of the brown hands seizing the wheel and taking control simply overwhelmed me. It seemed to parallel the strange event in my own life when I had been attacked by the dog, and experienced a strong sense of an intervening, redeeming entity who had saved my life.

But, even more moving to me was the fact that Vimalaji had once again seemed to read my thoughts. Her talk had moved my mind away from my small concerns.

It was at this same *satsang* that Vimalaji spoke about Krishnamurti and answered a question which has puzzled me ever since I had read her book, *On An Eternal Voyage,* a question which had emerged again after she had talked about Krishnamurti with me the previous week. I was wondering how it could have been that someone who was enlightened, and therefore filled only with universal unlimited love, could have behaved so cruelly towards Vimalaji. But now, as she began to speak about Krishnamurti, she addressed this precise question, as though once more she had read my mind.

'Today is Krishnaji's birthday. For the benefit of Christine, it is true that he was used by the Lord Maitreya, by the Christ. The Theosophical Society had found him, Leadbeater had found him as a small child, and they had taken him, as they needed a volunteer through which these Beings could halt the decay of moral values in a world which was growing increasingly corrupt. A change in direction was needed, and They succeeded in bringing a message of freedom from authority and nationalism. But Krishnamurti never had a childhood. He was manipulated and tortured. They almost succeeded in completely transforming him, but, unlike others who transformed themselves, there was always a seed of sadness, I could almost say, 'tragedy', remaining. So he gave his life that it could be used as a vehicle, and his message was revolutionary. This was his great gift,' she concluded. And when she said this, it was then that I was able to understand.

....

I had moved into a room at *Dakshinamurti*, for the rent was cheaper, and I was able to be with other friends of Vimalaji, including Sangeeta, after my three weeks alone in the wooden cabin on the mountain.

It was a large old rambling bungalow, with a roofed verandah onto which doors opened from all the front rooms, of which mine was one. From the window of my room I could see a white butterfly which hung in the air. Below, among the forest canopy were the roofs of other houses built along a ridge which ran at right-angles. From the house the cliff-face fell rapidly and its steep slopes were forested by firs, interspersed with other trees, the names of which I did not know. Far, far below, I could see a river, and on the other side, the forested ridges rose steeply until they reached a height which was above that at which I sat. There were several mountains along this ridge, the closest one having been partially cleared, and a small ribbon of road could be seen winding across it. Along this road some development had taken place. There were green patches of paddy field, like strips of striped velvet, and small villages scattered among the trees.

The view in the other direction, towards the plains of India, was largely blocked by trees, but if you maneuvered yourself into the right position you could see the burning yellow haze of the summer baking and glistening. Here, insulated from the buzz and glare of heat, the sun itself seemed to be absorbed into the dark pine and fir canopy, and the leaves and branches looked like the jade arrangements from antique Chinese pottery.

The house was cared for by Sangeeta. It contained a large
kitchen, dining room, and a meditation room, with an image
of Dr. Kaushik on the altar. In addition there were three
bedrooms, each with their own bathroom. In a small outer
house lived Premila. I did not know anything about Premila,
except that she was only about four feet high, and seemed
like a small bird. Vimalaji often asked her to sing, and
listened in rapture to her rich voice.

By moving to this house I was able to come to know some of
the people who had shared Vimalaji's life for much longer
than myself, particularly Sangeeta. As we became closer, I
gradually came to understand, through her, and through the
other friends whom I observed, that the real miracle was the
transformation which occurred in people's lives after they
had been exposed to the presence of Vimalaji. When we
talked together I learnt of the ways in which she had helped
them through difficult periods, predicted events, and uplifted
them.

One day Sangeeta and Premila took myself and a friend of
Vimalaji's who had come with her husband from Delhi to
see Vimalaji, and who was staying in *Dakshinamurti* for
only a few days, and her husband on a picnic in the
mountains. We were all exhilarated and happy and the friend
commented that she had perhaps never been happier in her
whole life. I also felt similarly.

A row of snow-laden mountains stretched across the horizon
from left to right for as far as we could see. They seemed to
float in the blue haze as if on a tray suspended in the sky,
with nothing connecting them to the earth except layer after
layer of grey ridges, each toned with darker colour at its
peak, with its foot in a haze of blue valley. On the closest

ridge one could see the roofs of houses and terraced paddy, but it too was so distant that it seemed to be of another world. Between the ridges and the steep rock path which we were following, there were sheets of forest canopy comprised of grey-green fir and pine. In the total silence the birds sang and an occasional insect buzzed past.

Behind us were mountain meadows, covered in daisies, strawberry flowers, agapanthus on rocks, blue flowers, pink tiny flowers, purple lantern-like flowers, maidenhair, fern fronds, an untouched, singing, rejoicing perfected stretching, which went on forever, and seemed unlimited, unstopped, unbound, without restriction, in which we were tiny figures, as fragile and ephemeral as the flowers.

We walked along the mountain ridge until we came to a Kali temple from which swung multifarious brass bells of all sizes and shapes, some stained with orange powder. Inside the simple cement structure, open to the sky, there was an orange-painted cement altar containing the God, Kalimata, silver with arrows. Sangeeta and the others lit incense which they had shaped from pine sap bought at a small shop, and placed white sweets in a plastic bag at the foot of the altar. Later they distributed these sweets as *prasad,* as blessed food. They prayed to Kalimata, Kalimata, mother of destruction and creation, the birth and death of nature, the ceaseless movement of dissolution and re-assemblance. Hundreds of rusted iron tridents, which had been placed by pilgrims of the past, towered in the clear air, the symbol of Shiva, the spirit which breathed over the face of the waters, and caused the world to form.

'The original trident was found by a villager on that small peak,' Sangeeta explained to me. 'He had a dream that it was buried there, and when he dug, it was unearthed.'

Then, when we had found a place to sit and had unpacked the lunch, and eaten the *parathas* which Sangeeta and Premila had prepared, and when we had walked back along the path, and almost reached the taxi, Sangeeta said, 'This is my favourite place. Shall we sit here awhile?'

It was a small hillock above the path, surrounded by trees, with a fir forest beneath. The earth was covered with thick grass, upon which we lay, staring heavenwards.

Soon Premila began to sing. From her small inadequate body the notes poured, and they were put on the air, and hung there, and each one matched the other, and was toned and modeled to its vibration, so that when they all were strung together, they were assorted gradings of the same emission, and were so blended and harmonious, and so pure and perfected, and rounded and filled, that we were breathless with the wonder of this sound which came from the crippled body.

'It's so beautiful,' I said to Premila. She had a vivid, affectionate smile.

'God gift,' she answered.

I was impressed with the way she sat so straight, so tidily and so collectedly, and said so. She did not understand my English and asked Sangeeta to explain.

Then Sangeeta explained, and Premila smiled, and Sangeeta told me that one of the disciples of Dr. Kaushik had met Premila, who was permanently in a bed, and who could not walk, nor move. And he taught her exercises, and she practiced the exercises, and began to walk. And he asked Dr. Kaushik where Premila could live, and Dr. Kaushik had given her the small room at the back, and she had found a job, and her life had become normal. And now she was always joyful, and she sung, because she was happy and grateful for all that had happened.

. . . .

I left *Dakshinamurti* a little early so that I would be sure to be on time for my interview with Vimalaji. When I arrived Kaiser met me at the door and said that she had phoned me, at Vimalaji's request,   as Vimalaji was feeling very exhausted. She had had meetings all afternoon, and had been talking to four different groups of people until the time I arrived, at five pm. I said I could come some other time, so Kaiser went into the room where Vimalaji was sitting, and told her this, but she insisted on seeing me. Kaiser looked quite worried so I said, 'Well, I'll just go in and say hello to her, and then I'll leave.'

She was sitting on the *asana*, so beautiful, I thought, and I said, 'Vimalaji, I'll just say hello, and I'm going now.'

'No,' she said. 'This is how it has happened, so let us flow with things. You are here, so we will talk now.'

I looked at Kaiser, who seemed anxious, but I did not like to argue with Vimalaji, as I trusted her to decide, but I said, 'The questions are all rather deep and complicated.'

'Well, we can just talk half an hour, and discuss a few of them, perhaps,' she answered.

I handed her the piece of paper, and she read the first question. I had a copy of the questions myself, and the first one said, 'There seem to be three major stages or dimensional shifts, in the process of total transmutation, the first being when one enters Silence, the second being when the Thatness descends or occupies the being, and thirdly, the final drawing of the curtain, as Vimalaji has called it. Would this be a correct understanding, and could Vimalaji comment please?'

'The two stages of silence and the first experiences of 'being occupied', occur in the same dimension,' she answered, 'But when It occupies permanently then the second dimensional shift, as you call it, takes place. There are many who cannot stand that overtaking, and they lose balance. If that 'being-possessed' crystallises at all levels, then total transformation has taken place.'

She then read the second question, which I had written; 'When the 'state of being possessed' first occurs it seems to be almost overwhelming with a fantastic velocity and energy, and then after a while, this sense of being swept away in the tides is replaced by a sense of bliss and communion. Would this be correct?'

She answered, 'Yes, the first time it is felt it is overwhelming, and you have to learn to assimilate and adjust to that Energy, not remaining a foreigner to it, nor letting it be foreign to you, but letting it become a part of you, and when that sense of it being normal happens, then the dimensional change has taken place. Until then it is a transitional stage with adjustment taking place. It is a learning phase.'

I was in such a state of dither and rapture that I was just blindly writing down whatever she said without really fully understanding the complexity of her answers. As she spoke I was thinking, 'Why am I asking her all these questions. What is the point of all this analysis? Am I just doing it to appear smart?' Because something else was taking place which seemed to be far more important. It was the exchange, I might even say, the transfer, of her being into my own being. It was as though a myriad of splodges of light arched in a stream between us, tearing at invisible speeds so that rocket-tails of energy billowed behind them and merged them into one high velocity ray which emerged from Vimalaji and vanished into myself. I adored her so much, and yet she was so far away at the source of this fantail of light, and Kaiser, sitting on her chair, seemed to be nodding off to sleep, her attention elsewhere as Vimalaji struggled valiantly with the complexity of questions which had nothing whatsoever to do with anything which was happening.

Vimalaji read out the third question. 'Is this state of actually being taken over, of being used, what is called the state of *bij samadhi*, which still contains a sense that the personality is being used?'

'Yes, this sense of 'being possessed' which you describe, this feeling that the whole being is used by the Cosmic, belongs to the Cosmic, which moves through it, feeling that one is stepping aside to allow It to move through one, this is *bij samadhi*. When it first permeates the being there is a sense of being possessed, but gradually it becomes a natural state, so there is nothing like perceiving it as being possessed.'

'There seems to be a further stage in which suddenly a shift takes place, and instead of a feeling that 'Christine is being used', it becomes 'I, the nothing, all this has come upon Me and which has got attached to me is outside me and there is nothing inside,' I said.

'Yes,' Vimalaji answered. 'It's the cosmic 'I', the cosmic 'Me', from which the whole universe proceeds. There is no sense of individuality in this 'I'. It is Infinite, unlimited.'

'Would this be what is experienced when the final downflow takes place?' I asked.

'It could be gradual. I don't know, but in Vimala's experience it happens in a timeless moment, a spreading, transforming, holistic event. But then again, who is to say – it could perhaps happen gradually and slowly.'

'Would *bij samadhi* be the state which is called the mystical marriage, which Vimalaji has referred to as the male and female energies blending? Is this *Shiva* and *Shakti* blending and is the consummation of this blending *nirbij samadhi*?'

'Yes,' she answered. 'It's called the 'mystic marriage' by the Sufis and other Indian mystic sects.'

She looked at my questions, and read out the next one: 'When *bij samadhi* occurs, what process is taking place – is it individual consciousness merging with universal consciousness, or is it the universal consciousness merging with the Absolute Source behind, and how does *shakti* relate to this process?'

'In *samadhi* it is not the individual and the universal consciousness getting blended together,' she answered. 'It is not the individual retaining the universal. The 'I' tries to resist the universal taking over, but if there is no resistance, and there is a sense of surrender and acceptance, then it comes upon you – we say 'merging'.'

Whilst she was talking I did not absorb this fully, but later, upon reflection, I realised that I had been seeing things back-to-front. The universal unlimitedness was the Reality which had always been there, and it was the small drops which became absorbed into It, through Its workings. The more I thought about her statement, the more crucial it seemed to be. It was a key to the successful continuation of the process.

Then she read out the next question which I had prepared: 'Which is the Energy which causes the final downflow of Spirit – I mean, in which state does it happen – in which state should the person be living – Silence, or *bij samadhi*, or does one need to be in that 'reversed' state?'

'What does this mean, dear?' she asked.

I felt my questions were all so futile. She also knew it was a futile question, and so had given this unplanned response, for surely she understood the question, which was really a repetition, in different words, of questions I had asked at other times. I looked at her. She appeared exhausted, although there was still the depth and intensity in the eyes, but I did not feel comfortable about continuing to impose my complex and pointless questions upon her.

'I don't know,' I answered. 'It doesn't really matter. I think you've answered already.'

Then she said, 'When the universal and individual consciousness merge, their blending is the ultimate *samadhi*. Even awareness, even assertion of universal consciousness is not there. It is sheer Isness, with nothing inside.'

'Is that what Vimalaji and Krishnamurti have called the Absolute Ground of Existence?'

'I don't understand, dear,' she answered. I was mumbling so much that she could not hear my words, so I proceeded to re-arrange the question.

'The Theosophists say that there is the consciousness and beyond the consciousness there is the Absolute, and when the state of Nirvana is lived, then even the consciousness ceases to exist, it is by-passed, and there is only Spirit, and this is why one should not get caught up in the extra-sensory powers, for they are part of the psyche, the soul, which ultimately is superceded.'

'Where do they say this?' Vimalaji asked.

'Well, it's in the Alice A. Bailey books,' I answered.

'And do they call this state the state of *Arhat*?'

'Yes,' I answered.

She looked deeply into my eyes and smiled. Neither of us said anything. That suspended moment seemed to last forever. She had told me everything in that simple sentence. I knew now that this was her state. She had left behind even the mind. I could not hope to understand.

Finally, after that magical, intimate moment had passed, she lifted up the piece of paper and read out the next question.

I looked at Kaiser, but she seemed to be dreaming in another world, no doubt also wearied by the influx of visitors and phone-calls, the letter-writing and other organizational procedures for which she was responsible.

'Is it necessary to live in the Silence for every minute of the waking hours, before the total transformation can occur?'

'It's a growth of your totality. The body/mind complex goes into abeyance in the same way that breathing in and breathing out continues automatically. So also the state of silence becomes automatic. In this state of silence the whole past is suspended, and the person lives in the Silence at the particular level which is a result of the intensity of their understanding.'

She was repeating the same thing to me over and over again in different words, in the hope that I might be able to grasp the extent and importance of what she was trying to convey – that all the experiences of my sojourn in Mt.Abu, all the intensities, all the fantastic, condensed, diluted, clashings of vacuums and voids and swellings and expansions, all the velocity which had blown me away like wind, when all this settled, and became normal, then one was getting somewhere. All this, she seemed to be saying was the first stage, the entering into the first altered dimension, and there was another even deeper dimension which would come upon the person, a revelation, a final veil to be drawn, and the state would become fixed.

The first stage, the stage of entering the silence, and of adjusting to the new energies was at the psychic level, and hence she called it the first change in dimension, for, even though one became aware of a Presence behind consciousness itself, a Seer behind the Seer, a presence behind the soul, this awareness all occurred initially in the realm of consciousness, it was consciousness that was changing and learning and adjusting. Hence, even though it had seemed to be to be two dimensions, as the outside world was seen first in the dimension of soul, and secondly in that abstracted dimension of void when everything was outside, she seemed to be suggesting that there was another dimension which I did not yet know, had not yet been shown.

'Is it necessary to live in the Silence every waking minute of the day before total transformation can occur?' I asked her again.

'To live in the silence is only the beginning,' she answered, patiently, slowly. 'Once the Silence lives in you, you're moved by It because you are an expression of that Silence. You don't live in that state. It takes over your life.'

Again I felt that the words were enormously significant, tremendously potent indicators of the way the enquiry would proceed, with Christine as an incidental appendage in the soup of space.

She then proceeded to read out my next question: 'Vimalaji
has talked about the silken thread which is Intelligence, and
that once this is built, nothing can destroy it. Would this be
the *antahkarana,* the conscious connection which the
enquirer builds whilst in the state of Silence and meditation,
and where does it connect, and to what?'

When she had finished reading the question, she was silent
for a moment, and then she began to talk on another subject.
'When Christine was in Mt. Abu,' she said, 'She was getting
self-educated, and when she began to live in the Silence, she
needed to be able to adjust her daily life to this, to be able to
move in the world, and at the same time to live in the
unconditioned energies. One needs to have at least twelve
hours per day alone – this means if you sleep eight hours per
night you would have four hours alone. You have seen how
Vimala goes into a room and shuts the door, and does not
open it for anybody or anything. As one needs to wash the
body every day to keep it clean, so also one needs to wash
the psyche in Silence every day to keep it pure. This practice
is especially necessary when one is leading a busy life of
social action.'

I wondered whether she had seen some glimpse of the future,
whether she was warning me, advising me of the essentials
of life, and trying to indicate to me gently that all the
questioning was not as important as living in the meditative
state. And when she said this, she answered a question which
had been troubling me for some time, namely, how I would
manage to adjust to life in the outside world now that I had
touched and tasted the blissful reality within my own being.

Again she returned to the written question, and proceeded to
answer it. 'If Vimala has mentioned the silken thread

somewhere – and I do not remember ...' She paused, then continued, 'Earth connects you to the interplanetary Life. The Consciousnesses have Their abode in that interplanetary system. The silken thread connects you to the whole interplanetary movement. Not only are we associated with it, we are connected to it. We talk about the Consciousness which moves through the seven orbs, if required, for global purposes. That relationship with the Interplanetary is there.'

I was so confounded I could hardly grasp the enormity, the vastness of what she was saying. Again she was lifting my mind into areas beyond my comprehension. She had managed, through a few words, to convey to Christine something which was, in reality, beyond the definition of words.

I suddenly began to realise that I had made a mistake in thinking that transformation of the human psyche was a step by step process on one level of existence. Rather, it was a happening occurring on all levels of the being. It was an awakening and purification of the consciousness that also affected all its lower vehicles, and in addition, it was a new extension of the *atma*, the individuated divinity, down into the gross matter of the material world.

With great effort I brought my mind back to the present. I myself felt utterly exhausted. Could it be that I was once more in connection with Vimalaji's mind, I wondered, and that I was actually feeling her exhaustion, because our consciousness had become one? I was ready to finish the interview. The production of words seemed to be an incredible labour, and incredible effort. But Vimalaji was able to rise above all this, and valiantly returned to my written questions, reading the next one out loud.

'How do you know when it is the final mutation, that is, the downflow of spirit which will permanently fix the state and after which, Vimalaji says, one does not need to be alone, because the state is constant?'

Her enormous eyes seemed heavy. Her face looked almost masculine, as though she could no longer be identified with either woman or man, as though that which overshadowed her, which had infused her being, had even moulded and shaped the pattern of her body.

'The evolution in consciousness is just a few thousand years old, it seems to me,' Vimalaji said. 'A new human race with mutated consciousness will occur, will have to inhabit the planet in order to restore it and re-organise it according to the need of the spiritual expression of the Great Life which is the consciousness of the cosmos.'

It was not at all what I wanted to know. She was still seeing huge and distant vistas of stars and spinning worlds, of space and moons, and I was worried about this little consciousness of Christine, and how it would arrive at some imagined goal.

'I was meaning in relation to total transformation of the human being,' I said.

'Why are you so anxious about the state being fixed?' she asked me. 'You have touched the Absolute. What more can Christine want? Nothing can be permanent, no state, no level of consciousness. There is only an inexpressible, infinite potential contained in divinity. To qualify it in any way would be damaging.'

'I understand,' I answered.

Kaiser was sitting with her head hanging forwards, and eyes closed, either asleep or dozing.

'These questions of Christine's are not really questions,' Vimalaji said to Kaiser. 'Rather, they are a recounting of what she has experienced.'

Kaiser looked up and smiled vaguely. There was thunder and rain outside.

'You'd better go,' Kaiser said.

I thanked Vimalaji for answering my questions when so many people had been asking for so much, and I went out the door. As I walked past the windows I could see into the room. Vimalaji was sitting on the *asana*, with her head hanging forwards, and her eyes closed. I made a vow that I would not again trouble her with any more questions. I felt ashamed that I had not been more definite, and refused to allow her to give so much, when so much had already been proffered.

The mountains had appeared again, because the wind had blown away the thick white curling clouds that had been gathered over the peaks all day, those same clouds drawn with squiggles and circular lines on Tibetan monastery murals. In their place were the mountains. They were deep grey for it was evening, and they were full of the same infinite power and majesty which seemed to stream from Vimalaji. They pointed to the endless infinity of sky, some of it turbulent, some of it still. I climbed the path.

I felt that I had learnt a great lesson in humility. I had gone with a great list of questions in order to confirm things which, as she had pointed out, I already understood. I had not needed to bother her at all. I had done the bothering only because she had previously referred to the 'integrity of the questions' and I was trying to better my own record. I had based my questions on the past, whereas she had been indicating I should be looking to the future. The questions had not come from the Silence, but from Christine's own ego. Ultimately they were unnecessary. I had burdened her for the purposes of duplication.

There was some rain, which splashed on the raincoat which Kaiser had lent me. I had unfolded it from its carry bag. I was grateful to have it. The rain soaked into the light brown crushed fabric, and I felt the wetness through my clothes underneath. I walked towards Gandhi Chowk, so moved and elated by the meeting that I traveled through the vividness and wonder of that world, seeing it, but not catching hold of it, rejoicing in it, but not being part of it.

I went to the Tibetan market. The tiny crowded booths, adjoining a long corridor covered with corrugated iron looked like a slum from the outside, but on the inside each shop was brightly lit, with clean glass cabinets, and neatly folded clothes. You forgot you were inside a shambles, a pretend edifice, except for the water which poured down through various places in the faulty roof, and which was being caught in bottles strategically placed underneath the major streams.

I bought a large mug with a lid and a blue dragon in it. Every time I had been with Vimalaji a great rapture filled me as the aftermath. I realised now that this was one of the crucial purposes of a Teacher: she could proceed, without any effort, to the core of the question, she could give the answers which were unasked, but needed, and ignore the questions which were asked but not needed. Through the vibration which she emitted, I was able to attempt to increase my own radio waves so that they would be able to synchronise with hers. Through being with her this became possible. Later perhaps it would be possible to do so without her immediate physical presence.

I walked past the one and only email shop. The owner could not download the mail. There had been a black-out. Two boys were playing pool. I sat with the keyboard on my lap on a roughly made wooden stool, and it seemed extraordinary that a message could travel across the world to this small booth in the mountains.

When I arrived at *Dakshinamurti*, Sangeeta was already in the kitchen cooking our dinner. I asked if I could help, but she said it was nearly ready.

I sat on the verandah and looked at the great river valley and the steeply rising ridges beyond. There was one patch of brilliant evening sunshine among the darkness of the rain. The sky and the earth were light and dark together, they existed in two states simultaneously. The roofs, sharp and highlighted by the late evening light, burnt with the golden sun on the ridge edge, and I stared at the patches of sunken grey, of receded forest, gone backwards beyond vision into the void of darkness. And I was transported still by Vimalaji's love, by her private, hidden gift, her endless giving, her light, and that which was behind the light.

There was only one more subject about which I wanted to question Vimalaji. It concerned the letter of which she had once given me a copy, in which she had written that she communicated with the ancient Vedic sages as well as others who had lived on this planet in different continents.

I went inside and sat at the typewriter which Kaiser had kindly lent me.

'Dear Vimalaji,' I wrote, 'The thing about which I have not been brave enough to ask you yet, is to do with who are the Rishis of whom Vimalaji is one, what is the means of communion between these Great Ones and their disciples, and so on. ... If you think that such things could be discussed, then I would like to ask about it ....'

I decided to ask Kaiser to give the letter to Vimalaji when we next met.

It was late when we ate dinner. Sonia had prepared the meal. She and her husband were fellow-enquirers, and they, together with myself and Sangeeta ate together at the round dining room table. We ate paneer cooked in tomato and cream, folded in chapatti. We spoke about Vimalaji in awed tones, that she had predicted the future so many times. 'She can speak on any level,' Sangeeta said. 'She can speak as a human about common things, or she can speak as a God.'

It was Buddha Purnima, the full moon of May. We sat together on the verandah. The night was still and we could hear dogs fighting on the distant ridge. Down the slopes of the mountains there were small lights twinkling. Behind a far mountain we could see a flare of light. It stained the sky and it made the selected horizon blessed with its presence, because it was defined and all the rest of everything was grey and vanished.

The moon was rising so fast that we saw the canopy of trees on the crest of the mountain begin to flare. It seemed as though there was fire between the dark outline of the firs and the sky itself. The gold went on bursting, swelling and rising until it exploded suddenly above the trees, a growing orb, which lined its chosen world with its borders of fire.

It had only half emerged above the mountain horizon, when a cloud descended upon it. The inside of the cloud was grey and the outside was coloured as if with a gold pencil, like children draw with magic sticks on greeting cards. And then, the moon burst from the cloud, and popped into itself, and shaped itself into a perfect white burning ball which rose more and more so that everything was gone in the blazing. Yet even this blazing was only reflected, and not real, and only a pretend thing, for it was the other, great fire of sun, consuming and contorting the air of space, which sent its own light that fell on this moon, and, if the sun was to come, then even this moon would go, and just be melted and faded.

. . . .

One day, Sangeeta asked me what had happened when I went away for three months.

'I sat in silence all the time. Finally, that energy came down. You could do it,' I said, 'But you need to be very determined.'

'I live in a place where it would be possible,' she answered. 'It's a big old house which was bought by Bhavna's father.

She wants it to be like an ashram, but not an ashram. She
asked Vimalaji what guidelines should be followed so we
could live together. It's very peaceful in a hill station of
Maharashtra.'

'Do you have a husband?'

'I do, but I don't live with him any more now.'

'In my situation I found it was easiest to go away because
there were no interruptions. If you do it in the place where
you normally live, you don't feel that there's this deadline,
you don't feel the same urgency.'

'Maybe I could do it,' Sangeeta said.

Now that we knew each other well she had said it would
'look very nice' if I dropped the honorific 'ji' at the end of
her name.

'You could ask Vimalaji,' I said. 'She seems to know past
and future without even thinking about it.'

'Maybe I will,' Sangeeta said, 'If there's a chance.'

I had learnt by now that most of Vimalaji's teaching came
through hints, even conveyed by other people. As an
example of this was a conversation which I had with
Sangeeta a few days later. She told me she had been visiting
Vimalaji and Vimalaji had asked her to come and sit and talk
to her. She had felt very privileged that Vimalaji should
invite her to sit and talk, and she said, 'Didi, you are very
busy, and have much work to do.'

Vimalaji replied, 'That's alright. It is my work,' So
Sangeeta, feeling as though she had won first prize, to have
this beaming power directed upon her personally and singly,
began to talk shyly in answer to Vimalaji's questions. As
was the custom, she did not initiate discussion, but rather,
responded. She said that she talked to Vimalaji for an hour
and twenty minutes.

'She talked about you, too,' Sangeeta said. 'She told me,
Christine is changing.'

I smiled.

'Did you ask Vimalaji about whether you should go **away** for
three months?'

'No, I didn't,' she answered.

It should have been obvious to me by then that I was pushing
Sangeeta into something about which she knew more than I,
and I decided to speak no more about it.

At the next *Satsang,* before everyone had arrived, Vimalaji
was talking to some of the newcomers. I could see Sangeeta
gathering up courage to ask a question as she edged herself
further forwards on the floor. I hoped that she was not going
to ask the question which I had bullied her into asking, but it
looked as though she had made up her mind to follow my
misguided advice.

'Vimalaji,' she asked. 'I've been talking to Christine, and
she said I should ask you that maybe I also should go away
for intensive *Sadhana* for three months.'

I felt extremely uncomfortable, because I knew that I had been quite wrong in suggesting such a thing. For all these years Vimalaji had known Sangeeta. Would she not have suggested it, if she had thought it to be appropriate? It was my own ego that had made me encourage Sangeeta. I had wanted to show to Vimalaji that I was able to encourage people by my own virtuous and dedicated example.

There was a long pause, while Vimalaji's antennae seemed to wait for a reply from outer space. I wondered how she could possibly answer such a question without being hurtful, for the room was now filled, and if she were to say to Sangeeta that she was not yet ready for such an encounter, it would have been very discouraging to her.

After a long time Vimalaji answered. 'Sangeeta has already a perfect place for the practice of Silence and Solitude,' she said. 'Have you seen it?' she asked me. 'Its so beautiful with lovely gardens and peace and serenity all around.'

Sangeeta looked relieved, and relaxed. She seemed to move backwards on her bottom, distancing herself again from Vimalaji without any effort, so flexible, so compliant, so lithe, able to sit cross-legged and straight-backed for hours on end, without a tremour of discomfort, whilst all my bones and joints creaked, and ached, and tingled.

The smell of incense in the room was heavy. Vimalaji began to cough. Looking around she noticed the smouldering incense on the bookcase to the right of the *asana*, and asked Achana to remove it.

There was much scuffling and sweeping past of saris and cottons, as the incense was hurried away by many eager and whispering women. Vimalaji sat, eyes closed, coughing into a handkerchief. When the flurry had subsided, and everyone was sitting still again, Vimalaji began to speak, amidst the coughs.

The talk was in Hindi and I could not understand it.

After she had finished speaking, the room sat in silence for a few moments, and then, when the three 'aums' had been sounded, Vimalaji spoke in Hindi to those present. Dispassionately and firmly she delivered a lecture, in which the word *agarbatti* (incense) was frequently repeated. There were indignant and muttered squeaks, crestfallen heads, and lips remorsefully bitten, by those who sat on the floor before her.

Everyone left the room in silence, and as I was walking up the path, Kaiser handed me a letter from Vimalaji. I opened it, and read it out loud to her, for I did not know whether Kaiser would have seen it or not.

'Dear Christine,' I read, 'I do not know the names of the Rishis. We never mention the name form or gender. The means of communication are perception, gestures, insight. With Vimalaji it is mostly Sanskrit. I regret inability to talk about *Arhats* and their lives beyond what has already transpired between us in our dialogues. It seems futile to try to speculate about the future of humanity. Let the sacred unknown reveal itself through the collective trends, aspirations and struggles of the global human community. With deep love, Vimala.'

By now I was no longer surprised. I had seen she was so different from an ordinary person, that only her physical body gave her any claims to being human, and even this was not like other bodies, for it did not seem to have anything inside it, but was rather like a screen or veil, or puppet, with some power behind a curtain, which moved and ruffled it, which lifted arms, and shone through eyes. And Kaiser also knew, and we shared this between us, and said nothing more.

As I walked home, I met Sangeeta buying mangoes.

After she had put them in her cloth bag, and after she had paid for them, we walked together along the narrow road, with hotels and tourists and troupes of monkeys.

She seemed abstracted and so I asked her if she was worried about the incense.

'Vimalaji was very angry with Achana. She said that Achana knew that she got asthma and bronchitis from incense smoke, and yet Achana had not removed the incense as Vimalaji had requested. But actually it was my fault, because I had said to Achana and the others that I would take responsibility for checking the room was ready for the *Satsang*, and I didn't go early today, because you and I went together to look at shawls.'

'I'm sure Vimalaji will understand,' I said.

But Sangeeta seemed doubtful. 'Sometimes she is very strict,' she said. 'Last year when we were here, she asked Achana to write to her mother. After a week she asked her, have you written to your mother? And Achana answered no, and so she sent her back to Mt Abu.'

'She must hate to do something like that.'

'She said it hurt her more than it hurt Achana.'

And I understood that she was trying to wake up people, and to speed their progress, and to make them jump so that they would not be sluggish, and would burn forwards and be faster. And to do this, she had to hurt herself.

When we arrived at *Dakshinamurti*, Sangeeta rang up Achana, and Achana said to her that she should not worry, and thus it was settled, and Sangeeta had learnt.

....

I walked along the winding road under the trees, past monkeys, which had invaded Dalhousie in such numbers that no-one could grow a garden, for they swung from roofs, ate flowers, raided kitchens, snatched food from hands, and made much mischief. We could not even hang out our clothes in front of the house without the monkeys taking them. Once Sangeeta found her new silk scarf hanging from the branch of a tree as high as a building. When I sat on the path outside my room, Huge male monkeys would stroll past, almost brushing my feet, causing me to start, as they came silently from the forest, padding on springing feet and spread hands, their muscular shoulders rolling, their small, yellow beady eyes vivid and full of challenge, and, if you looked at them, they would curl back their lips, flashing their teeth menacingly, making small noises of aggression. Sometimes, when a whole group of them sat on the stairs which led up to the road, we were afraid to pass, because we did not know if they would jump at us and bite us, and if they bit, then you had to have vaccinations against rabies.

There was a gate at the entrance to *Shiv Kul*, and a sign which said, 'Vimala Thakar', and which had the Sanskrit symbol of the sacred word '*Om*' painted on it. To the left of the gate and above the house was a hotel, the owners of which had constructed a new restaurant and ugly, misshapen outbuildings which hung over the path which led down to the house, and workmen spat chewing gum and threw paper out the windows onto the stairs. Tattered, faded clothes swung on string in the sun, items so worn that they looked more like washing rags than vestments, thus contributing to the general appearance of an expanding, looming slum.

There were not many people in the room on this occasion, and Vimalaji began her talk by saying, 'This is for Christine too, so she should come and sit nearer.'

I was sitting at the back on a chair, due to my rebellious legs which went numb and then devoid of any desire to obey instructions, after being folded for a period exceeding half an hour, but when Vimalaji invited me to move nearer, I went and sat on the floor, so close that I thought I would explode from the radiance which hurtled and jostled and punched and blotched and burnished the room and reduced me to a withered, empty thing just blowing in the wind.

'No, you should take a chair,' she said, aware of the recalcitrant legs, but I said it was fine on the floor.

Kaiser always sat near the wall close to a table on which was a large microphone, on a chrome stand, and some recording equipment. When Vimalaji was going to commence to speak, she would indicate to Kaiser as to whether the talk could be recorded, but hardly ever did she wish it. However, she often asked Kaiser to set up the microphone on a table in front of her so that she could speak without straining her voice.

'We need to understand,' she began, 'That there are various stages in the enquiry, like school education, there is the primary school and later there is the university education and so on. In the primary school there are three steps.'

She spoke slowly and carefully, and was looking at Sangeeta as she elaborated on her theme. 'The first step is to have physical discipline so that one's life is properly organized – not this dreadful word, routine, but regulation in one's life - so that the time is not wasted, and so that one can fully expressed the divinity, one of whose attributes is organization.'

'Having got this in order the second step is to have psychic discipline. Some people simply cannot live alone. They want to be in the company of other people and cannot not be quiet within themselves. They grow anxious if they're alone, and look for excuses to go out shopping, or to talk on the phone. But, if all these impulses to socialize can be overcome, if the person has the ability, the fearlessness, to live in solitude, then this second step can be accomplished.

'The third step is the ability to be able to leave behind the whole conditioned human past, to be able to live in the present only, not to be returning to the past and thinking over and over event in life which have finished, nor to be thinking of future details, such as who will come to visit me or what will I cook for dinner.

'When all these steps are accomplished, then there is the fourth step of living in the Silence. It is another dimension. In the Silence many occult powers start to manifest. You want to test it out. You use the excuse that you want to scientifically verify it. It is very, very difficult not become involved in these powers. When these energies begin to show themselves you want to do something with them. The temptation is to use them but you have to learn to contain them. These are not only the powers of clairaudience etc but also the other energies which become available which are of quite a different quality than the energies usually available. Only one in thousands reaches this stage, and it is very difficult to remain detached from all the energies which begin to move. But you have to move through this fourth stage also, and remain silent, and then the true Silence and Solitude will begin. Silence is the state in which there is no consciousness of the me. You do not ever have to take any effort to cause anything to happen. You can be absolutely sure that if the Cosmic wants to use you, it will use you, and even if you try to fight it, it will still use you, so you don't need to initiate anything but only respond.'

As Sangeeta and I walked home, we both felt that the talk had been directed at us, and we both felt very sober and humbled by its contents.

CHAPTER TEN

THE ISNESS OF LIFE

The orbit of Silence, the dimension of Silence, is a very romantic dimension. The conditioned energy goes into non-action, the unconditioned comes into play and a person sees many changes taking place. A new glow to the person's life, a new magnetism is expressed and if the person identifies with the magnetism, with that extraordinariness, then the inquiry comes to an end. Such persons render great service to the universe, yet the dimension of silence, where energies are still moving, is not the state of meditation.

If there is austerity of inquiry and humility not to identify, as one had not identified with thought and the movement of the 'I', if one does not identify with the movement of this non-I and unconditioned energy, then this movement of unconditioned energy also subsides. Please remember that meditation is a state of being where there is no movement at all, neither of the conditioned mind nor of the unconditioned mind. It is only ISNESS that remains, free of the cosmic intelligence or universal intelligence, free of the movement of even unconditioned energy[1].

One morning Kaiser and I took a taxi, and we asked the driver to drop us at a small tea shop. Behind the tea shop there was a path, and the path led into the forest. The forest was composed of deodar, and the deodar raised their straight trunks to the sky, so that the sun was taken by their greenery and we walked in the cool of their underneaths. But sometimes, where the canopy was broken by a fallen tree, or, where there was a hewn stump, there, where the sun came,

---

[1] Thakar, Vimala, 'Observation to Wholeness' talk from a conference Vimalaji addressed in Santiago, Chile, on February 20, 1983, *The Invincible,* Vol. XI, No. 3, July-September, 1995; 8-9.

there were fields of daisies which were like white thrown stars.

We walked through the forest until we came to a creek. The water was so pure that it could not be seen, and only the rocks, which slept under its coldness, were visible. The path split in two ways, and we wondered which direction to take.

A group of village men could be heard in the distance through the trees, their voices carrying, mixed with the sound of birds, of cicadas, and of the quiet passage of wind, which sounded like broken sea.

When the men came close to us, Kaiser asked them where the path went from which they had come, and they said that it came from a village, but that we should not go through the forest because there were bears in the forest which killed humans. But Kaiser did not mind about the bears, although she took her packet of matches from out of her ruksack and held it in her hand, because she said that bears were afraid of fire.

The path wound round the side of a hill, and then crossed another creek. There was a small cement tank built in the creek, and from the pipe the cold water burst onto the platform, which could be used for washing. Some of the water had also been piped, and was being carried in these pipes through the forest, to an unknown destination. But still there was enough, because of the trees, and the divided light, and the beds of golden pine needles. There was enough of everything, and we picked the fern fronds for later eating. Kaiser scraped the sap from the deodar with a knife. Some of the sap had hardened and looked like globules of amber among the rough bark, but some was still clear and semiliquid. She collected it in a small bottle, so that she could make incense, and it smelt of the fragrance of the forest, trapped in material substance.

Then we climbed a path, which was well-worn, and which rose up the side of a hill, further and further, until we were alone in the forest, and there was not the sound of nay person, but only the birds, and the wind, which was like the sea.

Finally we came to a ridge, and we walked along the ridge. It had been grazed, so that it had turned into a meadow of grasses, herbs and flowers And there were daisies, and wild violets, wild strawberry and ivy and buttercups, and maidenhair, and tiny pink flowers in clusters of buttons, and others which were blue. And even the weeds had wondrous flowers which were white and puffed like belled sleeves.

We sat on the ridge and the fir forest went backwards and backwards in lacings and plaitings of shades, retreating and shifting, according to distance and dimension There was wild rose, and wild sage which scented the air, with the deodar, and two crows which came from far away, and circles the sky because they had seen us on the ridge, and knew that with the people there would be food for the taking.

And there were so many birds, and they called and warbled, and whistled, and made soundings of bells and scales of song.

There were daisies which began as a tight green bud, and from the bud the white petals elongated until they formed a point, and then they pushed themselves outwards, at first in disarray, and then as discs of white, their faces to the sun,

fields of white discs, rejoicing and worshipping the golden
central balls of yellow spiraling dots which spun outwards
from a central depression, like a yellow vortex of the
universe, more and more multiplied, and more and more
bursting, more and more humming and singing and
expanding.

And Kaiser lay against the great old rough-trunked deodar,
in a blue dress with her white shawl tied round her head. She
was soft human flesh among the vibrancy and the growing
and being, and the forest did not ask anything but to be, not
even to be noticed or marked or seen, but just to be there
because it was, and had come and stood, and it was not
waiting for anything, but just present, and in a place, because
it had come there.

She had brought lunch of spiced potatoes, and flat bread, and
sweets, and we ate it. Then we walked again, through shade
and through sun and when we walked through the sun, the
faces of the daisies were singing, absorbing imbibing,
vibrating, and there was one tiny blue flower like a fallen eye
among them.

When we came out of the forest we saw two women with
curved knives who were slashing grasses and ferns, which
they stacked in large baskets on their backs. They were
collecting the products of the forest to feed to their cattle.

'Where have you been?' they asked.

'Into the forest, on the ridge,' Kaiser answered.

'But there are bears,' they said. 'They kill people. They have long claws like this.' They held up their hands and curled their fingers, and made faces so that they looked ferocious.

'So how do you protect yourselves?' Kaiser asked them.

'We never go alone, we go in groups,' they.answered.

But we had not seen a bear. We had only seen the celebration and the perfection, and the presence, and so we went from the place carrying within us the scent of flowers and of pine, and the sunlight and the sacredness of life.

That afternoon there was a storm, and when I arrived at the *Satsang* lightening was flashing. As we sat in silence, the room full of people, for there were many who had journeyed to sit with Vimalaji, there was a huge crash of thunder. At that moment both Vimalaji and myself instantaneously jumped, and she looked straight at me, noticing that no-one else in the room had jumped. She smiled, and said, 'The ecstasy of terror.' It was a small incident, but I somehow felt that I had jumped automatically when I heard the thunder because she had done so. Again I felt the Presence in the room. The atmosphere was thrilling. Every time I tuned into Vimalaji's mind I felt a great flood of bliss. Vimalaji's whole face was alive. Sometimes when she was in *samadhi* there seemed to be only an empty vehicle there, with an almost masculine expression, but today that body was alive, full of beauty, with the enormous brown eyes brimming with joy and vivaciousness.

....

At the next *Satsang*, I again learnt so much without having to
actually talk to Vimalaji. Before the singing started she
talked for about half an hour. There were many people who
had come to be with her, including a barrister from New
Delhi, who had a powerful presence, and sat with straight
back, one leg folded over the other, in unmoving silence
throughout the duration of her talk, except to sometimes nod
and smile, when she spoke his name. Although the talk was
directly specifically to him, she spoke in English. She said
that when you entered the silence, you had to stop trying to
analyse it, for all analysis related to the conditioned mind,
and silence could never be understood with the brain. We
relied on the brain and the mind, but we as a human race had
to learn to abandon these, as they had not got us anywhere,
and we had to go beyond, into the other realms of
consciousness. She said that the very difficult part was that
which occurred after the person had contacted the silence,
and tried to live it in daily life. If silence could be practiced
and maintained, it was our birthright as humans to undergo a
total transformation. There were no guidelines, no rules, no
techniques, because how could there be any restrictions on
the unconditioned, which was beyond time and space?

'I am not interested in the self or ego centred ambitions to
acquire occult experiences or to acquire, obtain
transformation or *samadhi* if at all it is obtainable. One
doesn't care for such petty little selfish concerns. One is
interested in meditation because it seems to provide a way
out of the thought structure that has become the obsession of
the human race .... Meditation is a psychic mutation which is
an holistic transformation in the quality of consciousness, its
mode of functioning and the character that it confers upon
the behaviour of the person.'

....

Sometimes Sangeeta and Premila also took me walking. We went into the forest which went backwards and backwards more and more, steepled and toppled and cut, staggered, shaped against a reducing sky, forever retreating in colour layered upon layer of grey shading, the sharp points and rock ridges, the glaciers and fields of snow, filling the valleys in one string with more behind, and also sky, but they were between sky and earth and heaven and not one nor the other but the link and joining, a necklace of clouds had spilled into one valley but the peak jutted beyond it. On an outcrop of rocks huge boulders jutted from the forest, surrounded by pine and fir needles, meadows of daisies. We brushed aside the prickling shrubs and climbed onto the rock, sitting in the silence where only birds could be heard and sometimes a buzzing insect, dry leaves between the rocks, ivy and flowering creepers, the fir path up the slope among the trees covered with pine needles, the fir trees with draping branches heavy with fronds and brushes of green needles, and the magical bursting of the uppermost growth, painted silver like green sticks of needles from showbags at festivals, to sway against the sky and cheer on heroes. The fantastic pine all bald branches with pompoms of long needles at the end of each branch and sub-branches with pompoms of long needles at the end of each branch an giving appearance of elaborate chandalier.

....

My relationship with Vimalaji now seemed to enter a new phase. It seemed to actually intensify as though not speaking to her had opened another avenue of communication. I had noticed that, ever since I had sat in the car with Vimalaji on the trip to Delhi, I was actually within her consciousness. During one *Satsang* I suddenly realised something very amazing. As usual, I sat in deep meditation trying to tune myself to the highest level possible of her vibration. I distinctly thought how, even when I was in the bathroom, if I was in the state of Silence, I felt she was knowing even that I was naked in the shower. I had thought this just before the *Satsang* started. During the *Satsang,* I received a distinct impression that I was embarrassed by the intimacy of the contact through consciousness with Vimalaji and this was because the contact was closer than any external, physical relationship. It reminded me somehow of my very early childhood, of one of my first memories, when I lay against the cardiganed bosom of my grandmother, and felt her love which glowed and radiated upon me. But this contact with Vimalaji was more intimate even than that, more intimate even than a sexual encounter. It was a complete and utter merging of mind in mind, devoid of any association with, or awareness of, the body.

Then suddenly I realised that my restlessness and inability to maintain contact with the ISNESS of Vimalaji was because I had a resistance. Somehow it did not seem right to be completely abandoned in unlimited love, even though this was not individual love, but it was a connection, through the *Buddhi* of Vimalaji to the one Unicity of the cosmos. All our lives in our human relationships we had been conditioned to love with reserve – there was something wrong with a person, so you could not love them fully; you could not love a woman fully or the intensity of the love might be considered unbalanced, even unexpressed homosexuality. You could not love another man fully and unconditionally, as he might suspect you were making overtures to him. And,

out of the habits of the past, because of my own inhibitions, I
was creating a screen or barrier in my mind, so that this
unrestrained, unlimited intimacy on the universal psychic
level could not occur between Vimala and myself.

I was actually embarrassed by my closeness to her, although
physically I was far distant, and nobody else could have
known what was happening in my mind. Yet I knew that she
knew. As the people in the room sat in silence, I actually
seemed to hear her voice say, 'There is only one
consciousness. There is no duality in consciousness.' I then
removed the screen which I had created in my mind, and
tried to be 'fearless' as Vimalaji had said. Then I was drawn
right into her being. I cannot describe what happened except
to say that she was Vimala and I was Christine and yet we
were one. There could not be any invasion, nor any
exclusion in the one consciousness. All was intimate, all was
shared, because it was all only one field of Energy, of mind,
of universal, unlimited love. It was not Christine submerged
in this mind, but merely a Mind. The barrier dropped, and I
saw or perceived that Vimala and I were separate and yet not
separate. We were in the Thatness and part of the Thatness,
and undivided from It and yet we were each an identity, but
what identity I could not say – Essence maybe, or just a point
of vibration.

. . . .

At the next two *Satsang* I was to be shown how Vimalaji
functioned in the state of *Samadhi*. I found it extraordinary
that I could learn so much just by being in her presence,
without needing to ask any questions. There were only seven
people at the *Satsang*, all close friends, and before the
chanting had even begun, Vimalaji had closed her eyes and

gone into *samadhi*. I could tell because her face became
blank, her eyelids and hands or arms sometimes twitched
unconsciously, as though in sleep. After a while she held up
her hands as though she was reading from a book. The palms
were upwards and she recited something I did now know.
Her eyes remained closed. After this, she lowered her hands
and remained silent again, but her lips seemed to be moving,
as though she was talking. She was sitting very straight,
without moving apart from the occasional involuntary
twitches. All through the singing she remained in this state
and after the singing, the meditation continued for a much
longer period than usual. Some people seemed to be growing
restless but I found it was a most blissful meditation and I
felt she was drawing me into her and I felt the incredibly fine
and rarified love which poured from the Nothing. I felt there
was just 'BEE-ING' as she often said. After about an hour
had passed, from the time she recited from the book, she
finally opened her eyes with great difficulty. She would open
them and then they would seem to close of their own accord
again, and then she would force them to open. Finally she
spoke, and she asked, in English, 'What was I singing?'

No-one in the room could answer. 'It was the Muslim
prayer,' she said, 'Which is used at the commencement of a
service.'

Then she asked, 'Why was it Muslim?'

Nobody knew, and nobody answered. 'Do you remember our
dear Muslim friend who came to Mt. Abu, and who was
campaigning for unity within the religions? Well, I heard
someone call, 'Ma, Ma', so I have been with him for twenty
minutes or so. They are in Calcutta. They are leaving on a
peace mission, to bring peace between Muslims and Hindus.

They were there together, at a prayer meeting. He built a Hindu temple, and his colleague, and Hindu, built a mosque. Then she described for us the service, and who had been there, and many of the details which she had observed.

From this I began to understand what hidden work she was performing, work of a nature which we could never comprehend, and I felt deeply privileged that I had been permitted to see a glimpse of the way a future humanity could function, if only we could open ourselves to the reality of life.

. . . .

When I arrived at the *Satsang*, Vimalaji was already sitting in the room with Kaiser, and she was saying a prayer in Sanskrit, although deeply unconscious. Her hands were moving. She had the thumb and index finger paced together for some time, with one palm facing up and the other facing down placed on the knees.

After a while she spoke in English, still seemingly unconscious, and said, as though talking in her sleep, some beautiful words, spoken in *Sanskrit*. She then translated them, so it seemed into English, for she spoke in the same distant, deep voice:

> Let humanity unite in love
> And live in harmony.
> With their feet on the earth
> And their heads in the sky,
> May they be compassionate
> To all living beings.

Then she fell silent again as other people entered the room. She started, and said, 'What time is it?' like someone who has dozed off in an armchair, and has an appointment. The *bhajans* were sung, and then the period of silence was held. I was trying in the meditation to solve the question of how I could get Christine out of the picture, as she was only a thought-form, and this seemed to be answered by a sudden understanding, which I had the distinct feeling was a projection from Vimalaji. 'There is nothing but Love,' the thought seemed to say, 'Nothing but one undivided sea of love, so how can there be any separation in such a state?'

The personality of Christine appeared in my mind's eye rather much as a pear which was swinging on a tree, the pear being an exudation, or expression of the vast, spreading unlimited branches of the tree.

After a while Vimalaji woke, with difficulty, and said, 'I'm sorry to interrupt your meditation,' as though something important had happened, and she wanted to share it, to allow us the privilege of knowing what happened in the consciousness of one so great.

She spoke in English, and as she spoke she looked penetratingly at me without once removing her gaze from my face. I felt my body and everything which was anything to do with Christine had vanished, and I was nothing but attention itself. I was utterly engrossed and absorbed by what she said. Every thought vanished from my mind as I heard the words and also at the same time seemed to understand the words, before they were spoken, or simultaneously to their speaking. It was as though the same words which were projected through her were also being projected through Christine and she seemed to know this.

'Let us wish the present Prime Minister of India a restful holiday in Manali,' she began. 'Vajpayee and Vimala have known each other since 1973. We were friends on different paths. Since he came to power in 1996 he has not had a moment's rest. He is seventy six years old, and let us hope he will have a few more years in him yet. He has held together a government with seventy three Cabinet Ministers from twenty four ideologies, castes, and regions, the youngest member being thirty years old, and he seems like an equal to all, has treated them all equally, has consulted them all on everything. This is a sign of his inner divinity, that he can keep so many together in harmony. In addition, he is very dignified in foreign affairs. With utter restraint he has allowed the Indian army to take back the bits of Kashmir which Pakistan annexed, but they did this in about a day, and they could easily have continued the battle and taken more of the land that Pakistan annexed fifty years ago. However, he said, no, this was the border at the moment, and if it was to be changed there would have to be international negotiations to do this. See the restraint, see the dignity, and he is very much aware of preserving Indian heritage also.

'In Fiji it is a very serious situation at the moment in which the Prime Minister and his colleagues have been kidnapped, and democracy is under threat. Many industrialists have asked Mr. Vajpayee to intervene but he has said he will not intervene in a domestic issue.

'The Prime Minister for Sri Lanka has offered to make Jaffna a separate province. See how he is unconditionally offering to concede a point according to his Buddhist philosophy. Again, Mr. Vajpayee was asked to intervene in Sri Lanka, but again he said, unless both parties, Tamils and the Sinhalese Government ask India to do so, we will not interfere because it is a domestic matter. See how the Americans bombed Iraq when they invaded a territory which belonged to them, or how the Americans had meddled in Afghanistan.

'So, Vimala is monitoring all this,' she continued, after a pause. 'She reads the papers, listens to the BBC and she is going there, and observing what is the state of things. So Vimala would ask that we could join in prayer for the needs of the world, so people can learn to live in harmony together.'

Again I was shown, through this information which she gave to us, an insight into the future destiny of humanity, a destiny in which we were no longer limited by space or time, in which we could merge our minds with other minds, in which we could work at the levels of cyberspace, with the brain as a biological computer, having abandoned mechanical email as a superceded historical technique no longer needed in the fluidity and creativity of a new world, which understood and worked with light, and the frequency of light.

During her talk, Vimalaji had been watching me almost continuously. It was as if she had directed images as well as words into my mind. And yet, she had not at all directed them, but rather, I felt that she was as surprised as I by the miraculous way in which these beautiful words had formed and been voiced, expressing a deeply optimistic view of the world.

A new person came into the room, and bowed before Vimalaji. 'Bow to your own inner God,' she said in Hindi.

When the *Satsang* had finished, a few people remained sitting, as Vimalaji had not yet left the room, and so I asked her, 'How is it that we can we pray effectively?'

'Christine knows the answer to this,' she responded. 'It is through the heart. Love is the way of prayer. In love are all answers. Why would you ask?'

'Sometimes people say that you should do it through creating an image or thoughtform.'

'No,' she answered. 'Love is complete in itself. No outcome is needed to be visualised. Every solution is already existent in the love; every answer is there. We can leave it to the love to find the right outcome.'

Then she added, 'The visualisation is used if we want to send a message.'

As I walked home I felt that I had again learnt an enormous lesson. Not only had she explained to me some of her secret work, but she had spoken the words about love which I had just been thinking during the meditation. I felt profoundly deeply connected to her, and now I understood, not only how I could begin to work for the world, but how I could leave Vimalaji, Dalhousie and all the love which was an expression of her appearance in the world.

We walked home together, Premila, Sangeeta and myself in a wild storm. Drops of hail pelted the road, the parked cars, our heads. Our dresses were soaked and our shoes wet. The monkeys climbed trees to find shelter and we ran into the reading room, welcomed by the man in charge. It was a small, wooden edifice, built on precarious pylons so that it extended from a small cliff outwards, and from its rows of windows a distant view of the valleys and plains could be seen. We read the daily paper, and waited, among the many refugees, for the wildness to pass.

When we arrived back at *Dakshinamurti*, I shed my wet clothes and sat in my room watching the lightening flash. In its light the trees would become white, before fading into darkness again. Christine could be dissolved through love alone, I thought, all healing, all solutions, all supply was in the love itself, was the expression of the love. Christine's task was only to move in that love, to let it swill and pour. There was no individual purpose. Every human being was essentially purposeless for we were not here to do anything, but rather to provide the cells in the eyes of God through which that Infinity could view the world. I was deeply, inexorably moved by the wonder of this, the enormity of the power of love, and our human purpose, to allow it to use us. I felt the sacredness of the task which was that of humanity, and the joy of the endlessness which was beginning. The *Satsang* had not been a matter of Vimalaji showing me what she did, but of her showing me the purpose of the whole of humanity.

....

Because I was soon to leave I wrote a farewell letter to Vimalaji which I planned to hand her at the last Satsang which I would be attending. I forgot to bring the letter, but as Vimalaji was talking to Kaiser when I entered the room, I went and sat on the floor near to the front, and explained that I would be leaving in a few days. She smiled and said, 'I have written you a letter,' and handed it to me.

I held it but did not open it. I was unsure if I should read it in her presence.

'You can read it now,' she said. I opened the envelope and read the letter.

> My Dear Christine,
> You will be leaving in a few days. Due to your long stay in Mt. Abu and Dalhousie, you have become a member of 'Friends of Vimala' group.
> It was very nice to go through our personal dialogues. It is very joyful to see you in the evening sessions.
> This is to wish you a comfortable and safe journey back to Australia. May you find congenial atmosphere to prepare the first draft of your book.
> Please feel free to visit us at Mt. Abu. May you be blessed with the Bliss of Meditative Life.
> With deep love and Blessings, Vimala.

After I had read it, I was greatly moved. To anyone else it would have appeared as a rather trite note, but to me every word had a second meaning.

'Vimalaji,' I said, loudly so that she could hear through her deafness, 'You have shown to me that great ocean of love. It is because of you that I am living in this bliss.'

No-one else was in the room except Kaiser, because I had arrived rather early.

'It is the Cosmic which has brought us together,' Vimalaji answered, 'And the Cosmic moves through the person who is ripe.'

'I feel that I am connected to you through that sea of love,' I said.

'You see dear, there is the river, and those who have the understanding, they can also merge themselves in that river.'

'And are you going to Australia now?' she asked.

'First I'm meeting Jeremy in Delhi, and we're going to our shelter in Kalimpong,' I said.

'Oh,' she said, 'I've been to Kalimpong. I stayed with one of my relations there in my youth. It was a very sacred place, a place of great silence and solitude.' Then she thought for a moment and added, 'But maybe it's changed.' Perhaps she knew of the political strife that now disrupted life in that area, the struggling of a group of Gorkha separatists and thugs who wanted a separate State in the north of West Bengal called Gorkhaland. But I felt I could not talk about these details. People were pressing round, waiting to have their moment of exchange with her.

'They don't have any electricity or road to their shelter,' Kaiser said.

'Oh, how do you manage?' Vimalaji asked, surprised.

'Its so beautiful,' I mumbled, and did not have anything to proffer.

So she thought for a moment, and then she said, 'Yes, it's true *Advaita* to be a citizen of the world, and to be at home in any country.'

And thus it was that I said goodbye to her, not knowing when we would again meet.

Premila arranged a taxi for me. She and Sangeeta handed me gifts of food as I climbed into the vehicle. They pressed their hands together in the traditional Indian gesture of greeting and parting, a prayer, an honour, a love, a *namaste*, all blended in that one graceful movement.

The taxi wound down through the hills. The air grew hotter. The landscape was parched and brown, waiting patiently for the monsoon, the worn, used landscape, trodden and tilled over the epocs, scratched, and planted, and dug and turned, used and reaped and cut, giving again and again, year after year, forever renewed, despite the exhaustion, despite the plundering.

I sat in a waiting room at the station. The ceiling was very high, and a large fan slowly turned in a vain attempt to circulate the burning air. There was a station attendant outside, dressed in a sari uniform of khaki, and she refused to let people past the door unless they could produce a ticket. Obviously this was an exclusive enclave, perhaps once used by the British. There was a green terrazzo floor, and an art deco fireplace with a black border. There were old wooden benches painted in brown, and a wooden table with a laminex top. There was a notice painted in wood, and affixed to the wall, which said, 'Notice. Bearers and ayes not responsible for looking after unattended luggage. There was a rippling wall mirror, and I sat in the quietness of the room, and looked through the door at the noise of the station outside, the dazzle of light, the *feriwalas* wheeling their dilapidated wooden carts with wobbling wheels, their offerings of suspect food, cooked before your eyes on flaming kerosene stoves, and the dog with cancer in its swollen, swinging penis, anxiously waiting for someone to drop some morsel of food which it could salvage.

And it seemed that Christine also was outside, and I was not at all Christine, for she was part of the movement and light, and far away. And there was a train journey, overnight, in a bunk with clean white sheets which the porter brought, and there was Jeremy, at the airport, and a flight to Siliguri, and a taxi up the hill, through the jungle, past the gushing River Teesta, filled with monsoonal mud. And there was this world, all there, and various, and it came and it went, and it was wondrous.